RANDOM
HOUSE

WEBSTER'S AMERICAN SIGN LANGUAGE

MEDICAL DICTIONARY

RANDOM HOUSE

WEBSTER'S AMERICAN SIGN LANGUAGE

MEDICAL DICTIONARY

Elaine Costello, Ph.D.

Illustrated by
Lois A. Lehman
Linda C. Tom

Random House
New York

Library of Congress Cataloging-in-Publication Data
Costello, Elaine.
    Random House Webster's American sign language medical dictionary Elaine
  Costello; illustrated by Lois A. Lehman, Linda C. Tom.
      p. cm.
    ISBN 0-375-70927-4
    1. American Sign Language—Dictionaries. 2. Medicine—Dictionaries—American
  Sign Language. I. Title: Webster's American sign language medical dictionary.
  II. Title: American sign language medical dictionary. III. Title.
  HV2475 .C663 2000
  610'.3—dc21   00-059172

Typeset and printed in the United States of America.

First Random House Large Print Edition
9 8 7 6 5
August 2000

ISBN: 0-375-70927-4

New York Toronto London Sydney Auckland

Contents

Introduction

Why This Dictionary?

Random House Webster's American Sign Language Medical Dictionary was created to help the Deaf and hearing communities cope with a real and widespread communication gap between deaf patients and hearing health-care professionals.

About 16 million people with some level of hearing loss form the largest disability group in the United States, and American Sign Language (ASL) is the native language of many in this group. It is the language learned first for some 300,000 to 500,000 users of ASL in North America—the standard means of communication in the Deaf community. For many Deaf people, it is the only language they are comfortably proficient in.

Fortunately, ASL is a growing language, with more than 13 million members of both the deaf and hearing populations currently using it or learning to use at least the basic signs. If we count all of these people, ASL is the fourth most commonly used language in the United States.

Even so, it is often difficult for deaf and hearing people to talk to each other, particularly when technical language is required. Nowhere is this more evident than in health care, where patients must be able to convey their fears and symptoms, and where doctors and nurses must be able to convey not only feelings of empathy, but accurate diagnoses and clear, understandable instructions for care.

Not surprisingly, Deaf people are often underserved by the health-care community—not because of negligence, but because the ability to exchange critical information is severely hampered. Many Deaf people would not understand English-language medical terminology even if it were fingerspelled, and most medical personnel lack sign language communication skills.

The 1990 Americans with Disabilities Act mandates the presence of a qualified interpreter during any medical procedure, but the interpreter may be delayed or may simply not be available in an emergency. Although such alternatives as writing notes or pointing to illustrations can help, more often than not, doctors and patients must struggle to express vital medical facts, even when friends or family members are there to help.

This book, virtually the only one of its kind available, is intended to help mitigate that struggle. It features over 1,000 signs—defined and described—that are commonly used for essential medical terms, with each sign illustrated with a full-torso line drawing. The signs are carefully broken down into their component parts, so that the unique syntax of American Sign Language is preserved.

Categories covered include:

Illnesses:	**arthritis** (JOINT/CAN'T MOVE), **astigmatism** (EYE/SHAPE/NOT/RIGHT)
Diagnostics:	**audiogram** (GRAPH/SHOW/HOW-MUCH/CAN/HEAR), **benign** (NOT/CANCER)
Treatments:	**antibiotic** (MEDICINE/INFECTION/DESTROY), **decongestant** (MEDICINE/FOR/COLD)
The Body:	**cartilage** (SAME-AS/ELASTIC/BETWEEN/BONE), **fontanel** (BABY/TOP-OF-HEAD/SOFT)

It is hoped not only that this book can serve as an introductory vocabulary resource for both the medical community and interpreters, but that Deaf people themselves can benefit from having a source for medical terms and definitions. The signs in this dictionary are used by interpreters in medical settings nationwide. By enabling and enhancing communication in such settings, use of these signs can sharply reduce the kinds of misunderstanding that English words alone might convey.

The presence of this book in a hospital emergency room or a doctor's office provides a key to communication, with drawings of medical terms that can be pointed to even by people who do not know American Sign Language. In short, *Random House American Sign Language Medical Dictionary* provides a comprehensive, reliable source of medical information for everyone who cares about helping each **patient** (PATIENT) to **recover** (AGAIN/HEALTHY).

Guide to the Dictionary

Guide: How to Use This Dictionary

How to Find a Sign

Alphabetization

All the entries in this book, whether complete entries, entries for alternate signs, or cross-reference entries, are shown in **large boldface type** in a single alphabetical listing—e.g., **accident, Ace bandage, acetominophen, ache, acid, acne**[1], **acne**[2]. Spaces and hyphens between words are taken into account, so that **Band-Aid** comes before **bandage,** as it would if the entry were simply **Band.**

Complete Entries

Each complete entry has at least one definition, a description of how to make the sign, and one illustration. However, many of the entries are more complex than that. It is not unusual for a medical term to be constructed of several signs put together, rather like a full sentence. The first entry for **allergy,** for example, is made up of the three sequential signs: **body | not | accept.** These component signs are shown in **small boldface type.**

Multiple Entries for the Same Word

When several entries are spelled the same way, each is marked with a small identifying superscript number. See, for example, the three entries for **confidential.** Note that the second and third of these are labeled "alternate sign." That is because they share the meaning of the first of the entries, **confidential**[1], which contains the definition. Although the second and third therefore lack definitions of their own, they have descriptions and illustrations for alternate signs that can be used instead of those shown at the earlier entry.

When identically spelled entries do have different meanings, each is defined, as at the two entries for **agree-with-one,** the first of which refers to the absorption of food and the second to the absorption of medicine.

Any group of these entries may include one that is simply a cross reference to one or more other signs elsewhere in the alphabet—e.g., **hurt**[2], which says, "See signs for PAIN[1,2]."

Cross References

Many entries include a list of other terms, shown in **smaller boldface,** for which the same sign (or compound sign) is applicable. Because the signs of ASL tend to represent broad concepts rather than specific English words, these additional terms are not always precise synonyms of the main entry. However, they share the entry's concept in some way, and their meanings can all be conveyed with the same sign. The sign at **body,** for example, is also used to express **physical.**

Where appropriate, these additional words are given usage labels (e.g., informal, slang) to indicate that in the context of certain social situations, the sign should be used with some caution.

A cross-reference entry at its own alphabetical listing does not show either a description or a sign. It may, however, give a definition when its meaning is not quite the same as that given for the main entry. A referential entry of this sort sends the reader to one or more complete entries by using small capital letters to point to the referent, where signs and descriptions will be found. Typical examples are the entry for **ABO system,** which says only "See sign for BLOOD TYPE," and the entry for **visible,** which first defines the word as "Able to be seen," and then directs the reader to the appropriate main entry with the instruction, "See sign for VISION."

How to Make a Sign

Illustrations

Every complete entry and every entry labeled "alternate sign" contain at least one illustration. All the drawings demonstrate how a right-handed signer would execute each sign as seen by the listener. The model's right hand is on the reader's left. A left-handed signer should transpose the hands, treating the picture as if it were a mirror image.

Descriptions

Each illustration is accompanied by a description. Within the description, italicized terms such as *A hand* and *C hand* refer to handshapes shown in the chart of the Manual Alphabet (p. xi). Terms such as *1 hand* or *10 hand* refer to handshapes for numbers (p. viii). Other special handshapes, such as *bent hand, open hand,* and *flattened C hand,* are shown on page xii.

An initialized sign (see, e.g., the entry for **centigrade**) is formed with one of the handshapes from the American Manual Alphabet (p. xi), and fingerspelled signs use the Manual Alphabet to spell out short words or abbreviations, as at **attention deficit disorder** or **ADD,** where the instruction reads, "Fingerspell abbreviation: A-D-D."

Using the above conventions, descriptions give detailed instructions on how to make the sign. Typically included in the description are a sign's four standard component parts: (1) handshape, (2) location in relation to the body, (3) movement of the hands, and (4) orientation of the palms. A component can appear more than once. The instructions at **hurt**[1], for example, are:

(1) Beginning with the thumb of the right *A hand*

(2) touching the chin,

(4) palm left,

(3) twist the wrist back,

(4) ending with the palm facing in.

Note that because the orientation of the palms changes during the course of making this sign, it is accounted for more than once.

American Manual Alphabet

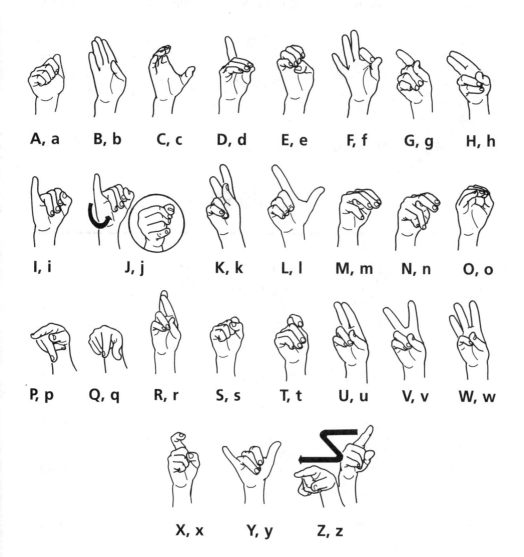

A, a   B, b   C, c   D, d   E, e   F, f   G, g   H, h

I, i   J, j   K, k   L, l   M, m   N, n   O, o

P, p   Q, q   R, r   S, s   T, t   U, u   V, v   W, w

X, x   Y, y   Z, z

Handshapes

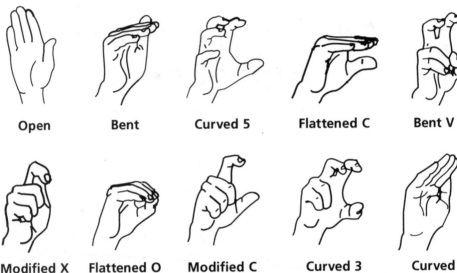

Open   Bent   Curved 5   Flattened C   Bent V

Modified X   Flattened O   Modified C   Curved 3   Curved

Numbers

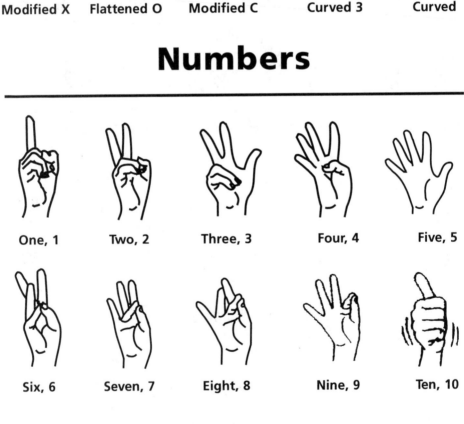

One, 1   Two, 2   Three, 3   Four, 4   Five, 5

Six, 6   Seven, 7   Eight, 8   Nine, 9   Ten, 10

---

abdomen[1] or **belly** (*informal*) The mid-part of the body between the chest and the hips. Same sign used for: **stomach**.

■ **abdomen** Pat the abdomen with the right *open hand*.

---

abdomen[2] or **belly** (*informal*) (alternate sign) Same sign used for: **stomach**.

■ **abdomen** Touch the abdomen with the extended index finger of the right *one hand*, palm up.

---

abdominal hernia See sign for RUPTURE.

---

aberration Any disturbance of the rays of a pencil of light such that they can no longer be brought to a sharp focus or form a clear image. See sign for AMBLYOPIA.

---

abnormal[1] or **unnatural** Not typical; deviating from the standard. Same sign used for: **deformity, dysplasia, malformation**. Related form: **abnormalities**.

■ **not** Bring the thumb of the right *10 hand* forward from under the chin with a deliberate movement.

■ **natural** Move the right *N hand* in a small circle and then straight down to land on the back of the left *open hand*.

---

abnormal[2] or **unnatural** (alternate sign) Same sign used for: **deformity, dysplasia, malformation**. Related form: **abnormalities**.

■ **not** Bring the thumb of the right *10 hand* forward from under the chin with a deliberate movement.

■ **right** Bring the little-finger side of the right *one hand* down sharply on the index-finger side of the left *one hand*.

---

abnormal[3] or **unnatural** (alternate sign) Same sign used for:
deformity, dysplasia, malformation. Related form: **abnormalities**.

- **something** Move the right *one hand* in a small circle in front of the right shoulder, palm facing back.

- **wrong** Bring the knuckles of the right *Y hand* back against the chin.

ABO system See sign for BLOOD TYPE.

---

abortion[1] The removal or expulsion of a fetus prior to natural birth before it can survive.

- **baby** With the right bent arm resting on the left bent arm, swing the arms from side to side with a double movement.

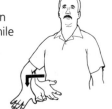

- **remove** Beginning with the fingers of the right *curved hand* on the right side of the abdomen, move the right hand outward while changing to an *A hand* and then opening to a *5 hand*.

---

abortion[2] (alternate sign)

- **remove** Move the right *curved hand* in to the abdomen. Change the right hand to an A hand and move it forward to the right while opening to a *5 hand*, palm facing down.

---

abrasion A scraped spot or area; the result of rubbing away the surface layers of the skin.

- **rough** Move the fingertips of the right *curved 5* hand from the heel to the fingertips of the left palm.

---

abscess¹ A collection of pus around inflamed tissue.

- **point-inside-hole** Insert the extended index finger of the right *one hand* into the hole formed by the left *O hand*.

- **poison** Hold both *bent V* hands in front of the opposite side of the chest, wrists crossed and palms facing in.

- **can't** Bring the extended index finger of the right *one hand* downward hitting the extended index finger of the left *one hand* as it moves.

- **outside** Beginning with the right *flattened O hand* inserted in the palm side of the left *C hand*, bring the right hand upward.

abscess² (alternate sign used for dental situations)

- **inside** Move the fingers of the right *flattened O* hand downward with a short double movement in the palm side of the left *C hand* held near the right side of the mouth.

- **poison** Place the palm sides of both *bent V* hands on the opposite side of the chest, wrists crossed.

- **closed** Beginning with the palms of both *B hands* facing each other in front of the right side of the mouth, fingers pointing up, twist the wrists to bring the index fingers sharply together, ending with palms forward.

- **can't** Bring the extended index finger of the right *one hand* downward hitting the extended index finger of the left *one hand* as it moves.

- **outside** Beginning with the right *flattened O hand* inserted in the palm side of the left *C hand* in front of the right side of the mouth, bring the right hand upward in an outward arc.

absorb

---

absorb **1.** To take in or suck up. **2.** To assimilate by chemical or molecular action. Same sign used for: **attract, magnet**. Related form: **absorption**.

- **attract** Beginning with both *5 hands* apart in front of the body, palms down, pull the hands back to the chest while changing into *flattened O hands*, fingers touching.

---

abstain[1] To refrain from sexual relations voluntarily. Related form: **abstinence**.

- **sex** Touch the index-finger side of the right *X hand*, first near the right eye and then to the right side of the chin.

- **none** Move both *flattened O* hands from in front of the chest outward to each side.

---

abstain[2] (alternate sign) Related form: **abstinence**.

- **sex** Touch the index-finger side of the right *X hand*, first near the right eye and then to the right side of the chin.

- **suspend** With the index fingers of both *X hands* hooked, pull the left hand upward with the right hand.

---

abstain[3] See signs for FAST[1,2].

---

abuse To use improperly; misuse.

- **wrong** Bring the knuckles of the right *Y hand* back against the chin.

- **use** Beginning with the heel of the right *U hand* on the back of the left *S hand*, move the right hand in a small upward circle.

---

accident An unexpected, undesired happening.

- **wrong** Bring the knuckles of the right *Y hand* back against the chin.

- **happen** Beginning with the extended index fingers of both *one hands* pointing forward in front of the body, palms up, flip the hands over toward each other, ending with palms down.

Ace bandage *Trademark.* See sign for ELASTIC BANDAGE.

acetaminophen See sign for ASPIRIN.

ache See signs for PAIN[1,2].

---

acid A compound having a sour taste and capable of neutralizing alkalis and turning blue litmus paper red. See sign for CANCER[2].

acne[1] A condition of the skin characterized by small inflamed swellings. Same sign used for: **pimple**.

- **pimple** Beginning with the right *S hand* near the right side of the chin and the left *S hand* in front of the face, both palms forward, alternatively move the right and left hands forward and back to the chin, flicking the index finger forward each time the hand moves forward.

---

acne[2] or **pimple** (alternate sign)

- **pimple** With the palm side of the right *S hand* against the right cheek, flick the index finger up with a double movement.

---

acquired immune deficiency syndrome[1] or **AIDS** A disease of the immune system characterized by increased susceptibility to opportunistic infections.

- Fingerspell abbreviation: A-I-D-S

---

acquired immune deficiency syndrome[2] or **AIDS** (alternate sign)

- **AIDS** Place the extended index finger of the right *one hand*, palm in, across the fingers of the left *V hand* pointing down.

---

acquired immune deficiency syndrome

acquired immune deficiency syndrome[3] or AIDS (alternate sign)

- **finish** With both *five hands* apart in front of the body, palms up, quickly turn the hands over toward each other, ending with palms down and fingers pointing forward.

- **have** Bring the fingertips of both *bent hands* in to touch each side of the chest.

- **body** Pat the palm side of both *open hands* first on each side of the chest and then on each side of the abdomen.

- **can't** Bring the extended index finger of the right *one hand* downward, hitting the extended index finger of the left *one hand* as it moves.

- **protect** With the wrists of both *S hands* crossed in front of the chest, palms facing in opposite directions, move the hands forward with a short double movement.

- **disease** Touch the bent middle finger of the right *5 hand* to the forehead while touching the bent middle finger of the left *5 hand* to the abdomen.

acrophobia A fear of heights.

- **look-down** Position both *V hands* in front of the chest, fingers pointing down, right hand somewhat lower than the left hand.

- **far-down** Beginning with the knuckles of the left *A hand* on the heel of the right *A hand* in front of the chest, move the right hand down at an angle.

- **fear** Move both *5 hands* toward each other with a short double movement in front of the chest, fingers pointing toward each other.

acupuncture A method of treatment of pain developed by the
Chinese whereby needles are inserted through the skin to
stimulate precise areas.

- **acupuncture** With a bouncing movement, touch the
fingertips of the right *F hand* on the bent left arm, moving
from the wrist to the upper arm.

acute^1 Characterized by the sudden appearance of a severe disease,
usually of short duration.

- **happen** Beginning with the extended index fingers of both
one hands pointing forward in front of the body, palms up,
flip the hands over toward each other, ending with palms down.

- **fast** Beginning with the extended index fingers of both *one
hands* pointing forward in front of the chest, pull the hands
back toward the chest while changing to *S hands*.

acute^2 (alternate sign)

- **hit** Strike the knuckles of the right *S hand* against the extended
index finger of the left *one hand* pointing up in front of the chest.

- **fast** Beginning with the extended index fingers of both *one
hands* pointing forward in front of the chest, pull the hands
back toward the chest while changing to *S hands*.

adapt^1 To adjust oneself to different conditions.

- **change** With the palm side of both *A hands* together, right
hand above left, twist the wrists in opposite directions in order
to reverse positions.

adapt

adapt² (alternate sign)

- **change** With the palm side of both *X hands* together, left hand above right, twist the wrists in opposite directions in order to reverse positions.

- **habit** With the heel of the right *C hand* on the back of the left *S hand*, palm down, move both hands downward while changing the right hand to an *S hand*.

ADD See sign for ATTENTION DEFICIT DISORDER.

addict A person who is physiologically or psychologically dependent on an addictive substance, such as alcohol or a narcotic.

- **addiction** Hook the index finger of the right *X hand* in the right corner of the mouth and pull outward a short distance.

- **person marker** Move both *open hands*, palms facing each other, downward along the sides of the body.

addiction¹ Being a slave to a habit. Same sign used for: **hooked** (*slang*).

- **addiction** Hook the index finger of the right *X hand* in the right corner of the mouth and pull outward a short distance.

addiction² (alternate sign)

- **become** With the palms of both *open hands* together, right hand on top of left, twist the wrists in opposite directions in order to reverse positions.

- **habit** With the heel of the right *C hand* on the back of the left *S hand*, palm down, move both hands downward while changing the right hand to an *S hand*.

addiction³ (alternate sign)

- **habit** With the heel of the right *C hand* on the back of the left *S hand*, palm down, move both hands downward while changing the right hand to an *S hand*.

- **can't** Bring the extended index finger of the right *one hand* downward, hitting the extended index finger of the left *one hand* as it moves.

- **stop** Hit the little-finger side of the right *open hand* on the palm of the left *open hand*.

adenoidectomy Surgery to remove the adenoids, the infection-fighting tissue in the upper throat.

- **adenoidectomy** Beginning with the bent fingers of the right *bent V* hand near each side of the nose, pull the hand forward.

ADHA See signs for ATTENTION DEFICIT HYPERACTIVITY DISORDER.

adhesive tape¹ or **tape** Tape coated with adhesive for holding a bandage in place. Same sign used for: **Band Aid** (*trademark*).

- **tape** Pull the extended fingers of the right *H hand* across the back of the left *open hand*.

adhesive tape² or **tape** (alternate sign) Same sign used for: **Band Aid** (*trademark*).

- **sticky** Touch the bent middle finger and thumb of each hand with a repeated movement, forming an *S hand* each time, palms up in front of each side of the body.

- **tape** Beginning with the extended fingers of the right *H hand* on top of the fingers of the left *H hand*, both palms down, move the hands apart.

administer

administer To dispense, give, or apply. Same sign used for: **feed.**

- **feed** Beginning with both *flattened O hands* in front of each side of the body, palms up and right hand somewhat forward of the left, push the hands forward with a short double movement.

admit-to-hospital

- **register** Tap the extended fingers of the right *R hand* on the palm of the left *open* hand, first to the fingers and then to the heel.

- **enter** Move the back of the right *open hand* forward in a downward arc under the palm of the left *open hand*, both palms down.

- **hospital** Bring the fingers of the right *H hand* first downward and then across from back to front on the upper left arm.

advance directive[1], living will, or physician's directive

A document in which a person stipulates that no extraordinary measures are to be used to prolong life in the event of terminal illness or other terminal circumstances.

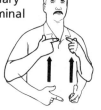

- **life** Move both *L hands*, index fingers pointing toward each other, upward on each side of the chest.

- **will** Bring the index-finger side of the right *W hand*, sharply against the palm of the left *open hand* held in front of the chest.

advance directive², living will, or physician's directive
(alternate sign)

■ **paper** Brush the heel of the right *open hand*, with a double movement on the heel of the left *open hand*, palms facing each other.

■ **tell** Bring the extended index finger of the right *one hand* from under the chin forward in an arc by bending the wrist forward.

■ **my** Place the palm of the right *open hand* on the chest.

■ **wish** Brush the fingertips of right *C hand* downward on the chest.

■ **life** Move both *L hands*, index fingers pointing toward each other, upward on each side of the chest.

■ **die** Beginning with both *open hands* in front of the body, right palm down and left palm up, flip the hands to the right, turning the right palm up and the left palm down.

adverse event See sign for SIDE EFFECT.

advise or counsel To give counsel or advice. Same
sign used for: **affect.**

■ **advise** Beginning with the fingertips of the right *flattened O hand* on the back of the left *open hand*, both palms down, move the right hand forward while opening into a *5 hand*.

affect

affect To attack or take control of a disease. See sign for ADVISE.

afterbirth The placenta expelled from the uterus after childbirth. See sign for PLACENTA.

aftercare The care and treatment of a convalescent patient.

- **from-now-on** Beginning with the palm of the right *bent hand* touching the back of the left *open hand*, both palms in, move the right hand forward a short distance.

- **take-care-of** With the little-finger side of the right *K hand* across the index-finger side of the left *K hand*, move the hands in a repeated flat circle in front of the body.

agree-with-one[1] To allow digestion without difficulty; used to refer to food.

- **food** Bring the fingertips of the right *flattened O hand* to the lips with a double movement.

- **agree** Move the extended right index finger from touching the right side of the forehead downward to beside the extended left index finger, ending with both fingers pointing forward in front of the body, palms down.

agree-with-one[2] To allow absorption without difficulty; used to refer to medicine.

- **medicine** With the bent middle finger of the right *5 hand* in the palm of the left *open hand*, palms facing each other, rock the right hand from side to side with a double movement while keeping the middle finger in place.

- **agree** Move the extended right index finger from touching the right side of the forehead downward to beside the extended left index finger, ending with both fingers pointing forward in front of the body, palms down.

aid¹, assist, or **help** To provide support for or relief to; help. Same sign used for: **rehabilitate.**

- **help** With the little-finger side of the left *A hand* in the palm of the right *open hand*, move both hands upward in front of the chest.

aid², assist, or **help** (alternate sign)

- **aid** Use the thumb of the right *A hand* under the little-finger side of the left *A hand* to push the left hand upward in front of the chest. Note: Add the person marker to this sign to form ASSISTANT or AIDE.

aide See signs for AID², ASSISTANT.

AIDS See signs for ACQUIRED IMMUNE DEFICIENCY SYNDROME[1,2,3].

AIDS virus See signs for HIV[1,2].

ailment A physical disorder or illness, especially of a minor or chronic nature.

- **pain** Beginning with the extended index fingers of both *one hands* pointing toward each other in front of the chest, both palms in, jab the fingers toward each other with a double movement.

- **disease** Touch the bent middle finger of the right *5 hand* to the forehead while touching the bent middle finger of the left *5 hand* to the abdomen.

airsickness Motion sickness caused by travel in an airplane.

- **airplane** Move the right hand with the thumb, index finger, and little finger extended, palm down, upward to the left in an arc beginning in front of the right shoulder.

- **disease** Touch the bent middle finger of the right *5 hand* to the forehead while touching the bent middle finger of the left *5 hand* to the abdomen.

airway A tube that is inserted in the trachea during surgery to maintain unobstructed air passage.

- **airway** Drag the extended index finger of the right *one hand* from the side of the nose down the right cheek to the base of the neck.

- **tube** Beginning with the index finger of the right *F hand*, palm left, on the index-finger of the left *O hand*, palm right, move the right hand up.

---

airway obstruction A blockage in the trachea that prevents the passage of air to and from the lungs.

- **airway** Drag the extended index finger of the right *one hand* from the side of the nose down the right cheek to the base of the neck.

- **prevent** With the little-finger side of the right *B hand* against the index-finger side of the left *B hand*, palms facing in opposite directions, move the hands forward a short distance.

---

alcoholic[1] or **intoxicated** Being in a state in which one's faculties are impaired by alcoholic liquor. Same sign used for: **dipsomaniac, drunkenness, inebriation.**

- **alcoholic** Move the thumb of the right *10 hand* in an arc from right to left past the chin.

---

alcoholic[2] or **intoxicated** (alternate sign) Same sign used for: **dipsomaniac, drunkenness, inebriation.**

- **addiction** Hook the index finger of the right *X hand* in the right corner of the mouth and pull outward a short distance.

- **cocktail** Beginning with the thumb of the right *modified C* hand near the mouth, palm left, tip the index finger back toward the face with a double movement.

Alcoholics Anonymous A self-help rehabilitation organization for alcoholics.

- Fingerspell abbreviation: A-A

---

alert[1], awake, or **wakeful** Fully aware; wide-awake. Same sign used for: **wake up.**

- **awake** Beginning with the index fingers and thumbs of each hand pinched together and all other fingers closed near the outside of each eye, quickly flick the index fingers and thumbs apart forming *bent L hands*.

alert[2] See signs for INSOMNIA[1,2].

allergen A substance that induces an allergy or allergic reaction. See signs for ALLERGY[1, 2, 3].

allergic reaction See signs for ALLERGY[1, 2, 3].

allergy[1] or **allergic reaction** An overreaction of the immune system to an ordinarily harmless substance, resulting in skin rash, sneezing, or other abnormal conditions. Same sign used for: **allergen, hay fever.**

- **body** Pat the palm side of both *open hands* first on each side of the chest and then on each side of the abdomen.

- **not** Bring the thumb of the right *10 hand* forward from under the chin with a deliberate movement.

- **accept** Beginning with both *5 hands* in front of the body, fingers pointing forward and palms down, pull both hands back to the chest while changing to *flattened O hands*.

allergy[2] or **allergic reaction** (alternate sign) Same sign used for: **allergen, hay fever.**

- **nose** Touch the nose with the extended index finger of the right *one hand*.

- **opposite** Beginning with the fingertips of the extended index fingers of both *one hands* touching in front of the chest, both palms in, move the right hand forward and downward, ending in front of the right side of the abdomen.

allergy

allergy³ or **allergic reaction** (alternate sign) Same sign used for: **allergen, hay fever.**

- **body** Pat the palm side of both *open hands* first on each side of the chest and then on each side of the abdomen.

- **opposite** Beginning with the fingertips of the extended index fingers of both *one hands* touching in front of the chest, right hand higher than left hand and both palms in, pull the hands apart, ending with the right hand in front of the right shoulder and the left hand in front of the left side of the abdomen.

alternative medicine or **holistic medicine** A group of health care and treatment practices that are outside the mainstream use of surgery and traditional drugs.

- **other** Beginning with the right *10 hand* in front of the chest, palm down, flip the hand over, ending with palm up.

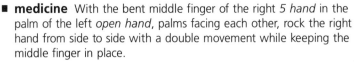

- **choice** Beginning with the bent index finger and thumb of the right *5 hand* touching the index finger of the left *5 hand*, pull the right hand outward while pinching the finger and thumb together. Repeat off the middle finger of the left hand.

- **medicine** With the bent middle finger of the right *5 hand* in the palm of the left *open hand*, palms facing each other, rock the right hand from side to side with a double movement while keeping the middle finger in place.

Alzheimer's disease See sign for DEMENTIA.

amblyopia Dimness of sight without an apparent natural defect. Same sign used for: **aberration.**

- **see** Move the fingers of the right *V hand,* pointing up in front of the eyes, forward a short distance.

- **blur** With the palms of both *5 hands* facing forward in front of the face, move both hands in from side to side going in opposite directions.

ambulance[1] A vehicle for carrying sick or injured people, usually to a hospital.

- **ambulance** Move the right *flattened O hand* in a circular movement near the right side of the head by repeatedly twisting the wrist and opening the fingers into a *5 hand* each time.

ambulance[2] (alternate sign)

- **ambulance** Move the right *curved 5 hand* in a circular movement near the right side of the head by repeatedly twisting the wrist.

ambulatory Not confined to bed; able or strong enough to walk.

- **can** Move both *S hands*, palms down, downward simultaneously with a short double movement in front of each side of the body.

- **walk** Beginning with both *3 hands* in front of each side of the body, palms down and fingers pointing forward, move the hands forward and back with an alternating double movement.

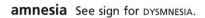

amnesia See sign for DYSMNESIA.

amniocentesis The extraction of a small amount of amniotic fluid in order to determine genetic or other disorders in a fetus.

- **pregnant** Beginning with both *5 hands* entwined in front of the abdomen, bring the hands forward.

- **draw-blood** Beginning with the knuckles of the right *curved 3 hand*, palm up, on the right side of the abdomen, pull the hand outward away from the body.

- **analyze** With both *V hands* pointing toward each other in front of the chest, palms down, move the fingers down and apart with a double movement, bending the fingers each time.

amnion

amnion, amniotic sac, or **bag of waters** The thin, transparent membrane filled with fluid in which the fetus lives until born.

- **baby** With the right bent arm resting on the left bent arm, swing the arms from side to side with a double movement.

- Point to abdomen: With the extended index finger of the right *one hand* touch the abdomen.

- **sac** Beginning with the little fingers of both *C hands* touching in front of the abdomen, palms up, bring the hands apart and upward a short distance, ending with the palms facing each other.

amniotic sac See sign for AMNION.

amphetamine, pep pill, or **stimulant** A habit-forming drug that stimulates the brain and central nervous system.

- **pill** Beginning with the thumb of the right *A hand* tucked under the right index finger, palm left, flick the thumb upward toward the mouth with a double movement.

- **upper** With the thumb of the right *10* hand pointing up, jerk the right hand upward with a short double movement.

amputate To cut off (all or part of a limb or digit) as by surgery. Related form: **amputation.**

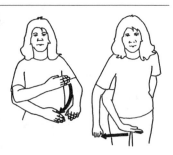

- **amputate-arm** Move the right *open hand*, palm in, downward with a deliberate movement near the extended left arm.
- **amputate-leg** Move the right *open hand*, palm up, from left to right across the top of the right leg.

analgesic A medication that relieves pain. See sign for ASPIRIN.

analyst or **psychoanalyst** A person who analyzes or
who is skilled in analysis of mental or emotional difficulties.

- **doctor** Tap the fingertips of the right *D hand* on the wrist of the
  upturned left *open hand* with a double movement.

- **specialty** Slide the little-finger side of the right *B hand*, palm left
  and fingers pointing forward, along the index-finger side of the left
  B hand held in front of the chest, palm right and fingers pointing
  forward.

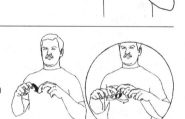

- **analyze** With both *V hands* pointing toward each other in front of
  the chest, palms down, move the fingers down and apart with a
  double movement, bending the fingers each time.

---

analyze **1.** To investigate or treat through
psychoanalysis. **2.** To make a chemical analysis of.
Related form: **analysis.**

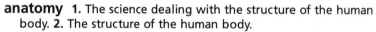

- **analyze** With both *V hands* pointing toward each
  other in front of the chest, palms down, move the
  fingers down and apart with a double movement,
  bending the fingers each time.

---

anatomy **1.** The science dealing with the structure of the human
body. **2.** The structure of the human body.

- **study** While wiggling the fingers, move the right *5 hand*, palm
  down, with a double movement toward the left *open hand* held
  in front of the body, palm up.

- **body** Pat the palm side of both *open hands* first on each side of the
  chest and then on each side of the abdomen.

- **structure** Beginning with the left *S hand* on the back of
  the right *S hand*, both palms down, move the right hand in
  a forward and upward arc to reverse positions. Repeat
  as the hands move upward in front of the chest.

anemia A condition of the blood, leading to weakness, dizziness, and other symptoms, and caused by red blood cells that are inadequate in one or more ways, including number, size, and the ability to carry oxygen. Related form: **anemic.**

- **tired** Beginning with the fingers of both *bent hands* on each side of the chest, palms facing in opposite directions, roll the hands downward on the fingertips, ending with the little-finger sides of both hands touching the chest.

- **not** Bring the thumb of the right *10 hand* forward from under the chin with a deliberate movement.

- **enough** Push the palm side of the right *open hand*, palm down, forward across the thumb side of the left *S hand*.

- **iron** Slide the base of the extended little finger of the right *I hand*, palm left, with a double movement across the extended left index finger, palm right and finger pointing left in front of the chest.

anesthesia[1] or **general anesthesia** Temporary loss of consciousness and inability to feel pain as induced by use of inhaled gases or injected anesthetics. Related form: **anesthetic.**

- **medicine** With the bent middle finger of the right *5 hand* in the palm of the left *open hand*, palms facing each other, rock the right hand from side to side with a double movement while keeping the middle finger in place.

- **go-to-sleep** Beginning with the right *curved 5 hand* in front of the face, move the hand down while drawing the fingertips and thumb together.

- **feel** Move the bent middle finger of the right *5 hand* upward on the chest.

- **none** Move both *O hands*, palms forward, from in front of the chest outward to each side.

- **pain** Beginning with the extended index fingers of both *one hands* pointing toward each other in front of the chest, both palms in, jab the fingers toward each other with a double movement.

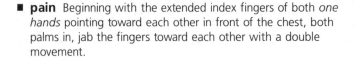

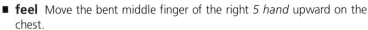
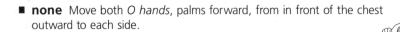
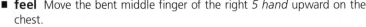

anesthesia[2] or **general anesthesia** (alternate sign used for injected anesthesia) Related form: **anesthetic.**

- **shot** Bend the thumb of the right *L hand* down while touching the left upper arm with the index finger.

- **go-to-sleep** Beginning with the right *curved 5 hand* in front of the face, move the hand down while drawing the fingertips and thumb together.

anesthesia[3] or **general anesthesia** (alternate sign used for inhaled anesthesia) Related form: **anesthetic.**

- **mask** Bring the right *curved hand*, palm in, toward the face with a deliberate movement to cover the nose and mouth.

- **go-to-sleep** Beginning with the right *curved 5 hand* in front of the face, move the hand down while drawing the fingertips and thumb together.

ankle The joint between the foot and the leg.

- **wrist** With the bent middle finger and thumb of the right *5 hand* grasp each side of the wrist of the left *S hand*, palm down, while bending the left hand up and down.

- **ankle** With the extended right index finger point downward toward the ankle.

anorexia nervosa See sign for MALNUTRITION.

anosmia The absence or loss of the sense of smell.

- **can't** Bring the extended index finger of the right *one hand* downward hitting the extended index finger of the left *one hand* as it moves.

- **smell** Move the palm side of the right *open hand* upward in front of the nose with a double movement.

- **nothing** Beginning with the index-finger sides of both *O hands* near the chin, palms facing each other, bring the hands forward and downward while opening into *5 hands*, palms angled down and fingers pointing forward.

---

anoxia or **asphyxia** Lack of oxygen.

- **oxygen** Shake the right *O hand* in front of the right shoulder.

- **none** Move both *O hands*, palms forward, from in front of the chest outward to each side.

- **can't** Bring the extended index finger of the right *one hand* downward hitting the extended index finger of the left *one hand* as it moves.

- **breathe** With the right *5 hand* in front of the chest above the left *5 hand*, fingers pointing in opposite directions and palms in, move both hands forward and back toward the chest with a double movement.

antidepressant medicine Any of several medications that help control depression.

- **medicine** With the bent middle finger of the right *5 hand* in the palm of the left *open hand*, palms facing each other, rock the right hand from side to side with a double movement while keeping the middle finger in place.

- **stop** Hit the little-finger side of the right *open hand* on the palm of the left *open hand*.

- **depression** Beginning with the bent middle fingers of both *5 hands* on each side of the chest, palms in and fingers pointing toward each other, move the hands downward with a simultaneous movement.

antiinflammatory A medication used to reduce inflammation.

- **medicine** With the bent middle finger of the right *5 hand* in the palm of the left *open hand*, palms facing each other, rock the right hand from side to side with a double movement while keeping the middle finger in place.

- **stop** Hit the little-finger side of the right *open hand* on the palm of the left *open hand*.

- **burn** Wiggle the fingers of both *curved 5 hands* with a repeated movement in front of each side of the body, palms up.

antibiotic Any of a group of medications that attack germs and fight infection. Same sign used for: **antibody**.

- **medicine** With the bent middle finger of the right *5 hand* in the palm of the left *open hand*, palms facing each other, rock the right hand from side to side with a double movement while keeping the middle finger in place.

- **infection** Move the right *I hand*, palm forward, from side to side with a repeated movement in front of the right shoulder.

- **destroy** Beginning with both *curved 5 hands* in front of the chest, right hand over the left, palms facing each other, bring the right hand over the left while closing both hands into *A hands*. Then bring the knuckles of the right hand past the left knuckles as the right hand moves forward to the right with a deliberate movement.

antibody Any of numerous Y-shaped protein molecules produced by B cells in the body as a primary immune defense. See sign for ANTIBIOTIC.

antiseptic 1. Free from germs or other microorganisms. 2. An antiseptic drug or chemical capable of freeing an area of the body from germs or other microorganisms.

- **keep** Tap the little-finger side of the right *K hand* across the index-finger side of the left *K hand*, palms facing in opposite directions.

- **clean** Slide the palm of the right *open hand* from the heel to the fingers of the upturned palm of the left *open hand*.

antitoxin The antibody formed in immunizations with a given toxin, used in treating or immunizing against certain infectious diseases.

- **medicine** With the bent middle finger of the right *5 hand* in the palm of the left *open hand*, palms facing each other, rock the right hand from side to side with a double movement while keeping the middle finger in place.

- **against** Hit the fingertips of the right *bent hand* into the left *open hand*, palm right and fingers pointing forward.

- **infection** Move the right *I hand*, palm forward, from side to side with a repeated movement in front of the right shoulder.

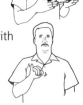

anus or **rectum** A muscular band at the end of the rectum that expands to allow passage of feces or the rectum itself. Same sign used for: **rectal.**

- **anus** Point the extended right index finger first to the thumb side of the left *F hand*, palm facing forward, and then to behind the right hip.

anxiety 1. Extreme unease and apprehension.
2. Agitation and nervousness. Related form: **anxious.**

- **concern** Beginning with the bent middle fingers of both *5 hands* pointing to each side of the chest, left hand closer to the chest than the right hand and palms facing in, bring the hands forward and back to the chest with a repeated alternating movement.

anxiolytic See sign for TRANQUILIZER.

apnea Suspension of breathing.

- **stop** Hit the little-finger side of the right *open hand* on the palm of the left *open hand.*

- **breathe** With the right *5 hand* in front of the chest above the left *5 hand*, fingers pointing in opposite directions and palms in, move both hands forward and back toward the chest with a double movement.

apothecary¹ See sign for DRUGGIST.

apothecary² See sign for PHARMACY.

appendix¹ or **vermiform appendix** A small wormlike tube attached to the intestine.

- **appendix** Bend the extended right index finger, palm back, forward and back with a double movement near the right side of the waist.

appendix

appendix² or **vermiform appendix** (alternate sign

- **appendix** Beginning with the thumb side of the exten right index finger under the palm side of the left *A han* the right index finger up and down with a double movement.

appetite¹ A desire for food.

- **hungry** Beginning with the fingertips of the right *C hand* touching th chest, palm in, move the hand downward a short distance.

appetite² (alternate sign)

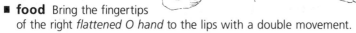

- **hungry** Beginning with the fingertips of the right *C hand* touching the chest, palm in, move the hand downward a short distance.

- **food** Bring the fingertips of the right *flattened O hand* to the lips with a double movement.

- **none** Move both *O hands*, palms forward, from in front of the chest outward to each side.

appetite³ (alternate sign)

- **hungry** Beginning with the fingertips of the right *C hand* touching the chest, palm in, move the hand downward a short distance.

- **want** Beginning with both *curved 5 hands* in front of the body, both palms up and fingers pointing forward, bring the hands back toward the chest while constricting the fingers toward the palms.

- **eat** Bring the fingertips of the right *flattened O hand* to the lips.

apply To smooth on something, such as a salve, ointment, or the like. Related form: **application**.

- **use** Move the right *U hand*, palm forward and fingers pointing up, in a repeated circle over the back of the left *S hand* held in front of the chest, palm down, hitting the heel of the right hand on the back of the left hand each time it passes.

---

appointment¹ A mutually agreed upon time and place to meet, as between doctor or hospital and patient, for medical tests, examination, or the like.

- **appointment** Move the right *S hand* in a small circle and then down to the back of the left *A hand*, both palms down.

---

appointment² (alternate sign)

- **time** Tap the bent index finger of the right *X hand* with a double movement on the back of the wrist of the left *S hand* held in front of the chest, both palms down.

- **must** Move the bent index finger of the right *X hand* downward with a deliberate movement in front of the right side of the body by bending the wrist down.

- **go-to** Beginning with both extended index fingers pointing up in front of the chest, right hand closer to the chest than the left and both palms facing forward, move both hands forward simultaneously while bending the wrists so the fingers point forward.

- **doctor** Tap the fingertips of the right *D hand* on the wrist of the upturned left *open hand* with a double movement.

---

arm or **brachial** The upper limb of the human body extending from the shoulder to the wrist.

- **arm** Slide the palm of the right *curved hand* up the length of the extended left arm beginning at the wrist.

---

armpit The hollow under the arm at the shoulder.
- **armpit** Point the extended right index finger under the raised left arm.

---

aromatic A plant, drug, or medicine yielding a fragrant aroma and used for medicinal purposes.
- **smell** Move the palm side of the right *open hand* upward in front of the nose with a double movement.

- **good** Beginning with the fingertips of the right *open hand* near the mouth, palm in and fingers pointing up, bring the hand downward, ending with the back of the right hand across the palm of the left *open hand*, both palms up.

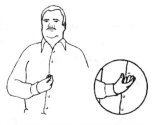

---

arouse To stimulate sexually.
- **arouse** Beginning with the little-finger side of the right *flattened O hand* against the chest, palm up, open and close the fingers to the thumb.

---

arsenic A poison. See sign for TOXIC.

---

artery[1] Blood vessels that carry blood from the heart to the body. Related form: **arterial**
- **blood** While wiggling the fingers, move the right *5 hand* downward with a double movement past the back of the left *open hand* held in front of the chest, both palms in and fingers pointing in opposite directions.

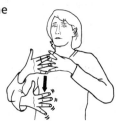

- Point to artery: Move the right extended index finger from the crook of the left elbow to the wrist.

---

artery[2] (alternate sign) Related form: **arterial.**

- **blood** While wiggling the fingers, move the right *5 hand* downward with a double movement past the back of the left *open hand* held in front of the chest, both palms in and fingers pointing in opposite directions.

- **tube** Beginning with the index-finger sides of both *F hands* together in front of the chest, pull the hands apart to the sides.

- **artery** Bring the fingertips of the right *G hand* from the upper chest up the length of the neck.

arthritis, degenerative joint disease, osteoarthritis, or **rheumatoid arthritis** Inflammation of one or more joints.

- **joint** Cup the right *curved hand* over the thumb side of the left *S hand*.

- **can't** Bring the extended index finger of the right *one hand* downward hitting the extended index finger of the left *one hand* as it moves.

- **move** Beginning with both *flattened O hands* apart in front of the body, palms down, move the hands simultaneously in an arc to the right.

articulation The union or the joint between bones.

- **connect** Beginning with both *curved 5 hands* apart in front of the body, bring the hands together to intersect with each other by closing the thumb to the index finger of each hand.

artificial or **synthetic** Made by human skill; not natural.

- **fake** With a double movement, brush the extended right index finger across the tip of the nose from right to left by bending the wrist.

aseptic See sign for STERILE[1].

asexual **1.** Having no sex or sexual organs. **2.** Unaffected by sexuality.

- **not** Bring the thumb of the right *10 hand* forward from under the chin with a deliberate movement.

- **male** Beginning with the thumb of the right *10 hand* on the right side of the forehead, bring the hand downward while opening into a *5 hand*, ending with the thumb touching the chest.

- **not** Bring the thumb of the right *10 hand* forward from under the chin with a deliberate movement.

- **female** Beginning with the thumb of the right *A hand* on the chin, bring the hand downward while opening into a *5 hand*, ending with the thumb touching the chest.

asphyxia See sign for ANOXIA.

aspirin, acetaminophen, or **ibuprofen** A white, crystalline substance used as an antiinflammatory and to relieve pain and fever. Same sign used for: **analgesic.**

- **medicine** With the bent middle finger of the right *5 hand* in the palm of the left *open hand*, palms facing each other, rock the right hand from side to side with a double movement while keeping the middle finger in place.

- **for** Beginning with the extended right finger touching the right side of the forehead, twist the hand forward, ending with the index finger pointing forward.

- **pain** Beginning with the extended index fingers of both *one hands* pointing toward each other in front of the chest, both palms in, jab the fingers toward each other with a double movement.

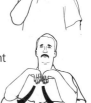

assimilate To convert ingested food to substances suitable for incorporation into the body and its tissues. Related form: **assimilation.**

- **food** Bring the fingertips of the right *flattened O hand* to the lips with a double movement.

- **spread-in-body** Beginning with both *flattened O hands* in front of the chest, fingers pointing down, move the hands downward while opening into *5 hands*.

- **body** Pat the palm side of both *open hands* first on each side of the chest and then on each side of the abdomen.

assist See signs for AID[1,2].

assistant or **aide** A helper, especially a confidential one. See also sign for AID[2].

- **assistant** Use the thumb of the right *L hand* under the little-finger side of the left *A hand* to push the left hand upward in front of the chest.

asthma

---

asthma¹ A disease that makes breathing difficult.

- **asthma** Rub the thumb sides of both *A hands* up and down on each side of the chest with a double movement.

---

asthma² (alternate sign)

- **breathe** With the right *5 hand* in front of the chest above the left *5 hand*, fingers pointing in opposite directions and palms in, move both hands forward and back toward the chest with a double movement.

- **hard** Strike the little-finger side of the right *bent V hand* sharply against the index-finger side of the left *bent V hand*, palms facing in opposite directions.

---

astigmatism An unevenness on the retina causing external rays of light not to converge on a single point as on a normal retina.

- **eye** Tap the extended right index finger at the outward side of the right eye with a double movement.

- **shape** Bring both *10 hands*, palms forward, downward with a wavy movement from in front of the chest to in front of each side of the waist.

- **not** Bring the thumb of the right *10 hand* forward from under the chin with a deliberate movement.

- **right** Bring the little-finger side of the right *one hand* down sharply on the index-finger side of the left *one hand*.

---

asymptomatic Showing no evidence or symptoms of disease.

- **show** With the extended right index finger touching the palm of the left *open hand*, palm right and fingers pointing forward, move both hands forward a short distance.

- **none** Move both *O hands*, palms forward, from in front of the chest outward to each side.

ataxia Loss of coordination of the muscles, especially of the limbs and digits.

- **muscle** Tap the fingertips of the right *M hand* against the upper part of the bent left arm with a double movement.

- **can't** Bring the extended index finger of the right *one hand* downward hitting the extended index finger of the left *one hand* as it moves.

- **control** Beginning with both *modified X hands* in front of each side of the body, right hand forward of the left hand and palms facing each other, move the hands forward and back with a repeated movement.

atrial fibrillation See sign for VENTRICULAR FIBRILLATION.

attack Seizure by a disease, illness, or other condition. Same sign used for: **bout.**

- **a modified form of hit** Bring the knuckles of the right *S hand*, palm in, from in front of the right shoulder to hit the extended left index finger held up in front of the chest, palm forward, forcing the left finger downward to point forward.

attending doctor 1. A doctor having primary responsibility for a patient. 2. A doctor holding a staff position in an accredited hospital.

- **senior** Place the palm of the right *5 hand*, palm down and fingers pointing left, on the thumb of the left *5 hand*, palm in and fingers pointing right.

- **doctor** Tap the fingertips of the right *flattened D hand* on the wrist of the upturned left *open hand* with a double movement.

attention deficit disorder or **ADD** An older name for a condition, usually in children, marked by inattentiveness, dreaminess, and passivity.
- Fingerspell abbreviation: A-D-D

attention deficit hyperactivity disorder[1] or **ADHD** A condition, usually in children, marked by inattentiveness, dreaminess, and passivity.
- Fingerspell abbreviation: A-D-H-D

attention deficit hyperactivity disorder[2] or **ADHD** (alternate sign)
- **attention** Move both *open hands* from near each cheek, palms facing each other, straight forward simultaneously.

- **short** Rub the middle-finger side of the right *H hand* back and forth with a repeated movement on the index-finger side of the left *H hand*.

- **frantic** With the back of the right *bent V hand* on the upturned palm of the left *open hand*, move the right hand around randomly with a twisting movement.

attention Focus of the mind on an object or thought. See sign for CONCENTRATE.

attract See sign for ABSORB.

audiogram The graphic record produced by an audiometer showing a person's hearing levels.

- **graph** Beginning with the left *open hand* held in front of the left shoulder, palm right and fingers pointing forward, bring the fingers of the right *4 hand* down across the left palm, and then drag the back of the right fingers across the length of the left palm from the heel to the fingertips.

- **show** With the extended right index finger touching the palm of the left *open hand*, palm right and fingers pointing forward, move both hands forward a short distance.

-- [sign continues] ---------------------------->

- **how-much** Beginning with the fingertips of both *curved 5 hands* touching each other in front of the body, palms facing each other, bring the hands outward to in front of each side of the chest.

- **can** Move both *S hands*, palms down, downward simultaneously with a short double movement in front of each side of the body.

- **hear** Bring the extended right index finger to touch the right ear.

---

audiologist A person who is skilled in testing hearing levels.

- **person marker** Move both *open hands*, palms facing each other, downward along the sides of the body.

- **specialty** Slide the little-finger side of the right *B hand*, palm left and fingers pointing forward, along the index-finger side of the left *B hand* held in front of the chest, palm right and fingers pointing forward.

- **hear** Bring the extended right index finger to touch the right ear.

---

audiology[1] The study of hearing and hearing measurement.

- **audiology** Move the thumb of the right *A hand* in a circular movement, palm forward, around the ear.

audiology² (alternate sign)

- **audiology** Move the thumb of the right *A hand* in a circular movement, palm forward, around the ear.

- **earphones** Tap the fingertips of both *curved 5 hands* on each side of the head around each ear with a double movement.

audiometer An instrument for gauging and recording acuity of hearing.

- **machine** With the fingers of both *curved 5 hands* loosely meshed together, palms in, move the hands up and down in front of the chest with a repeated movement.

- **show** With the extended right index finger touching the palm of the left *open hand*, palm right and fingers pointing forward, move both hands forward a short distance.

- **hear** Bring the extended right index finger to touch the right ear.

auditory Of or pertaining to hearing. See sign for HEAR.

aural Of or pertaining to the ear or the sense of hearing. See sign for HEAR.

autism A developmental disorder characterized by impaired communication, extreme self-absorption, and detachment from reality. Related form: **autistic**.

- **autism** Move the palm side of the right *5 hand* up and down with a repeated movement in front of the face.

autoimmune Of or pertaining to a disease in which a person's immune system attacks its own tissues.

- **inside** Move the fingers of the right *flattened O* hand downward with a short double movement in the thumb side of the left *O hand* held in front of the chest.

- **body** Pat the palm side of both *open hands* first on each side of the chest and then on each side of the abdomen.

- **protect** With the wrists of both *S hands* crossed in front of the chest, palms facing in opposite directions, move the hands forward a short distance.

- **disease** Touch the bent middle finger of the right *5 hand* to the forehead while touching the bent middle finger of the left *5 hand* to the abdomen.

autopsy or **necropsy** Inspection and dissection of a body after death to determine cause of death.

- **die** Beginning with both *open hands* in front of the body, right palm up and left palm down, flip the hands to the left, turning the right palm down and the left palm up.

- **a modified form of operate** Move the thumbs of both *10 hands* downward in short alternating movements on various parts of the body.

avulse To pull off or tear off forcibly. Related form: **avulsion**.

■ **tear** Beginning with the index-finger sides of both *modified X hands* touching in front of the chest, palms down, pull the right hand back toward the body with a deliberate movement.

awake[1] See sign for ALERT[1].

awake[2] Unable to sleep. See signs for INSOMNIA[1,2].

---

baby A very young child. See signs for NEWBORN[1,2].

---

baby tooth See sign for MILK TOOTH.

---

back[1] The rear upper portion of the body below the neck. Same sign used for: **dorsal, lumbar.**
- **back** Pat the fingertips of the right *open hand* behind the right shoulder with a double movement.

---

back[2] (alternate sign) Same sign used for: **dorsal, lumbar.**
- **back** With the extended right index finger of the right *one hand*, palm up, point to the lower back.

---

back rub A massage intended to relax muscles and improve circulation.
- **back** Pat the fingertips of the right *open hand* behind the right shoulder with a double movement.

- **massage** With both *open hands* apart in front of the body, palms down, move the hands down with a repeated movement closing the fingers to *A hands* each time.

---

backache or **lumbago** A pain or ache in the back, usually in the lumbar region.
- **backache** Beginning with the extended index fingers of both *one hands* pointing toward each other near the right side of the body, right palm down and left palm up, twist the wrists in opposite directions, ending with the right palm up and the left palm down.

---

backbone See signs for SPINE[1,2].

bag of waters See sign for AMNION.

balance To be or hold steady.
- With an alternating movement, bring the right *open hand* and the left *open hand*, both palms down, up and down in front of each side of the chest, shifting the entire torso slightly with each movement.

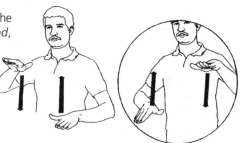

Band-Aid *Trademark.* An adhesive bandage with a gauze pad in the center used to cover minor cuts and abrasions. See signs for ADHESIVE TAPE[1,2].

bandage or **dressing** A strip of material used in dressing a wound.
- **bandage** Beginning with the fingers of the right *H hand*, palm in, touching the little-finger side of the left hand, palm down, move the right hand in a circular movement completely around the left hand.

barbiturate See sign for DEPRESSANT.

basal or **baseline** The measured state of the body or psyche prior to intervention or the onset of disease.
- **base** Move the right *B hand*, palm left, in a flat circle under the left *open hand*, palm down.

bear See sign for HURT[1].

bed rest See sign for CONFINEMENT.

bed ridden See sign for CONFINEMENT.

bedpan A shallow toilet pan used by persons confined to bed.

- **bed** Rest the right cheek at an angle on the palm of the right *open hand*.

- **toilet** Shake the right *T hand*, palm forward, with a small repeated movement in front of the right shoulder.

- **bowl** Beginning with the little fingers of both *C hands* touching, palms up, bring the hands apart and upward a short distance, ending with the palms facing each other.

bedside manner The attitude and approach of a doctor toward patients.

- **doctor** Tap the fingertips of the right *D hand* on the wrist of the upturned left *open hand* with a double movement.

- **behavior** Move both *B hands*, palms forward, simultaneously from side to side in front of the body with a repeated swinging movement.

belch 1. The noisy expulsion of air from the stomach through the mouth. 2. To pass gas from the stomach through the mouth. See sign for REFLUX.

belly *Informal.* See signs for ABDOMEN[1,2].

belly button See sign for UMBILICUS.

bellyache

bellyache See sign for STOMACHACHE.

benign Not cancerous or malignant; harmless.

- **not** Bring the thumb of the right *10 hand* forward from under the chin with a deliberate movement.

- **cancer** Open and tightly close the fingers of the right *curved 5 hand* as it moves with a crawling movement from the heel to the fingertips of the left *open hand*, palm right.

better See sign for IMPROVE.

beverages See sign for FLUIDS.

binocular vision Vision involving both eyes.

- **eye** Tap the extended right index finger at the outward side of the right eye with a double movement.

- **focus** Beginning with both *F hands* in front of the face, right hand closer to the face than the left hand, palms facing in opposite directions, twist the hands downward in opposite directions.

biological See sign for GENETIC.

biology The scientific study of living matter in all its forms and processes.

- **biology** Move both *B hands*, palms forward, in large alternating circles toward each other in front of the chest.

biopsy or **dissection** Removal of a small amount of tissue or cells, such as fluid from a cyst, for laboratory examination that aids in diagnosis. Same sign used for: **specimen.**

- **operate** Move the thumb of the right *A hand*, palm down, across the upturned palm of the left *open hand* held in front of the chest.

- **examine** Beginning with the fingertips of the right *9 hand* touching the palm of the upturned left *open hand* held in front of the chest, turn the right hand over, ending with the right palm facing up.

- **analyze** With both *V hands* pointing toward each other in front of the chest, palms down, move the fingers down and apart with a double movement, bending the fingers each time.

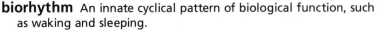

---

biorhythm An innate cyclical pattern of biological function, such as waking and sleeping.

- **body** Pat the palm side of both *open hands* first on each side of the chest and then on each side of the abdomen.

- **regular** Brush the little-finger side of the right *one hand* across the index-finger side of the left *one hand*, as the right hand moves in a double circular movement toward the chest.

---

birth[1] or **born** A coming into life or having come into life.

- Beginning with the back of the right *open hand* against the palm of the left *open hand*, both palms in and fingers pointing in oppo: directions, move the right hand down under the little-finger side of the left hand, ending with the right palm facing down.

birth

birth² or born (alternate sign)

- Bring the right *open hand*, palm in, from the abdomen forward and down, ending with the back of the right hand in the upturned palm of the left *open hand*.

birth control¹, contraception, or contraceptives Control of the number of children conceived or prevention of conception, especially by use of planned contraceptive methods.

- Fingerspell abbreviation: B-C

birth control², contraception, or contraceptives (alternate sign)

- **prevent** With the little-finger side of the right *B hand* against the index-finger side of the left *B hand*, palms facing in opposite directions, move the hands forward a short distance.

- **pregnant** Beginning with both *5 hands* entwined in front of the abdomen, bring the hands forward.

birth defect Any physical, mental, or biochemical abnormality present at birth.

- **baby** With the right bent arm resting on the left bent arm, swing the arms from side to side with a double movement.

- **something** Move the right *one hand* in a small circle in front of the right shoulder, palm facing back.

- **wrong** Bring the knuckles of the right *Y hand* back against the chin.

birthing room An area, whether in a hospital or a birthing center, equipped for delivering babies. See sign for DELIVERY ROOM.

birthmark A spot on the skin that was there at birth.

- **birth** Bring the right open hand, palm in, from the body forward and down, ending with the back of the right hand in the upturned palm of the left open hand.

- **spot** Note: Substitute the location of the birthmark being discussed. Place the index-finger side of the right *F hand*, palm forward, against the right cheek.

black out See signs for PASS OUT[1,2].

bladder or **urinary bladder** An organ that holds urine.

- Beginning with the fingers of both *C hands* overlapping in front of the abdomen, palms facing each other, pull the hands apart a short distance.

- **urine** Tap the middle finger of the right *P hand* against the nose with a double movement.

- **inside** Move the fingers of the right *flattened O* hand downward with a short double movement in the thumb side of the left *O hand* held in front of the bladder.

bleed To lose or discharge blood.

- **red** Brush the extended right index finger downward on the lips.

- **blood** While wiggling the fingers, move the right *5 hand* downward with a double movement past the back of the left *5 hand* held in front of the chest, both palms in and fingers pointing in opposite directions.

bleeder Someone who suffers from hemophilia. See sign for HEMOPHILIA.

blind Not able to see.

- **blind** Jab the fingertips of the right *bent V hand* back toward the eyes with a short, deliberate movement.

blister A thin, rounded swelling of the skin containing watery matter.

- **lump** Place the knuckles of the right *bent hand* on the back of the left *open hand* held in front of the chest, palm down.

- **water** Tap the index-finger side of the right *W hand*, palm left and fingers pointing up, against the chin with a double movement.

bloat To expand or swell, as with air or water.

- **water** Tap the index-finger side of the right *W hand*, palm left and fingers pointing up, against the chin with a double movement.

- **swell** Raise the right *curved 5 hand* a short distance above the back of the bent left arm.

blockage[1] An interruption of normal function due to an obstruction. See signs for CHOKE[1,2].

blockage[2] An obstruction that prevents normal function. See sign for PREVENT.

blood The red fluid flowing through veins and arteries. Same sign used for: **plasma.**

- **blood** While wiggling the fingers, move the right *5 hand* downward from the chin with a double movement past the back of the left *open hand* held in front of the chest, both palms in and fingers pointing in opposite directions.

blood bank A place where blood or plasma is collected, processed, stored, and distributed.

- **place** Beginning with the middle fingers of both *P hands* touching in front of the body, palms facing each other, move the hands apart in a circular movement back until they touch again near the chest.

- **blood** While wiggling the fingers, move the right *5 hand* downward from the chin with a double movement past the back of the left *open hand* held in front of the chest, both palms in and fingers pointing in opposite directions.

- **store** Insert the fingertips of the right *flattened O hand* into the thumb side of the left *O hand* held in front of the chest.

---

blood clot A thick mass that is formed when blood thickens and coagulates. Same sign used for: **thrombus, thrombosis.**

- **blood** While wiggling the fingers, move the right *5 hand* from the chin downward with a double movement past the back of the left *5 hand* held in front of the chest, both palms in and fingers pointing in opposite directions.

- **freeze** Beginning with both *5 hands* in front of each side of the body, palms down and fingers pointing forward, pull the hands back toward the body while constricting the fingers.

---

blood group See sign for BLOOD TYPE.

---

blood poisoning See sign for TOXEMIA.

---

blood pressure, BP, or **pressure** The pressure of the blood against the arterial walls. See also HYPERTENSION, HYPOTENSION.

- **blood** While wiggling the fingers, move the right *5 hand* downward with a double movement past the back of the left *5 hand* held in front of the chest, both palms in and fingers pointing in opposite directions.

- **compress** With the right *C hand* grasp the upper left arm.

blood stream

blood stream See signs for CIRCULATION[1,2].

blood sugar Glucose in the blood.

- **sugar** Bring the fingers of the right *U hand* downward on the chin with a double movement, bending the fingers each time.

- **in** Insert the fingertips of the right *flattened O hand* into the thumb side of the left *O hand* held in front of the chest.

- **blood** While wiggling the fingers, move the right *5 hand* from the chin downward with a double movement past the back of the left *5 hand* held in front of the chest, both palms in and fingers pointing in opposite directions.

blood test A test of a blood sample used to determine blood group, presence of infection or other pathology, or parentage.

- **blood** While wiggling the fingers, move the right *5 hand* from the chin downward with a double movement past the back of the left *5 hand* held in front of the chest, both palms in and fingers pointing in opposite directions.

- **inspect** Move the extended right index finger from near the right eye down to the upturned palm of the left *open hand*, moving from the heel to the fingers.

blood transfusion or **transfusion** The injection of blood or plasma received from one person into the bloodstream of another.

- **blood** While wiggling the fingers, move the right *5 hand* from the chin downward with a double movement past the back of the left *5 hand* held in front of the chest, both palms in and fingers pointing in opposite directions.

- **exchange** Beginning with both *modified X hands* in front of the body, right hand somewhat forward of the left hand, move the right hand back toward the body in an upward arc while moving the left hand forward with a downward arc.

-- [sign continues] --➤

- **other** Beginning with the right *10 hand* in front of the chest, palm down, flip the hand over to the right, ending with palm up.

- **blood** While wiggling the fingers, move the right *5 hand* from the chin downward with a double movement past the back of the left *5 hand* held in front of the chest, both palms in and fingers pointing in opposite directions.

blood type, ABO system, or blood group Any of several distinct, genetically determined classes of human blood.

- **blood** While wiggling the fingers, move the right *5 hand* from the chin downward with a double movement past the back of the left *5 hand* held in front of the chest, both palms in and fingers pointing in opposite directions.

- **what** Bring the extended right index finger downward across the left *open hand* held in front of the chest, palm up.

- **kind** Beginning with both *K hands* in front of the chest, palms facing in opposite directions, bring the right wrist in a circle around the right hand, ending with the little-finger side of the right *K hand* on the thumb side of the left *K hand*.

- Fingerspell blood types: A-B-O

bloodshot eyes Red and irritated eyes caused by dilated blood vessels.

- **red** Brush the extended right index finger downward on the lips, bending the finger as it moves down.

- **eyes** With the extended index fingers of both *one hands* point to the bottom of each eye.

blush See sign for FLUSH.

BM See signs for BOWEL MOVEMENT[1,2].

body The trunk or torso of a person, excluding the head and limbs. Same sign used for: **physical.**
- **body** Pat the palm side of both *open hands* first on each side of the chest and then on each side of the abdomen.

bonding A relationship, especially one that begins at the time of birth between a parent and baby that establishes the basis for an ongoing mutual attachment.
- **relationship** With the thumbs and index fingers of both *F hands* intersecting, move the hands forward and back toward the chest with a double movement.

bone[1] One of the structures forming the skeleton of a vertebrate animal.
- With a double movement, tap the back of the right *bent V hand*, palm up, on the back of the left *S hand*, palm down.

bone[2] (alternate sign)
- **rock** With a double movement, tap the knuckles of the right *A hand* on the back of the left *S hand* held in front of the chest, both palms down.

- **skeleton** With the hands crossed at the wrists, tap the fingers of both *bent V hands* on the opposite side of the chest.

booster See sign for BOOSTER SHOT.

booster dose See sign for BOOSTER SHOT.

booster shot, booster, or **booster dose** A dose of an immunizing substance given to maintain or renew the effect of a previous one.
- **shot** Bend the thumb of the right *L hand* down while touching the left upper arm, with the index finger.

-- [sign continues] ---➤

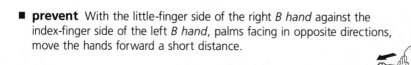

- **additional** Beginning with the right *H hand*, palm up, slightly lower than the left *H hand*, palm down, flip the right hand over, ending with the extended right fingers across the extended left fingers.

- **prevent** With the little-finger side of the right *B hand* against the index-finger side of the left *B hand*, palms facing in opposite directions, move the hands forward a short distance.

- **disease** Touch the bent middle finger of the right *5 hand* to the forehead while touching the bent middle finger of the left *5 hand* to the abdomen.

---

born See signs for BIRTH[1,2].

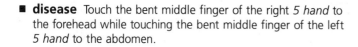

botulism A sometimes fatal disease of the nervous system acquired from spoiled foods in which botulin is present. Same sign used for: **food poisoning, ptomaine poisoning, salmonellosis.**

- **food** Bring the fingertips of the right *flattened O hand* to the lips with a double movement.

- **cause** Beginning with both *S hands* near the body, palms up, move the hands forward while opening into *5 hands*.

- **disease** Touch the bent middle finger of the right *5 hand* to the forehead while touching the bent middle finger of the left *5 hand* to the abdomen.

---

bout The period of time a person has a disease or illness. See sign for ATTACK.

---

bowel movement[1], **BM,** or **defecation** The voiding of excrement from the bowels through the anus; defecation. Same sign used for: **excrement, feces, stool.**

- Fingerspell abbreviation: B-M

---

bowel movement

bowel movement[2], **BM,** or **defecation** (alternate sign) Same sign used for: **excrement, feces, stool.**

- **bowel movement** Beginning with the thumb of the right *10 hand* inserted in the little-finger side of the left *A hand*, palms facing in opposite directions, bring the right hand deliberately downward.

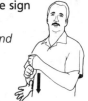

BP See sign for BLOOD PRESSURE.

brace An orthopedic appliance for supporting a weak joint or joints.

- **strong** Move both *S hands* forward with a deliberate movement from each shoulder.

- Grasp the wrist of the right *S hand*, palm in, with the left *C hand*, and move the right arm forward slightly.

braces An oral appliance consisting of wires and bands, used to correct misalignment of the teeth and jaws. Same sign used for: **retainer.**

- **braces** Bring the fingertips of the right *bent V hand* from left to right in front of the teeth.

brachial See sign for ARM.

brain See signs for MIND[1,2,3].

brain damage

- **mind** Touch the index finger of the right *one hand* against the right side of the forehead.

- **damage** Beginning with both *curved 5 hands* in front of the chest, right hand over the left, palms facing each other, bring the right hand in a circular movement over the left. Then close both hands into *A hands* and bring the knuckles of the right hand past the left knuckles as the right hand moves forward to the right with a deliberate movement.

break See sign for FRACTURE.

breakdown or **collapse** A loss of mental health; collapse. See also NERVOUS BREAKDOWN.

- **mind** Touch the index finger of the right *one hand* against the right side of the forehead.

- **breakdown** Beginning with the fingertips of both *curved 5 hands* touching in front of the chest, palms facing each other, allow the fingers to loosely drop, ending with the palms down.

breast 1. Either of the two mammary organs on the upper front part of the female body. 2. The female chest. Same sign used for: **mammary**.

- **breast** Touch the fingertips of the right *bent hand* first on the right side of the chest and then on the left side of the chest.

breast examination examination of one's breasts by manipulation for signs of lumps or other irregularities. Same sign used for: **self-examination**.

- **myself** Bring the thumb side of the right *A hand*, palm left, against the chest with a double movement.

- **breast** Touch the fingertips of the right *bent hand* first on the left side of the chest and then on the right side of the chest.

- While keeping the fingertips of both *bent hands* on the right side of the breast, move the hands around simultaneously with a short movement.

breast feed

breast feed[1] or **nurse** To nurse a baby at the breast; suckle.

- **breast** Touch the fingertips of the right *bent hand* first on the left side of the chest and then on the right side of the chest.

- **feed** Beginning with both *flattened O hands* in front of each side of the body, palms up and right hand somewhat forward of the left, push the hands forward with a short double movement.

breast feed[2] or **nurse** (alternate sign)

- **baby** With the right bent arm resting on the left bent arm, swing the arms from side to side with a double movement.

- **suck-breast** Beginning with the fingertips of the right *5 hand* on the right side of the chest, bring the hand forward with a double movement, closing into a *flattened O hand* each time.

breath analyzer, Breathalyzer (*trademark*), or breath test An instrument into which a motorist breathes as a test for intoxication.

- **breathe** With the right *5 hand* in front of the chest above the left *5 hand*, fingers pointing in opposite directions and palms in, move both hands forward and back toward the chest with a double movement.

- **analyze** With both *V hands* pointing toward each other in front of the chest, palms down, move the fingers down and apart with a double movement, bending the fingers each time.

-- [sign continues] -->

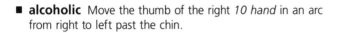

- **for** Beginning with the extended right finger touching the right side of the forehead, twist the hand forward, ending with the index finger pointing forward.

- **alcoholic** Move the thumb of the right *10 hand* in an arc from right to left past the chin.

breath test See sign for BREATH ANALYZER.

Breathalyzer *Trademark.* A brand of BREATH ANALYZER.

breathe or **respire** To inhale air into the lungs and exhale it from the lungs. Related form: **breath.** Same sign used for: **dyspnea, exhale, expel, expire, respiration.**

- With the right *5 hand* in front of the chest above the left *5 hand*, fingers pointing in opposite directions and palms in, move both hands forward and back toward the chest with a double movement.

bridge[1] A partial denture attached to adjacent teeth.

- **tooth** Touch a front tooth with the index finger of the right *one hand*.

- **false** Brush the extended right index finger across the tip of the nose from right to left by bending the wrist.

- Mime putting bridge in mouth: Move the right *modified C hand*, palm up, up to the mouth, ending with the thumb and index finger on each side of the mouth.

bridge

bridge² (alternate sign)

- **bridge** Beginning with both *10 hands* near each side of the chin, palms facing each other, push the extended thumbs upward against each side of the upper teeth.

bridge³ The upper bony ridge of the nose.

- **nose-bridge** Move the extended right index finger from the top of the nose to its tip.

bronchitis Inflammation in the bronchial tubes. Related form: **bronchial.**

- Bring the index-finger sides of both *B hands*, palms facing each other and fingers pointing up, straight down the center of the chest with a double movement.

bruise or contusion A usually painful discolored spot on the skin, as from a blow.

- **purple** Swing the right *P hand* from side to side in front of the right side of the body.
- **spot** Place the fingers of the right *bent L hand,* palm back, on the left upper arm.

bulimia nervosa or hyperphagia An eating disorder characterized by bouts of excessive eating followed by self-induced vomiting, purging with laxatives, strenuous exercise, or fasting. Shortened form: **bulimia.**

- **eat** Bring the fingertips of the right *flattened O hand* to the lips.

- **gag** Insert the extended right index finger a short distance into the open mouth.

- **vomit** Beginning with the right *4 hand* near the mouth, palm left and fingers pointing up, move the hand forward in a large arc.

-- [sign continues] ------------>

■ **decrease** Beginning with the fingers of the right *H hand* across the fingers of the left *H hand*, palms down, flip the right hand over with a double movement.

■ **weight** With the middle-finger side of the right *H hand* across the index-finger side of the left *H hand*, palms angled toward each other, tip the right hand up and down with a repeated movement.

bump See signs for LUMP[1,2,3].

burn[1] An injury caused by heat, abnormal cold, chemicals, poison gas, or electricity characterized by a painful reddening and swelling of the skin.

■ **burn** Wiggle the fingers of both *curved 5 hands* with a repeated movement in front of each side of the body, palms up.

burn[2] (alternate sign)

■ **feel** Move the bent middle finger of the right *5 hand* upward on the chest.

■ **burn** Wiggle the fingers of both *curved 5 hands* with a repeated movement in front of each side of the body, palms up.

■ With a repeated movement, rub the palm of the right *curved hand* up and down on the left forearm.

burp

burp 1. The noisy expulsion of air from the stomach through the mouth. 2. To pass gas from the stomach through the mouth. See sign for REFLUX.

---

bursa A cavity or sac between joints.

- **bone** With a double movement, tap the back of the right *bent V hand*, palm up, on the back of the left *S hand*, palm down.

- **muscle** Tap the fingertips of the right *M hand* against the upper part of the bent left arm with a double movement.

- **soft** Beginning with both *curved 5 hands* in front of each side of the chest, palms up, bring the hands down with a double movement while closing the fingers to the thumbs each time.

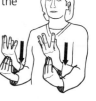

- **between** Brush the little-finger side of the right *open hand*, palm left, back and forth with a short repeated movement on the index-finger side of the left *open hand*, palm right.

---

bursitis Inflammation of a bursa.

- **shoulder** Pat the palm of the right *curved hand* on the left shoulder.

- **joint** Cup the right *curved hand* over the thumb side of the left *S hand*.

-- [sign continues] --➤

buttocks

- **can't** Bring the extended index finger of the right *one hand* downward hitting the extended index finger of the left *one hand* as it moves.

- **move** Beginning with both *flattened O hands* apart in front of the right side of the body, palms down, move the hands simultaneously in an arc to the left.

- **stuck** Bring the fingertips of the right *V hand* back with a deliberate movement to touch the neck.

buttocks[1] or gluteus maximus The fleshy lower hind part of the body.
- **buttocks** Pat the right *open hand* on the right buttock with a double movement.

buttocks[2] or gluteus maximus (alternate sign)
- **buttocks** Touch the extended index finger of the right hand to the right buttock.

59

C-section See signs for CESAREAN[1,2].

cadaver, corpse, or **corpus** A dead body.

- **die** Beginning with both *open hands* in front of the body, right palm up and left palm down, flip the hands to the right, turning the right palm down and the left palm up.

- **body** Pat the palm side of both *open hands* first on each side of the chest and then on each side of the abdomen.

callus A thick, horny skin layer. Related form: **callous.**

- **skin** Pinch and shake the loose skin on the back of the left *open hand* with the bent thumb and index finger of the right *5 hand*.

- **hard** Strike the little-finger side of the right *bent V hand* sharply against the index-finger side of the left *bent V hand*, palms facing in opposite directions.

canal See sign for VESSEL.

cancer[1] A malignant and invasive growth or tumor.

- Fingerspell: C-A-N-C-E-R

cancer[2]**, carcinoma,** or **sarcoma** (alternate sign) Same sign used for: **acid, malignant.**

- **cancer** Open and tightly close the fingers of the right *curved 5 hand* as it moves with a crawling movement from the heel to the fingertips of the left *open hand*, palm right.

cancer[3] or **carcinoma** (alternate sign)

- **cancer** Shake the right *C hand*, palm left, in front of the right shoulder.

---

cane A stick used to aid in walking. Same sign used for: **crutch, walking stick.**

- **stick** Beginning with the index-finger sides of both *F hands* together in front of the chest, palms forward, bring the hands apart.

- **mime using a cane** With the right *A hand*, palm left, near the right hip, move the right hand forward in a series of arcs.

---

cap See signs for crown[1,2].

---

caplet See signs for pill[1,2].

---

capsule See signs for pill[1,2].

---

carbohydrate A group of compounds containing starches, sugars, cellulose, and gums found in whole grains, fresh fruits, and fresh vegetables.

- **food** Bring the fingertips of the right *flattened O hand* to the lips with a double movement.

- **become** With the palms of both *open hands* together, right hand on top of left, twist the wrists in opposite directions in order to reverse positions.

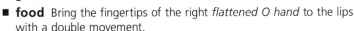

- **sugar** Bring the fingers of the right *U hand* downward on the chin with a double movement, bending the fingers each time.

carcinogen Any agent or substance that tends to produce a cancer.

- **something** Move the right *one hand* in a small circle in front of the right shoulder, palm facing back.

- **cause** Beginning with both *S hands* near the body, palms up, move the hands forward while opening into *5 hands*.

- **cancer** Open and tightly close the fingers of the right *curved 5 hand* as it moves with a crawling movement from the heel to the fingertips of the left *open hand*, palm right.

---

carcinoma See signs for CANCER[2,3].

---

cardiac Of the heart. See sign for HEART.

---

cardiac arrest, coronary or **heart attack**
Abrupt cessation of heartbeat.

- **heart** Touch the bent middle finger of the right *5 hand* on the left side of the chest.
- **hit** Bring the back of the right *S hand* forward to strike the palm of the left *open hand*, both palms in.

---

cardiology The study of the heart, its diseases, and its functions. Note: Add the person marker before this sign to form the medical professional: **cardiologist.**

- **medical** Touch the fingertips of the right *flattened O hand* on the wrist of the upturned left *open hand*.

- **specialty** Slide the little-finger side of the right *B hand*, palm left and fingers pointing forward, along the index-finger side of the left *B hand* held in front of the chest, palm right and fingers pointing forward.

-- [sign continues] ---►

■ **heart** Touch the bent middle finger of the right *5 hand* on the left side of the chest.

cardiopulmonary resuscitation See signs for MOUTH-TO-MOUTH RESUSCITATION[3,2].

care for See sign for MONITOR.

care giver One who assists sick or disabled people.

■ **take-care-of** With the little-finger side of the right *K hand* across the index-finger side of the left *K hand*, move the hands in a repeated flat circle in front of the body.

■ **person** Move both *P hands*, palms facing each other, downward along the sides of the body.

caries See sign for DENTAL CARIES.

carpal Pertaining to the wrist bone.

■ **bone** With a double movement, tap the back of the right *bent V hand*, palm up, on the back of the left *S hand*, palm down.

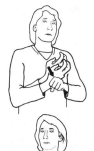

■ **wrist** With the bent middle finger and thumb of the right *5 hand* grasp each side of the left wrist .

carpus See sign for WRIST.

cartilage Rubbery, dense connective tissue that permits smooth movement of the joints. See also PULLED CARTILAGE, TORN CARTILAGE.

- **same-as** Move the right *Y hand*, palm forward, from side to side with a double movement in front of the right side of the body.

- **elastic** Beginning with the bent index fingers of both *X hands* touching in front of the chest, palms in, pull the hands apart to in front of each side of the chest with a double movement.

- **between** Brush the little-finger side of the right *open hand*, palm left, back and forth with a short repeated movement on the index-finger side of the left *open hand*, palm right.

- **bone** With a double movement, tap the back of the right *bent V hand*, palm up, on the back of the left *S hand*, palm down.

cast A rigid surgical dressing usually made of bandages treated with plaster of Paris.

- **rock** With a double movement, tap the knuckles of the right *A hand* near the wrist of the left *open hand* held in front of the chest, both palms down.

- **arm** Note: Substitute location of cast as appropriate. Slide the palm of the right *curved hand* up the length of the extended left arm beginning at the wrist.

castrate To remove the testicles; emasculate.

- **testicles** Shake both *C hands* near each other in front of the abdomen, palms up.

- **slice-off** Move the back of the right *open hand*, palm up, with a sweeping movement across the thumb side of the left *O hand*, palm right, held in front of the abdomen.

casualty See sign for FATALITY.

CAT scan See sign for CT SCAN.

cataract[1] Opacity of the eye lens, causing total or partial blindness.

- **inside** Move the fingers of the right *flattened O hand* downward with a short double movement in the thumb side of the left *O hand* held near the eye.

- **eye** Tap the extended right index finger at the outward side of the right eye with a double movement.

- **vague** With the palms of both *5 hands* together in front of the face, move the right hand from side to side.

- **cover-eye** While holding the bent index finger and thumb of the right *F hand* in front of the right eye, twist the wrist of the left *curved hand* to move the left hand from in front of the little-finger side of the right hand, palm in, to near the nose, palm right.

cataract² (alternate sign)

- **eye** Tap the extended right index finger at the outward side of the right eye with a double movement.

- **white** Beginning with the fingertips of the right *curved 5 hand* on the chest, pull the hand forward while closing the fingers into a *flattened O hand*.

- **spot** Beginning with the right *S hand*, in front of the right eye, palm left, quickly open the fingers to form an *F hand*.

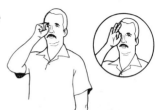

---

catheter A thin flexible tube inserted into the body for the purpose of withdrawing or introducing substances.

- **tube** Beginning with the index-finger of the right *F hand*, palm left, on the index finger of the left *F hand*, palm right, move the right hand up.

- **insert-up** Push the fingertips of the right *flattened O hand*, palm up and fingers pointing up, up in the little-finger side of the left *O hand* held in front of the abdomen.

- **for-for** Beginning with the extended right finger touching the right side of the forehead, twist the hand forward, ending with the index finger pointing forward. Repeat.

- **urine** Tap the middle finger of the right *P hand* against the nose with a double movement.

-- [sign continues] --→

- **drain** Move the right *4 hand*, palm in and fingers pointing left, from near the left *O hand* downward with a double movement.

cauterize[1] To destroy small areas of diseased tissue by burning it with an electric needle or laser beam, freezing with low-temperature instruments, or using a caustic chemical. Same sign used for: **electrocautery.**

- **burn-with-instrument** Point the right extended index finger, palm in, toward the left forearm.

- **stop** Hit the little-finger side of the right *open hand* on the palm of the left *open hand*.

- **blood** While wiggling the fingers, move the right *5 hand* downward with a double movement past the back of the left *5 hand* held in front of the chest, both palms in and fingers pointing in opposite directions.

cauterize[2] (alternate sign) Same sign used for: **electrocautery.**

- **burn-with-instrument** Point the right extended index finger, palm in, toward the left forearm.

- **remove** Beginning with the palm of the right *A hand* on the palm of the left *open hand*, move the right hand upward to the right and then down while opening to a *5 hand*.

- **easy** Brush the fingertips of the right *curved hand* upward on the back of the fingertips of the left *curved hand* with a double movement, both palms up.

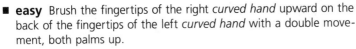

cavity

cavity See sign for DENTAL CARIES.

cell¹ The smallest unit of an organism that is capable of independent functioning.
- Fingerspell: C-E-L-L

cell² (alternate sign)
- **cell** Move the right F hand, palm left, multiple places in front of the head and body.

Celsius See sign for CENTIGRADE.

centigrade or **Celsius** A temperature scale divided into 100 degrees on which the freezing point of water is 0° and the boiling point is 100°.
- **temperature** Slide the extended right index finger, palm down and finger pointing left, up and down with a repeated movement on the extended index finger of the left hand, palm right and finger pointing up.
- Initialize: C

central nervous system The part of the nervous system that controls the body's involuntary acts, composed of the brain and the spinal column.
- Fingerspell abbreviation: C-N-S

cephalic Of or pertaining to the head or the brain. See sign for HEAD.

cerebral Of or pertaining to the head or the brain. See sign for HEAD.

cerebral palsy Impaired muscle control due to brain damage that occurs before birth.
- Fingerspell abbreviation: C-P

cerebrum See signs for MIND[1,2,3].

cervical Of or pertaining to the bone in the neck at the top of the spinal column.
- **spine** Beginning with the little-finger side of the right F hand on the index-finger side of the left F hand, bring the right hand up with a wavy movement.
- **neck** Touch the extended right index finger to the right side of the neck.

-- [sign continues] -------------------------------------->

■ **bone** With a double movement, tap the back of the right *bent V hand*, palm up, on the back of the left *S hand*, palm down.

Cesarean[1], C-section, or **Cesarean Section** 1. Designating a surgical operation for the delivery of a baby. **2.** A Cesarean operation.

■ Initialize: C

■ **operate** Move the extended thumb of the right *10 hand*, palm down, from left to right across the abdomen.

Cesarean[2], C-section, or **Cesarean Section** (alternate sign)

■ **pregnant** Beginning with the right *curved hand* on the stomach, palm in and fingers pointing down, bring the hand forward a short distance.

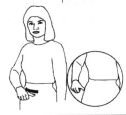

■ **operate** Move the extended thumb of the right *10 hand*, palm down, from left to right across the abdomen.

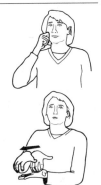

Cesarean Section See signs for CESAREAN[1,2].

chafe To make sore by rubbing.

■ **skin** Pinch and shake the skin on the right cheek with the modified right *X hand*.

■ **rough** Move the fingertips of the right *curved 5* hand from the heel to the fingertips of the left palm with a repeated movement.

change of life See sign for MENOPAUSE.

chapped hands Hands with skin that is dry, roughened, red, and often cracked, especially from wind and cold.

- **hand** Slide the little-finger side of the right *open hand*, palm left, at an angle across the palm of the left *open hand*.

- **dry** Drag the index-finger side of the right *X hand*, palm down, from left to right across the chin.

- **crack** Move the extended right index finger, palm in, across the palm of the left *open hand*, palm angled forward, with a jagged movement.

chapped lips Lips that are dry and cracked, especially from wind and cold.

- **dry** Drag the index-finger side of the right *X hand*, palm down, from left to right across the chin.

- **lip** Move the extended right index finger, palm in, across the lips from side to side.

- **crack** Move the extended right index finger, palm in, across the lips while bending the fingers several times as the hand moves.

charley horse A muscle cramp in an arm or leg.

■ **leg** Beginning with the left *open hand* on the upper leg, bend the leg sliding the left hand downward toward the knee.

■ **cramp** Beginning with the thumb side of right *S hand*, palm right, on the thumb side of the left *S hand*, palm in, twist the right hand forward, ending with palm in.

chart See sign for MEDICAL CHART.

check See sign for EXAMINE.

check up See signs for EXAMINATION[1,2].

cheek The side of the face below the eye.

■ **cheek** Touch the fingertips of the right *flattened C hand* against the cheek.

chemical 1. a substance produced by or used in chemistry. 2. of, used in, produced by, or concerned with chemistry or chemicals. See signs for CHEMISTRY[1,2].

chemistry[1] or **science** The scientific study of the composition, structure, properties, and reactions of matter. Same sign used for: **chemical**.

■ **chemistry** Beginning with the right *10 hand* in front of the right shoulder and the left *10 hand* in front of the left side of the chest, palms forward, move the hands in large alternating circles toward each other.

chemistry[2] or **science** (alternate sign)

■ **chemistry** Beginning with the right *C hand* in front of the right shoulder and the left *C hand* in front of the left side of the chest, palms forward, move the hands in large alternating circles toward each other.

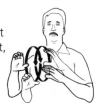

chemotherapy The treatment of cancer by injecting chemicals that kill cancer cells without harming healthy tissue. Shortened form: **chemo.**

- **chemistry** Beginning with the right *10 hand* in front of the right shoulder and the left *10 hand* in front of the left side of the chest, palms forward, move the hands in large alternating circles toward each other.

- **therapy** Beginning with the little-finger side of the right *T hand*, palm in, on the upturned palm of the left *open hand*, move both hands upward in front of the chest.

- **stop** Hit the little-finger side of the right *open hand* on the palm of the left *open hand*.

- **cancer** Open and tightly close the fingers of the right *curved 5 hand* as it moves with a crawling movement from the heel to the fingertips of the left *open hand*, palm right.

chest The top, front part of the body. Same sign used for: **pectoral.**

- **chest** Rub the fingertips of both *open hands*, palms in and fingers pointing toward each other, up and down on the chest with a repeated movement.

chicken pox A contagious viral disease, usually in children, characterized by a low fever and small watery blisters.

- **bird** Close the index finger and thumb of the right *G hand*, palm forward, with a repeated movement in front of the mouth.

- **measles** Beginning with the fingertips of both *curved 5 hands* on each lower cheek, touch the fingers several places on the cheeks as the hands move upward.

childbirth or **parturition** The process of giving birth to children.

- **baby** With the right bent arm resting on the left bent arm, swing the arms from side to side with a double movement.

- **birth** Beginning with the back of the right *open hand* against the palm of the left *open hand*, both palms in and fingers pointing in opposite directions, move the right hand down under the little-finger side of the left hand, ending with the right palm facing down.

childhood diseases A series of diseases that children commonly experience.

- **grow-up** Bring the right *open hand*, palm down, from in front of the right side of the body upward.

- **disease** Touch the bent middle finger of the right *5 hand* to the forehead while touching the bent middle finger of the left *5 hand* to the abdomen.

- **measles** Beginning with the fingertips of both *curved 5 hands* on each lower cheek, touch the fingers to several places on the cheeks as the hands move upward.

- **mumps** Beginning with both *curved 5 hands* on each side of the neck, palms facing in, bring the hands outward a short distance while spreading the fingers slightly.

- **what** Shake both *open hands*, palms up, with a short, repeated side to side movement in front of each side of the body.

chill See sign for RIGOR.

chin The front of the lower jaw below the mouth.

- **chin** Touch the extended right index finger on the chin, palm in and finger pointing up.

---

chiropody See sign for PODIATRY.

---

chiropractic[1] Treatment of bodily ailments through a system of healing based on massage and manipulations to restore normal body functions. Same sign used for: **osteopathic, osteopathy.**

- **medical** Touch the fingertips of the right *flattened O hand* on the wrist of the upturned left *open hand*.

- **specialty** Slide the little-finger side of the right *B hand*, palm left and fingers pointing forward, along the index-finger side of the left *B hand* held in front of the chest, palm right and fingers pointing forward.

- **spine** With the extended right index finger of the right *one hand*, palm up, point to the right side of the lower back. Beginning with the right *F hand* on the thumb side of the right *F hand*, bring the left hand straight up.

---

chiropractic[2] (alternate sign) Same sign used for: **osteopathic, osteopathy.**

- **medical** Touch the fingertips of the right *flattened O hand* on the wrist of the upturned left *open hand*.

- **specialty** Slide the little-finger side of the right *B hand*, palm left and fingers pointing forward, along the index-finger side of the left *B hand* held in front of the chest, palm right and fingers pointing forward.

- **massage** With both *C hands* apart in front of the chest, palms in, twist the hands forward, turning the palms forward. Repeat in front of the abdomen.

---

chlamydia See signs for SEXUALLY TRANSMITTED DISEASE[1,2].

choke[1] To have or cause to have the windpipe blocked. Same sign used for: **blockage.**

- **choke** Touch the fingertips of the right *flattened C hand* against the neck.

- **stuck** Bring the fingertips of the right *V hand* back with a deliberate movement to touch the neck.

choke[2] (alternate sign) Same sign used for: **blockage.**

- **choke** Bring the palm sides of both *C hands* around the opposite sides of the neck, ending with each thumb on one side of the neck and the fingers on the other side and the wrists crossed.

cholesterol A waxy, fatty substance present in many foods, especially meat and eggs, that when eaten collects in the arteries and gall badder.

- **good** Beginning with the fingertips of the right *open hand* near the mouth, palm in and fingers pointing up, bring the hand downward, ending with the back of the right hand across the palm of the left *open hand*, both palms up.

- **bad** Move the fingers of the right *open hand* from the mouth, palm in and fingers pointing up, downward while flipping the palm quickly down as the hand moves.

- Fingerspell: F-A-T

- **inside** Move the fingers of the right *flattened O* hand downward with a short double movement in the thumb side of the left *O hand* held in front of the chest.

- **blood** While wiggling the fingers, move the right *5 hand* from the chin downward with a double movement past the back of the left *5 hand* held in front of the chest, both palms in and fingers pointing in opposite directions.

chronic Of or pertaining to long-term, continuing illnesses that are usually not curable, although symptoms can be controlled.

- **disease** With elliptical repeated movements, bring the bent middle finger of the right *5 hand* in a circular movement toward the forehead while bringing the bent middle finger of the left *5 hand* in a circular movement toward the abdomen.

chronic fatigue syndrome A viral disease of the immune system, usually characterized by debilitating fatigue and flu-like symptoms.

- **always** Move the extended right index finger, palm and finger angled up, in a repeated circle in front of the right side of the chest.

- **tired** Beginning with the fingers of both *bent hands* on each side of the chest, palms facing in opposite directions, roll the hands downward on the fingertips, ending with the little-finger sides of both hands touching the chest.

cicatrix See sign for SCAR.

circulation[1] or **blood stream** The movement of blood through the body in a system of veins and arteries to and from the heart, which acts as a pump.

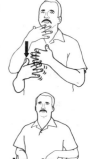

- **blood** While wiggling the fingers, move the right *5 hand* from the chin downward with a double movement past the back of the left *5 hand* held in front of the chest, both palms in.

- **spread** Beginning with both *flattened O hands* on each side of the waist, fingers pointing down, move the hands downward while changing into *5 hands* and wiggling the fingers as the hands move.

circulation[2] or **blood stream** (alternate sign)

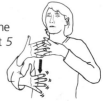

- **blood** While wiggling the fingers, move the right *5 hand* from the chin downward with a double movement past the back of the left *5 hand* held in front of the chest, both palms in.

- **circulate** Beginning with both *5 hands* in front of the chest, fingers pointing toward each other and right hand higher than the left hand, move the hands up and down with alternating double movements.

circumcise¹ To remove the foreskin of (a male) surgically.
- **operate** Move the thumb of the right *10 hand* in a circle around the thumb of the left *10 hand*, palms down.

circumcise² (alternate sign)
- **operate** Move the thumb of the right *10 hand* around the extended left index finger, palms down.

clamp A device used to block blood flow during surgery.
- **clamp** Close the fingers of the right *open hand* firmly around the index-finger side of the left *B hand*, palms down.

claustrophobia An abnormal fear of being in closed or narrow places.
- **close-in** Bring both *open hands*, palms facing each other and fingers pointing up, in to near each side of the head.

- **fear** Move both *5 hands* toward each other with a short double movement in front of the chest, fingers pointing toward each other.

clavicle or **collarbone** Either of two bones, on either side, that join the breast bone and the shoulder blade.
- **bone** With a double movement, tap the back of the right *bent V hand*, palm up, on the back of the left *S hand*, palm down.

- **clavicle** Move both extended index fingers from near each other at the bottom of the neck outward to near each shoulder.

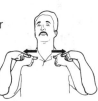

cleanse, disinfect, sanitize or **sterilize** To make clean; free from bacteria.

- **rub** Rub the fingers of the right *open hand*, palm down, back and forth with a quick repeated movement on the upturned palm of the left *open hand*.

- Fingerspell: G-E-R-M

- **none** Move both *O hands,* palms forward, from in front of the chest outward to each side.

climax[1] or **orgasm** The intense physical and emotional sensation experienced at the peak of sexual excitement.

- **climax** With the thumb of the right *curved 3 hand* on the chest, palm left, curl the extended index finger and middle finger downward toward the palm.

climax[2] (alternate sign)

- **climax** Hold the right *C hand* in front of the right shoulder, palm left.

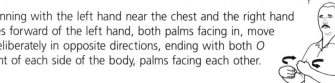

clinic[1] A medical facility for the treatment of outpatients, sometimes at a reduced cost.

- **medical** Touch the fingertips of the right *flattened O hand* on the wrist of the upturned left *open hand*.

- **office** Beginning with the left hand near the chest and the right hand several inches forward of the left hand, both palms facing in, move the hands deliberately in opposite directions, ending with both *O hands* in front of each side of the body, palms facing each other.

clinic[2] (alternate sign)

- **clinic** Bring the fingers of the right *C hand* first downward and then across from back to front on the upper left arm.

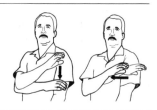

clitoris A small female organ at the end of the vulva corresponding to the male penis. Same sign used for: **vulva.**

- **vagina** Touch the index fingers and thumbs of both *L hands*, palms in and index fingers pointing down, together in front of the body.

- **clitoris** With the extended right index finger, palm left, flick the bent middle finger of the left *5 hand*, palm down, back and forth with a short double movement.

cocaine or **coke** (*slang*) A bitter, addictive narcotic and illicit drug. Also used as a local anesthetic to deaden pain. Same sign used for: **crack.**

- **cocaine** Push the extended thumb of the right *10 hand*, palm left, first upward on the right nostril and then the left nostril.

cochlear implant[1] A surgically implanted hearing device that converts sound reaching the cochlea into electrical impulses that are transmitted by wire to the auditory nerve.

- Touch the fingertips of the right *bent V hand*, palm left, to behind the right ear.

cochlear implant[2] (alternate sign)

- Bring the thumb of the right *C hand* to touch the right side of the head.

- **wire** Bring the extended little finger of the right *I hand* outward from behind the right ear with a wavy movement.

coherent Speaking with logical consistency.

- **awake** Beginning with the index fingers and thumbs of each hand pinched together and all other fingers closed near the outside of each eye, quickly flick the index fingers and thumbs apart forming *bent L hands*.

- **okay** Form an *O hand* and then a *K hand* with the right hand in front of the right shoulder.

coitus See signs for INTERCOURSE[1,2].

coitus interruptus[1] or **withdrawal** Intercourse that is intention-
   ally interrupted by withdrawal before ejaculation.

- **coitus interruptus** Beginning with the extended index finger of
   the right *one hand* inserted in the thumb side of the left *S hand*,
   palm, pull the right hand upward to the right.

coitus interruptus[2] or **withdrawal** (alternate sign)

- **stop** Hit the little-finger side of the right *open hand* on the palm of
   the left *open hand*.

- **intercourse** Bring the right *V hand* downward in front of the chest
   to tap against the heel of the left *V hand* with a double movement,
   palms facing each other.

coke Slang. See sign for COCAINE.

Cold, common cold, or **head cold** A common respiratory illness
   characterized by a runny nose and often a cough and sore throat.

- **cold** Grasp the nose with the thumb and index finger of the right
   A hand and pull the hand forward off the nose with a double
   movement.

colic[1] A condition in young infants characterized by loud and
   prolonged crying, for which no physiological or other cause has
   been found. Related form: **colicky**.

- **baby** With the right bent arm resting on the left bent arm, swing
   the arms from side to side with a double movement.

- **cry** Bring both extended index fingers, palms in and fingers pointing
   up, downward from each eye.

-- [sign continues] --->

- **continue** Beginning with the thumb of the right *10 hand* on the thumbnail of the left *10 hand*, both palms down in front of the chest, move the hands forward.

- **none** Move both *O hands*, palms forward, from in front of the chest outward to each side.

- **wrong** Bring the knuckles of the right *Y hand* back against the chin.

---

colic^2 See sign for STOMACHACHE.

---

collapse See sign for BREAKDOWN.

---

collarbone See sign for CLAVICLE.

---

colon The last major part of the large intestine where waste material is formed into feces and held for elimination.

- **intestine** Move with the right *F hand*, palm in, in a wavy movement from the middle of the abdomen to the right side.

- **bowel movement** Beginning with the thumb of the right *10 hand* inserted in the little-finger side of the left *A hand*, palms facing in opposite directions, bring the right hand deliberately downward, while opening into a *5 hand*.

---

color-blind Afflicted with an often hereditary condition where a person is unable to distinguish certain colors, such as red and green, often seeing only shades of gray, black, and white. Related form: **color-blindness.**

- **color** Wiggle the fingers of the right *5 hand* in front of the mouth, fingers pointing up.

-- [sign continues]

coma

■ **blind** Jab the fingertips of the right *bent V hand* back toward the eyes with a short, deliberate movement.

coma A prolonged state of unconsciousness, including a lack of response to stimuli. Same sign used for: **comatose, faint, unconscious.**

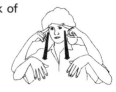

■ Touch both extended index fingers, palms down, to each side of the forehead. Then drop the hands down while opening into *5 hands*, ending with both palms facing in and fingers pointing down in front of each side of the chest.

comatose Affected with or characterized by coma. See sign for COMA.

common cold See sign for COLD.

communicable Able to be spread from person to person, such as a disease. See sign for EPIDEMIC.

compatible Able to be mixed or blended without rejection, such as *compatible blood* or *compatible drugs*.

■ **match** Beginning with both *curved 5 hands* in front of each side of the chest, palms in, bring the hands together, ending with the bent fingers of both hands meshed together in front of the chest.

■ **none** Move both *O hands*, palms forward, from in front of the chest outward to each side.

■ **problem** Beginning with the knuckles of both *bent V hands*, touching in front of the chest, twist the hands in opposite directions with a deliberate movement, rubbing the knuckles against each other.

complete fracture The breaking entirely through of a bone. See also FRACTURE, GREENSTICK, OPEN FRACTURE, SIMPLE FRACTURE.

■ **bone** With a double movement, tap the back of the right *bent V hand*, palm up, on the back of the left *S hand*, palm down.

-- [sign continues] ---➤

- **break** Beginning with both *S hands* in front of the body, index fingers touching and palms down, move the hands away from each other while twisting the wrists with a deliberate movement, ending with the palms facing each other.

- **full** Slide the palm of the right *open hand*, palm down, from right to left across the index-finger side of the left *S hand*, palm right.

complication An undesired event during treatment of a disease that causes additional symptoms or delays in recovery.

- **problem** Beginning with the knuckles of both *bent V hands* touching in front of the chest, twist the hands in opposite directions with a deliberate movement, rubbing the knuckles against each other.

- **increase** Beginning with the right *H hand*, palm up, slightly lower than the left *H hand*, palm down, flip the right hand over, ending with the extended right fingers across the extended left fingers. Repeat in front of the chest at a higher level.

compound The combination of two or more elements or ingredients mixed chemically.

- **mix** Beginning with the right *curved 5 hand* over the left *curved 5 hand*, palms facing each other in front of the chest, move the hands in circles moving in opposite directions.

- **chemistry** Beginning with the right *10 hand* in front of the right shoulder and the left *10 hand* in front of the left side of the chest, palms forward, move the hands in large alternating circles toward each other.

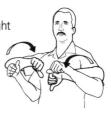

compound fracture See sign for OPEN FRACTURE.

compress, constrict, or squeeze To apply pressure to the surface of the body, usually to stop bleeding. Related form: **compression**.

- **compress** Beginning with both *5 hands* in front of the chest, right hand above the left hand and fingers pointing in opposite directions, bring the hands toward each other while squeezing the fingers together, ending with the little-finger side of the right *S hand* on top of the thumb side of the left *S hand*.

conceive¹ To become pregnant. Related form: **conception**. Same sign used for: **impregnate**.

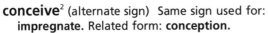

- **conceive** Bring both *5 hands* from in front of each side of the body, palms in, toward each other, ending with the fingers meshed together in front of the abdomen.

conceive² (alternate sign) Same sign used for: **impregnate**. Related form: **conception**.

- **sperm** While touching the wrist of the right *S hand* with the left extended index finger, palms facing in opposite directions, move the right hand forward while opening into a *4 hand*, ending with the right palm left and fingers pointing forward. Beginning with the fingertips of the right *curved 5 hand* on the chest, pull the hand forward while closing the fingers into a *flattened O hand*.

- **egg** Beginning with the middle-finger side of the right *H hand* across the index-finger side of the left *H hand*, palms angled toward each other, bring the hands downward and away from each other with a double movement by twisting the wrists each time.

- **connect** Beginning with both *curved 5 hands* apart in front of the body, bring the hands together to intersect with each other by closing the thumb to the index finger of each hand.

- **pregnant** Beginning with both *5 hands* entwined in front of the abdomen, bring the hands forward.

concentrate To direct one's thoughts on one thing. Same sign used for: **attention**.

- **attention** Move both *open hands* from near each cheek, palms facing each other, straight forward simultaneously.

conception See signs for CONCEIVE[1,2].

concussion An injury to the brain or spinal cord caused by jarring from a blow, fall, or the like.

- **head** Touch the fingertips of the right *bent hand* first to the right side of the forehead and then to the right side of the chin.

- **Locational form of hit** Strike the knuckles of the right *A hand* against the right side of the head, pushing the head to the left.

- **fall-down** Beginning with the extended index finger of the right *one hand* pointing up in front of the chest, move the right hand down to land on the palm of the left *open hand*.

- **pass-out** Beginning with the right *P hand* in front of the right shoulder, palm left, move the right hand down while changing to an *O hand*, ending with the little-finger side of the right *O hand* on the palm of the left *open hand* held in front of the chest, palm up.

condom See sign for PROPHYLACTIC.

condyloma See sign for GENITAL WARTS.

confidential[1] Imparting or consisting of private matters that are entrusted to one in strict secrecy.

- **not** Bring the thumb of the right *10 hand* forward from under the chin with a deliberate movement.

- **tell** Bring the extended index finger of the right *one hand* from under the chin forward in an arc by bending the wrist forward.

confidential[2] (alternate sign)

- **secret** Tap the thumb side of the right *A hand*, palm left, against the mouth with a double movement.

confidential[3] (alternate sign)

- **shut-up** Beginning with the thumb of the *flattened C hand* touching the chin, close the fingers to the thumb, forming a *flattened O hand*.

confinement or bed rest The state of being kept indoors with certain restrictions, often including having to stay in bed. Related form: **bed ridden.**

- **lie-down** With the back of the right *V hand* on the palm of the left *open hand*, both palms up, move the hands forward in a repeated circular movement.

- **must** Move the bent index finger of the right *X hand* downward with a deliberate movement in front of the right side of the body by bending the wrist down.

- **stay** Move the right *Y hand*, palm down, downward in front of the right side of the body with a deliberate movement.

- **bed** Rest the right cheek at an angle on the palm of the right *open hand*.

confusion, delirium, or disorientation A temporary disturbance of consciousness, often accompanied by hallucinations or delusions.

- **think** Touch the right side of the forehead with the extended right index finger.
- **mix** Beginning with the right *curved 5 hand* over the left *curved 5 hand*, palms facing each other in front of the chest, move the hands in circles moving in opposite directions.

congenital Of or pertaining to abnormalities that are present at birth, either inherited or caused by conditions occurring as the fetus grows in the uterus.

- **birth** Beginning with the back of the right *open hand* against the palm of the left *open hand*, both palms in and fingers pointing in opposite directions, move the right hand down under the little-finger side of the left hand, ending with the right palm facing down.

- **up-to-now** Move both extended index fingers from touching the upper right chest, palms in, forward in an arc, ending with the index fingers pointing forward and the palms up.

congestion Clogging of the nasal passage due to an accumulation of fluid and mucus.

- **cold** Grasp the nose with the thumb and index finger of the right *A hand* and pull the hand forward off the nose.

- **can't** Bring the extended index finger of the right *one hand* downward hitting the extended index finger of the left *one hand* as it moves.

- **breathe** With the right *5 hand* in front of the chest above the left *5 hand*, fingers pointing in opposite directions and palms in, move both hands forward and back toward the chest with a double movement.

conjunctivitis[1] or **pinkeye** Inflammation of the outmost surface of the eye.

- **red** Brush the extended right index finger downward on the lips, bending the finger as it moves down.

- **eye** Tap the extended right index finger at the outward side of the right eye with a double movement.

- **infection** Move the right *I hand*, palm forward, from side to side with a repeated movement in front of the right shoulder.

conjunctivitis² or **pinkeye** (alternate sign)

- **pink** Brush the middle finger of the right *P hand* downward on the lips bending the middle finger as the hand moves down.

- **eye** Tap the extended right index finger at the outward side of the right eye with a double movement.

conscious Mentally alert or active. Related form: **consciousness.**

- **awake** Beginning with the index fingers and thumbs of each hand pinched together and all other fingers closed near the outside of each eye, quickly flick the index fingers and thumbs apart forming *bent L hands*.

- **aware** Tap the fingertips of the right *bent hand* against the right side of the forehead with a double movement.

constipation¹ An abnormally difficult bowel movement or infrequent bowel movements.

- **can't** Bring the extended index finger of the right *one hand* downward hitting the extended index finger of the left *one hand* as it moves.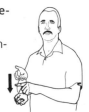

- **bowel movement** Beginning with the thumb of the right *10 hand* inserted in the little-finger side of the left *A hand*, palms facing in opposite directions, bring the right hand deliberately downward.

constipation² (alternate sign)

- **constipation** Firmly hold the thumb of the right *10 hand* in the little-finger side of the left *A hand* held in front of the abdomen.

constrict See sign for COMPRESS.

consultation Deliberation between physicians on a case or its treatment.

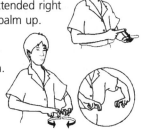

- **discuss** With a double movement, tap the side of the extended right index finger, palm in, on the palm of the left *open hand*, palm up.

- **sit-down-together** Position the knuckles of both *bent V hands* near each other in front of the body, palms down. Then bring the hands away from each other in outward arcs while turning the palms out, ending with the hands in front of each side of the body.

contact lens[1] One of a pair of small plastic lenses worn on the eyes to correct nearsightedness, farsightedness, or astigmatism.

- Fingerspell abbreviation: C-L

contact lens[2] (alternate sign)

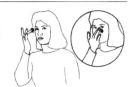

- Bring the bent middle finger of the right *5 hand* first toward the right eye and then toward the left eye.

contact or **exposure** The act or state of touching or being in close proximity to an infected person.

- **close** Bring the back of the right *open hand* from near the chest forward toward the left *open hand*, palms in and fingers pointing in opposite directions.

- **disease** Touch the bent middle finger of the right *5 hand* to the forehead while touching the bent middle finger of the left *5 hand* to the abdomen.

- **maybe** Beginning with both *open hands*, palms up and fingers pointing forward, in front of each side of the chest, one hand higher than the other, alternately move the hands up and down with a double movement.

- **give-me** Beginning with both *flattened O hands* in front of the body, palms up, bring the hands up to touch the fingertips on the chest, palms in.

contagious

contagious or **infectious** Of or pertaining to a disease or condition that spreads from one person to another.

- **disease** Touch the bent middle finger of the right *5 hand* to the forehead while touching the bent middle finger of the left *5 hand* to the abdomen.

- **easy** Brush the fingertips of the right *open hand* upward on the back of the fingertips of the left *curved hand* with a double movement, both palms up.

- **spread** Beginning with the fingers of both *flattened O hands* together in front of the chest, palms down, move the hands forward and apart while opening into *5 hands*.

---

contaminate 1. To infect by contact. 2. To make impure or unfit for use.

- **become** With the palms of both *open hands* together, right hand on top of left, twist the wrists in opposite directions in order to reverse positions.

- **dirty** With the back of the right *5 hand* under the chin, palm down and fingers pointing left, wiggle the fingers.

---

contraception See signs for BIRTH CONTROL[1,2].

---

contraceptives See signs for BIRTH CONTROL[1,2].

---

contraction See sign for CRAMP.

---

control or **manage** To direct the medical treatment of a patient.

- **control** Beginning with both *modified X hands* in front of each side of the body, right hand forward of the left hand and palms facing each other, move the hands forward and back with a repeated movement.

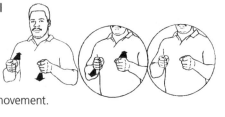

control group A group that closely resembles an experimental group but does not receive the active medication or other intervention, thereby serving as a comparison for evaluation of results.

- **experiment** Beginning with both *E hands* in front of the chest, palms forward and right hand higher than the left hand, move the hands up and down with alternating movements.

- **compare** With both *curved hands* in front of each side of the chest, alternately turn one hand and then the other toward the face while turning the other hand in the opposite direction, keeping the palms facing each other and the fingers pointing up.

- **group-group** Beginning with both *C hands* in front of the right side of the chest, palms facing each other, bring the hands away from each other in outward arcs while turning the palms in, ending with the little fingers near each other. Repeat in front of the left side of the chest.

---

controlled substance Any of a category of addictive or mind-altering drugs, such as heroin or cocaine, whose possession and use is restricted by law.

- **can't** Bring the extended index finger of the right *one hand* downward hitting the extended index finger of the left *one hand* as it moves.

- **buy** Beginning with the back of the right *flattened O hand* in the palm of the left *open hand*, both palms up, move the right hand forward in an arc.

- **medicine** With the bent middle finger of the right *5 hand* in the palm of the left *open hand*, palms facing each other, rock the right hand from side to side with a double movement while keeping the middle finger in place.

- **without** Beginning with the palms of both *A hands* together in front of the chest, bring the hands apart while opening into *5 hands*, fingers pointing forward.

-- [sign continues] --➤

- **doctor** Tap the fingertips of the right *D hand* on the wrist of the upturned left *open hand* with a double movement.

- **permit** Beginning with both *P hands* in front of the body, palms down, swing the wrists to move both hands upward and forward in small arcs.

---

contusion See signs for BRUISE.

---

convalescence Recovery from an illness or surgery.

- **rest** With the arms crossed at the wrists, lay the palm of each *open hand* near the opposite shoulder.

- **become** With the palms of both *open hands* together, right hand on top of left, twists the wrists in opposite directions in order to reverse positions.

- **healthy** Beginning with the fingertips of both *curved 5 hands* touching near each shoulder, bring the hands downward and forward with a deliberate movement while closing into *S hands*.

---

convalescent home See signs for NURSING HOME[1,2,3].

---

convulsion or fit Contortion of the body caused by violent, involuntary muscular contractions. Related form: **convulse.**

- **shake** With both *5 hands*, palms in and fingers pointing down, hanging limply in front of the body, shake the hands with a short, repeated movement.

- **drool** Beginning with the index finger of the right *4 hand* near the right side of the mouth, palm in and fingers pointing left, bring the hand downward with a slow, deliberate movement.

---

coordination Interaction of body parts to move or function properly.

- **coordinate** With the thumbs and index fingers of both *F hands* intersecting, move the hands in a flat circle in front of the body.

- **body** Pat the palm side of both *open hands* first on each side of the chest and then on each side of the abdomen.

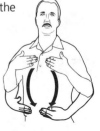

copulate To engage in sexual intercourse. See signs for INTERCOURSE[1,2].

coronary 1. Of the heart. 2. A heart attack. See signs for HEART, CARDIAC ARREST.

coroner or **medical examiner** A public official whose chief duty it is to discover the causes of any death not due to natural causes. Same sign used for: **inquest**.

- **person** Move both *P hands*, palms facing each other, downward along the sides of the body.

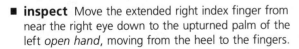

- **inspect** Move the extended right index finger from near the right eye down to the upturned palm of the left *open hand*, moving from the heel to the fingers.

- **cause** Beginning with both *S hands* near the body, palms up and left hand nearer the body than the right hand, move the hands forward in an arc while opening into *5 hands*.

- **die** Beginning with both *open hands* in front of the body, right palm down and left palm up, flip the hands to the right, turning the right palm up and the left palm down.

corpse

corpse or **corpus** See sign for CADAVER.

corpulent See sign for FAT.

cortisone A medication similar to natural hormones used chiefly in the treatment of autoimmune and inflammatory diseases. Related form: **corticosteroid.**

- **shot** Bend the thumb of the right *L hand* down while touching the left elbow with the index finger.

- **open-joint** Beginning with the palm side of the left *curved 5 hand* over the back of the right *S hand,* both plams down, slowly raise the right hand while forming a *5 hand*.

- **reduce** Move the right *bent hand* from in front of the chest downward to a few inches above the left *bent hand*, palms facing each other.

- **pain** Beginning with the extended index fingers of both *one hands* pointing toward each other in front of the chest, both palms in, jab the fingers toward each other with a double movement.

cosmetic surgery or **plastic surgery** Surgery to improve one's appearance.

- **operate face** Move the extended thumbs of both *10 hands*, palms facing forward, in repeated short movements outward on each cheek.

- **help** With the little-finger side of the left *A hand* in the palm of the right *open hand*, move both hands upward in front of the chest.

- **looks** Move the extended index finger of the right *one hand* in a circle around the face.

-- [sign continues] --→

- **young** Beginning with the fingers of both *bent hands* on each side of the chest, brush the fingers upward with a double movement.

cough[1] or **croup** 1. To force air from the lungs with a sharp noise. 2. The act or sound of coughing.
  - **cough** With the fingertips of the right *curved 5 hand* on the chest, lower the wrist with a repeated movement while keeping the fingertips in place.

cough[2] or **croup** (alternate sign)
  - **cough** Bring the index-finger side of the right *S hand*, palm left, back against the chest with a double movement.

cough drop A small medicinal lozenge for relieving a sore throat or cough.
  - **cough** Bring the index-finger side of the right *S hand*, palm left, back against the chest with a double movement.

  - **pill** Beginning with the thumb of the right *A hand* tucked under the right index finger, palm left, flick the thumb upward toward the mouth with a double movement.

cough syrup A medicated, syrup-like fluid, usually flavored and nonnarcotic or mildly narcotic, for relieving coughs or soothing irritated throats.
  - **cough** Bring the index-finger side of the right *S hand*, palm left, back against the chest with a double movement.

  - **syrup** Wipe the extended right index finger, palm down, across under the nose and then shake it downward.

counsel See sign for ADVISE.

CPR See signs for MOUTH-TO-MOUTH RESUSCITATION[1,2].

crab louse A crablike louse that infests body hair in humans, especially pubic hair. See signs for PEDICULOSIS[1,2].

crack A highly addictive, purified cocaine in the form of pellets prepared for smoking. See sign for COCAINE.

cramp, contraction, the cramps, or **spasm** An involuntary, usually painful, contraction or spasm of a muscle in the wall of the abdomen, uterus, or other origin.

- **abdomen** Pat the abdomen with the right *open hand*.

- **cramp** Beginning with the thumb side of right *S hand*, palm right, on the thumb side of the left *S hand*, palm in, twist the right hand forward, ending with the palm in.

cramps, the See sign for CRAMP.

cranium See sign for HEAD.

cremation Reduction of a dead body to ashes by fire or heat.

- **body** Pat the palm side of both *open hands* first on each side of the chest and then on each side of the abdomen.

- **burn** While moving upward, wiggle the fingers of both *curved 5 hands* with a repeated movement in front of each side of the body, palms up.

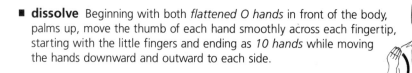

- **dissolve** Beginning with both *flattened O hands* in front of the body, palms up, move the thumb of each hand smoothly across each fingertip, starting with the little fingers and ending as *10 hands* while moving the hands downward and outward to each side.

crippled, lame, or **limp** Being physically disabled, especially in a way that
interferes with use of the legs.

- **limp** Beginning with both extended
index fingers pointing down in front
of each side of the body, palms in,
move the hands up and down with
an alternating uneven movement.

crisis[1], critical point, or **turning point** The point in the course
of a serious disease at which a decisive change occurs, leading either
to recovery or death.

- **serious** With the fingertip of the extended right index finger on the
right side of the chin, twist the hand back and forth with a small
double movement.

- **time** Tap the bent index finger of the right *X hand*, palm down, with
a double movement on the wrist of the downturned left hand.

crisis[2], critical point, or **turning point** (alternate sign)

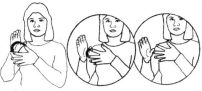

- **crisis** Bring both *C hands*, palms facing each other, upward from
each side of the chest to meet in front of the neck.

critical or **dangerous** Important at a time
of crisis or other turning point.

- **critical** Touch the thumb of the right *C hand*,
palm forward, first to the thumb, then to the
index finger, and then to the middle finger
of the left *5 hand*, palm right.

critical point See signs for CRISIS[1,2].

cross-eyed Having a squint or crossed eyes. See sign for STRABISMUS.

croup See signs for COUGH[1,2].

crown[1] or **cap** 1. An artificial covering for a tooth.
2. The part of a tooth that is covered by enamel.

- **crown** Place the right *curved 5 hand* down over the
extended left index finger, palm in and finger pointing up.

crown² or cap (alternate sign)

- **crown** Push the fingertips of the right index finger, middle finger, and thumb upward on one of the upper front teeth.

crowning The point during the birthing process when the top of the infant's head is visible emerging from the birth canal.

- **baby** With the right bent arm resting on the left bent arm, swing the arms from side to side with a double movement.

- **crowning** Push the right *S hand* forward under the palm side of the left *C hand* held in front of the chest, both palms down.

crutch¹ A support usually fitted under the arm, used to aid in walking.

- **crutch** Beginning with the right *S hand* extended down and the left *S hand* near the right armpit, move the right arm stiffly forward in a series of arcs.

crutch² (alternate sign) See sign for CANE.

CT scan or CAT scan (*Computerized Tomography*) A computerized X-ray that produces exceptionally clear images of parts of the body providing an aid for diagnosis.

- **(Locational form of lie-down)** Move the right *H hand* under the palm side of the left *C hand* held in front of the chest, both palms down.

- **picture** Move the right *C hand*, palm forward, from near the right side of the face downward, ending with the index-finger side of the right *C hand* against the palm of the left *open hand* held in front of the chest, palm right.

-- [sign continues] -- ►

■ **body** Pat the palm side of both *open hands* first on each side of the chest and then on each side of the abdomen.

culture See sign for SPECIMEN.

cure 1. A course of remedial treatment. 2. Successful remedial treatment; restoration to health.

■ **become** With the palms of both *open hands* together, right hand on top of left, twist the wrists in opposite directions in order to reverse positions.

■ **healthy** Beginning with the fingertips of both *curved 5 hands* touching near each shoulder, bring the hands downward and forward with a deliberate movement while closing into *S hands*.

cut See sign for INCISION.

cyanide A poison. See sign for TOXIC.

cyanosis Blueness of the skin caused by a deficiency of oxygen.

■ **can't** Bring the extended index finger of the right *one hand* downward hitting the extended index finger of the left *one hand* as it moves.

■ **breathe** With the right *5 hand* in front of the chest above the left *5 hand*, fingers pointing in opposite directions and palms in, move both hands forward and back toward the chest with a double movement.

■ **skin** Pinch and shake the skin on the right cheek with the right *modified X hand*.

-- [sign continues] ---➤

cyst

- **blue** Move the right *B hand* back and forth by twisting the wrist in front of the right side of the chest.

---

cyst or **wen** An abnormal sac or cavity filled with fluid or diseased matter. Related form: **cystoid.**

- **lump** Place the knuckles of the right *bent S hand* on the back of the left *open hand* held in fron of the chest, palm down.

- **inside** Move the fingers of the right *flattened O* hand downward with a short double movement in the thumb side of the left *O hand* held in front of the chest.

- **full** Slide the palm of the right *open hand*, palm down, from right to left across the index-finger side of the left *S hand*, palm right.

- **bad** Move the fingers of the right *open hand* from the mouth, palm in and fingers pointing up, downward while flipping the palm quickly down as the hand moves.

- **blood** While wiggling the fingers, move the right *5 hand* from the chin downward with a double movement past the back of the left *open hand* held in front of the chest, both palms in and fingers pointing in opposite directions.

D and C or **dilatation and curettage** A procedure that involves stretching of the cervix so that a scraping process can be used to obtain tissue from the lining of the uterus for laboratory analysis to aid in diagnosis.

- ■ Fingerspell abbreviation: D-C

dangerous See sign for CRITICAL.

dB See sign for DECIBEL.

dead See sign for DIE.

deaf[1] Being partially or wholly unable to hear.

- ■ **deaf** Touch the tip or side of the extended right index finger first to near the right ear and then to near the right side of the mouth.

deaf[2] (alternate sign)

- ■ **hear** Touch the extended right index finger to near the right ear.
- ■ **closed** Bring the index fingers of both *B hands* sharply together in front of the chest, palms forward.

death See sign for DIE.

debility A general weakening or deterioration in health. Same sign used for: **feeble, weak.**

- ■ **weak** Beginning with the fingertips of the right *5 hand* touching the palm of the left *open hand* held in front of the chest, collapse the right hand downward with a double movement, bending the fingers each time.

decay, erosion, or **rot** Decline in soundness, health, strength, or vigor.

- ■ **wear-out** Beginning with both *S hands* together in front of the chest, palms up, move the hands forward with a sudden movement while opening into *5 hands*.

decibel

decibel or **dB** A unit for measuring the relative loudness of sound.
- Fingerspell abbreviation: D-B

deciduous tooth See sign for MILK TOOTH.

decline[1], deteriorate, or **worse** A gradual failing in health or strength; wasting away. Same sign used for: **regress, regression.**
- **decline** Touch the little-finger side of the right *open hand* first near the shoulder, then near the elbow, and finally near the wrist of the extended left arm.

decline[2], deteriorate, or **worse** (alternate sign) Same sign used for: **regress, regression.**
- **decline** Move the right *bent hand* from near the right side of the head, palm down and fingers pointing forward, downward and forward in an arc.

decongestant Treatment to relieve mucus congestion of the upper respiratory tract.
- **medicine** With the bent middle finger of the right *5 hand* in the palm of the left *open hand*, palms facing each other, rock the right hand from side to side with a double movement while keeping the middle finger in place.

- **for** Beginning with the extended right index finger touching the right side of the forehead, twist the hand forward, ending with the index finger pointing forward.

- **cold** Grasp the nose with the thumb and index finger of the right *A hand* and pull the hand forward off the nose with a double movement.

decrease[1], lessen, or **reduce** The act or process of reducing something, such as an activity, and the resulting state or the amount of the reduction.
- **decrease** Beginning with both extended index fingers pointing forward in front of the chest, right hand over left hand and palms facing each other, bring the hands toward each other.

decrease[2], lessen, or reduce (alternate sign)

■ **less** Move the right *open hand*, palm down and fingers pointing left, from in front of the chest downward, stopping a few inches above the left *open hand*, palm up and fingers angled forward.

decrease[3], lessen, or reduce (alternate sign)

■ **decrease** Beginning with the fingers of the right *H hand* across the fingers of the left *H hand*, palms down, flip the right hand over with a double movement.

defecation See signs for BOWEL MOVEMENT[1,2].

defect An abnormality or imperfection.

■ **wrong** Bring the knuckles of the right *Y hand* back against the chin.

defend See sign for PROTECT.

deformity See signs for ABNORMAL[1,2,3], DYSPLASIA.

degeneration Passing to a lower condition of vitality or health.

■ **decline** Touch the little-finger side of the right *open hand* first near the shoulder, then near the elbow, and finally near the wrist of the extended left arm.

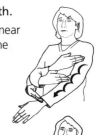

■ **wear-out** Beginning with both *S hands* together in front of the chest, palms up, move the hands forward with a sudden movement while opening into *5 hands*.

degenerative joint disease See sign for ARTHRITIS.

dehydrate[1] To lose an abnormal amount of water from the body. Related form: **dehydration**.

■ **dry** Drag the index-finger side of the right *X hand*, palm from left to right across the chin.

-- [sign continues] --➤

dehydrate

- **thirsty** Move the extended index finger of the right *one hand* down the length of the neck, bending the finger as it moves.

dehydrate[2] (alternate sign) Related form: **dehydration.**

- **none** Move both *O hands*, palms forward, from in front of the chest outward to each side.

- **water** Tap the index-finger side of the right *W hand*, palm left and fingers pointing up, against the chin with a double movement.

- **inside** Move the fingers of the right *flattened O hand* downward with a short double movement in the thumb side of the left *O hand* held close to the chest.

delirious See signs for DELIRIUM[1,2].

delirium[1] or delirious A disordered mental condition marked by confusion, disordered speech, and hallucinations.

- **mind** Touch the index finger of the right *one hand* against the right side of the forehead.

- **not** Bring the thumb of the right *10 hand* forward from under the chin with a deliberate movement.

- **right** Bring the little-finger side of the right *one hand* down sharply on the index-finger side of the left *one hand*.

delirium² or **delirious** (alternate sign)

- **vision** Beginning with the left hand cupped over the right *S hand* in front of the forehead, palms facing each other, move the hands apart while opening into *C hands*.

- **fake** Beginning with the index-finger side of the right *4 hand* touching the right side of the forehead, palm left, move the hand forward in an arc.

delirium³ See sign for CONFUSION.

delivery The act or process of giving birth. Related form: **deliver**.

- **baby** With the right bent arm resting on the left bent arm, swing the arms from side to side with a double movement.

- **birth** Beginning with the back of the right *open hand* against the palm of the left *open hand*, both palms in and fingers pointing in opposite directions, move the right hand down under the little-finger side of the left hand, ending with the right palm facing down.

- **bring** Move both *open hands*, palms up, from in front of the right side of the body in large arcs to the left side of the body.

delivery room An area of a hospital equipped for delivering babies. Same sign used for: **birthing room**.

- **baby** With the right bent arm resting on the left bent arm, swing the arms from side to side with a double movement.

-- [sign continues] --➤

■ **birth** Beginning with the back of the right *open hand* against the palm of the left *open hand*, both palms in and fingers pointing in opposite directions, move the right hand down under the little-finger side of the left hand, ending with the right palm facing down.

■ **room** Beginning with both *R hands* in front of each side of the body, palms facing each other and fingers pointing forward, turn the hands sharply in opposite directions, ending with both palms in and fingers pointing in opposite directions.

---

delusion See sign for HALLUCINATION.

---

dementia or **Alzheimer's disease** Severely impaired memory and reasoning ability, usually with disturbed behavior, associated with damaged brain tissue. Same sign used for: **senile, senility.**

■ **old** Move the right *C hand* from near the chin, palm left, downward a short distance while closing into an *S hand*.

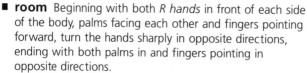

■ **mind** Touch the index finger of the right *one hand* against the right side of the forehead.

■ **decline** Touch the little-finger side of the right *open hand* first near the shoulder, then near the elbow, and finally near the wrist of the extended left arm.

---

dental Pertaining to the teeth. See also sign for TOOTH.

■ **connect** Beginning with both *curved 5 hands* apart in front of the body, bring the hands together to intersect with each other by closing the thumb to the index finger of each hand.

-- [sign continues] --->

■ **tooth** Touch a front tooth with the index finger of the right *one hand*.

dental caries, caries, or **cavity** A hole hollowed out in a tooth, caused by bacteria and decay.

■ **tooth** Touch a front tooth with the index finger of the right *one hand*.

■ **decline** Touch the little-finger side of the right *open hand* first near the shoulder, then near the elbow, and finally near the wrist of the extended left arm.

dentist[1] A person whose profession is treating diseases of and damage to the teeth and gums.

■ **dentist** Tap the fingertips of the right *D hand* against the right side of the teeth with a double movement.

dentist[2] See sign for TEETH.

dentures[1], **false teeth,** or **plate** An artificial replacement for one or more teeth.

■ **false** Brush the extended right index finger across the tip of the nose from right to left by bending the wrist.

■ **teeth** Move the curved index finger of the right *X hand* from right to left across the top front teeth.

dentures

dentures², false teeth, or plate (alternate sign)

- **insert-in-mouth** Push upward on the front teeth with the fingers of the right *flattened O hand*, palm in and fingers pointing up.

deoxyribonucleic acid or DNA A nucleic acid having a very complicated structure and forming the main constituent of the chromosomes of living cells.

- Fingerspell abbreviation: D-N-A

dependence The state of being psychologically or physiologically dependent on either a legal or illegal drug.

- **medicine** With the bent middle finger of the right *5 hand* in the palm of the left *open hand*, palms facing each other, rock the right hand from side to side with a double movement while keeping the middle finger in place.

- **habit** With the heel of the right *C hand* on the back of the left *S hand*, palm down, move both hands downward while changing the right hand to an *S hand*.

depressant, barbiturate, or downer (*informal*) A drug that reduces irritability or excitement; a sedative. See also sign for TRANQUILIZER.

- **pill** Beginning with the thumb of the right *A hand* tucked under the right index finger, palm left, flick the thumb upward toward the mouth with a double movement.

- **downer** Jerk the extended thumb of the right *10 hand*, palm forward, downward with a double movement.

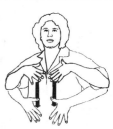

depression¹ A condition of general emotional dejection and withdrawal. Related form: depressed.

- **depression** Beginning with the fingertips of both *5 hands* on each side of the chest, palms in and fingers pointing toward each other, move the hands downward with a simultaneous movement.

depression[2] (alternate sign) Related form: **depressed.**

■ **depression** Beginning with the bent middle fingers of both *5 hands* on each side of the chest, palms facing in and fingers pointing toward each other, move the hands downward with a simultaneous movement.

dermatitis Inflammation of the skin.

■ **red** Brush the extended right index finger downward on the lips, bending the finger as it moves down.

■ **skin** Pinch and shake the skin on the right cheek with the right *modified X hand*.

■ **scratch** Move the fingertips of the right *curved 5 hand* up and down with a double movement on the other hand.

dermatologist See sign for DERMATOLOGY.

dermatology The branch of medicine dealing with the skin and its diseases. Note: Add the person marker before this sign to form the medical professional: **dermatologist.**

■ **medical** Touch the fingertips of the right *flattened O hand* on the wrist of the upturned left *open hand*.

■ **specialty** Slide the little-finger side of the right *B hand*, palm left and fingers pointing forward, along the index-finger side of the left *B hand* held in front of the chest, palm right and fingers pointing forward.

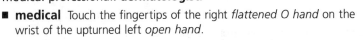

■ **skin** Pinch and shake the loose skin on the back of the left *open hand* with the bent thumb and index finger of the right *5 hand*.

dermis

dermis The thick layer of skin directly under the epidermis.

- **layer** Slide the thumb of the right *G hand*, palm left, from the wrist to off the fingers of the back of the left *open hand* held in front of the chest, palm down.

- **under** Move the right *B hand* from in front of the chest downward and forward under the left *open hand* held in front of the chest, palm down and fingers pointing right.

- **skin** Pinch and shake the loose skin on the back of the left *open hand* with the bent thumb and index finger of the right *5 hand*.

desiccant Completely dried up. Related form: **desiccate.**

- **become** With the palms of both *open hands* together, right hand on top of left, twist the wrists in opposite directions in order to reverse positions.

- **dry** Drag the index-finger side of the right *X hand*, palm down, from left to right across the chin.

detect To observe; become aware of.

- **notice** Bring the curved index finger of the right *X hand* from touching the cheek near the right eye downward to touch the palm of the left *open hand*, palm right in front of the chest.

deteriorate See signs for DECLINE[1,2].

detoxification The process of withdrawing a person from dependence on alcohol. Related forms: **detox** (*informal*), **detoxify.**

- **quit** Beginning with the extended fingers of the right *H hand* inside the opening of the left *O hand* held in front of the body, palm right, bring the right hand upward, ending in front of the right shoulder, palm left and fingers pointing up.

-- [sign continues] --->

■ **addiction** Hook the index finger of the right *X hand* in the right corner of the mouth and pull outward a short distance.

■ **habit** With the heel of the right *C hand* on the back of the left *S hand,* move both hands downward while changing the right hand to an *S hand*.

develop[1] To go through a process of natural growth. Related form: **development**.

■ **grow** Bring the right *flattened O hand*, palm in and fingers pointing up, up through the left *C hand*, palm right, while spreading the right fingers into a *5 hand*.

develop[2] (alternate sign) Related form: **development**.

■ **develop** Move the fingertips of the right *D hand*, palm left, upward from the heel to the fingers of the left *open hand*, palm right and fingers pointing up.

developmentally disabled See signs for MENTAL RETARDATION[1,2].

deviant Characterized as different from an accepted standard.

■ **different** Beginning with both extended index fingers crossed in front of the chest, palms forward, bring the hands apart from each other with a deliberate movement.

dexfenfluramine See sign for DIET PILLS.

diabetes or **diabetes mellitus** Disorders characterized by high levels of glucose in the blood.

■ **blood** While wiggling the fingers, move the right *5 hand* from the chin downward with a double movement past the back of the left *5 hand* held in front of the chest, both palms in and fingers pointing in opposite directions.

-- [sign continues]

diabetes mellitus

- **exceed** Beginning with the fingers of the right *bent hand* on the back of the left *bent hand*, both palms down, bring the right hand upward in an arc.

- **sugar** Bring the fingers of the right *U hand* downward on the chin with a double movement, bending the fingers each time.

---

diabetes mellitus See sign for DIABETES.

---

diagnosis¹ The process of finding out the nature of a disease by a medical examination. Related form: **diagnose.**

- **medical** Touch the fingertips of the right *flattened O hand* on the wrist of the upturned left *open hand*.

- **analyze** With both *V hands* pointing toward each other in front of the chest, palms down, move the fingers down and apart with a double movement, bending the fingers each time.

- **decide** Move both *F hands,* palms facing each other, downward. in front of each side of the body.

---

diagnosis² The decision as to the nature of a disease as determined by a medical examination. Related form: **diagnose.**

- **explain** Beginning with the fingers of both *F hands* in front of the chest, palms facing each other and finger pointing forward, move the hands forward and back with an alternating movement.

-- [sign continues] ---→

- **problem** Beginning with the knuckles of both *bent V hands* touching in front of the chest, twist the hands in opposite directions with a deliberate movement, rubbing the knuckles against each other.

- **your** Push the palm of the right *open hand*, palm forward and fingers pointing up, toward the person being talked to.

diagnosis[3] (alternate sign) Related form: **diagnose**.

- **diagnosis** Bring the right *D hand* from near the right cheek, downward to the palm of the left *open hand* and then across the left palm off the fingertips.

dialysis[1] The removal of natural wastes from the bloodstream of a person suffering from kidney failure.

- **machine** With the fingers of both *curved 5 hands* loosely meshed together, palms in, move the hands up and down in front of the chest with a repeated movement.

- **exchange** Beginning with both *modified X hands* in front of the body, right hand somewhat forward of the left hand, move the right hand back toward the body in an upward arc while moving the left hand forward with a downward arc.

- **clean** Slide the palm of the right *open hand* from the heel to the fingers of the upturned palm of the left *open hand*.

- **blood** While wiggling the fingers, move the right *5 hand* from the chin downward with a double movement past the back of the left *5 hand* held in front of the chest, both palms in and fingers pointing in opposite directions.

dialysis

dialysis[2] (alternate sign)

- **dialysis** Brush the fingertips of the right *D hand* on the bent left arm as the right hand moves upward in a double circular movement.

diaphragm[1] The wall of muscle separating the chest and the abdominal cavities.

- **muscle** Tap the fingertips of the right *M hand* against the upper part of the bent left arm with a double movement.

- **between** Brush the little-finger side of the right *open hand*, palm left, back and forth with a short repeated movement on the index-finger side of the left *open hand*, palm right.

- **chest** Place the fingertips of both *open hands*, palms in and fingers pointing toward each other, on the chest.

- **abdomen** Place the fingertips of both *open hands*, palms in and fingers pointing toward each other, on each side of the upper abdomen.

diaphragm[2] A thin, dome-shaped device worn during sexual intercourse to prevent pregnancy.

- **sex** Touch the index-finger side of the right *X hand*, first near the right eye and then to the right side of the chin.

- **round** Place the curved thumb and index finger of the right *5 hand* on the curved thumb and index finger of the left *5 hand*, palms facing each other.

-- [sign continues] -->

■ **inside** Beginning with the fingertips of the right *flattened O hand*, palm up and fingers pointing up, inserted up in the little-finger side of the left *O hand*, push the right hand up through the left hand.

---

diarrhea[1] An abnormally frequent or abundant discharge of loose or fluid matter from the bowels.

■ **nausea** Move the fingertips of the right *curved 5 hand* in a repeated circle on the stomach.

■ **bowel movement** Beginning with the thumb of the right *10 hand* inserted in the little-finger side of the left *A hand*, palms facing in opposite directions, bring the right hand deliberately downward.

---

diarrhea[2] (alternate sign)

■ **toilet** Shake the right *T hand*, palm forward, with a small repeated movement in front of the right shoulder.

■ **back-and-forth** Move the right *10 hand*, palm left, forward and back with a repeated movement in front of the right side of the chest.

---

die, expire, perish, or **succumb** To stop living. Same sign used for: **dead, death.**

■ **die** Beginning with both *open hands* in front of the body, right palm down and left palm up, flip the hands to the right, turning the right palm up and the left palm down.

---

diet

diet[1] A special selection of foods and drinks consumed in consideration of the effects on one's health.

- **precise** Beginning with the right *modified X hand* over the left *modified X hand,* move the right hand in a small circle and then down to touch fingertips together in front of the chest.

- **eat** Bring the fingertips of the right *flattened O hand* to the lips.

- **avoid** Beginning with the knuckles of the right *A hand*, palm left, near the base heel of the left *A hand*, palm right, bring the right hand back toward the body with a wavy movement.

- **disease** Touch the bent middle finger of the right *5 hand* to the forehead while touching the bent middle finger of the left *5 hand* to the abdomen.

diet[2] (alternate sign)

- **limit** Beginning with both *bent hands* in front of the chest, right hand above the left hand and both palms down, move the hands forward simultaneously.

- **food** Bring the fingertips of the right *flattened O hand* to the lips with a double movement.

- **right** Bring the little-finger side of the right *one hand* down sharply on the index-finger side of the left *one hand*.

-- [sign continues] ---→

■ **food** Bring the fingertips of the right *flattened O hand* to the lips with a double movement.

diet³ (alternate sign)

■ **eat** Bring the fingertips of the right *flattened O hand* to the lips.

■ **drink** Beginning with the thumb of the right *C hand* near the chin, palm left, tip the hand up toward the face.

■ **you** Point the right extended index finger forward toward the referent.

diet⁴ A limitation of the amount or kind of food a person eats in order to lose weight.

■ Beginning with both L hands in front of each side of the chest, palms up, swing the hands downward by twisting the wrists, ending with hands in front of each side of the waist, both palms facing down.

diet⁵ (alternate sign)

■ **decrease** Beginning with the fingers of the right *H hand* across the fingers of the left *H hand*, palms down, flip the right hand over the left fingertips with a double movement.

-- [sign continues] --➤

diet pills

- **regular** Brush the little-finger side of the right *one hand* across the index-finger side of the left *one hand*, as the right hand moves in a double circular movement toward the chest.

- **weight** With the middle-finger side of the right *H hand* across the index-finger side of the left *H hand*, palms angled toward each other, tip the right hand up and down with a repeated movement.

---

diet pills or **dexfenfluramine** Medication that helps to treat obesity by curbing one's appetite.

- **pill** Beginning with the index finger of the right *A hand* tucked under the right thumb, palm in, flick the index finger toward the mouth with a double movement.

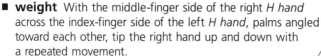

- **hungry** Beginning with the fingertips of the right *C hand* touching the chest, palm in, move the hand downward a short distance.

- **less** Move the right *bent hand*, palm down and fingers pointing left, from in front of the chest downward, stopping a few inches above the left *open hand*, palm up and fingers angled forward.

---

dietician A person who is an expert in nutrition and dietetics.

- **person** Move both *P hands*, palms facing each other, downward along the sides of the body.

- **specialty** Slide the little-finger side of the right *B hand*, palm left and fingers pointing forward, along the index-finger side of the left *B hand* held in front of the chest, palm right and fingers pointing forward.

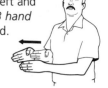

-- [sign continues] ------------------>

■ **eat** Bring the fingertips of the right *flattened O hand* to the lips.

■ **regular** Brush the little-finger side of the right *one hand* across the index-finger side of the left *one hand*, as the right hand moves in a double circular movement toward the chest.

difficulty See sign for DISORDER.

digestion The processing of food for absorption into the blood stream. Same sign used for: **peptic.**

■ **food** Bring the fingertips of the right *flattened O hand* to the lips with a double movement.

■ **chew** With the palm sides of both *A hands* together, right hand on top of the left hand in front of the abdomen, move the right hand in small repeated circles, causing the knuckles of the two hands to rub together.

digitalis[1] A drug used to treat congestive heart failure and some other heart diseases.

■ **medicine** With the bent middle finger of the right *5 hand* in the palm of the left *open hand*, palms facing each other, rock the right hand from side to side with a double movement while keeping the middle finger in place.

■ **increase** Beginning with the right *H hand*, palm up, slightly lower than the left *H hand*, palm down, flip the right hand over, ending with the extended right fingers across the extended left fingers. Repeat several times moving the hands upward each time.

■ **heartbeat** Touch the bent middle finger of the right *5 hand* on the left side of the chest. Then tap the palm side of the right *A hand* against the chest with a double movement.

digitalis

digitalis[2] (alternate sign)

■ **heart** Touch the bent middle finger of the right *5 hand* on the left side of the chest.

■ **medicine** With the bent middle finger of the right *5 hand* in the palm of the left *open hand*, palms facing each other, rock the right hand from side to side with a double movement while keeping the middle finger in place.

dilatation and curettage See sign for D AND C.

dilate[1] To enlarge the pupil of the eye through medicine for the purpose of examination. Related form: **dilation.**

■ **spot** Beginning with the right *S hand*, palm left, in front of the right eye, quickly open the fingers to form an *F hand*.

dilate[2] To enlarge the cervix during labor, whether through normal processes or artificially, for the purpose of making space for the birth of a baby. Related form: **dilation.**

■ **dilate** Beginning with the left *C hand* around the right *S hand*, palms facing each other in front of the abdomen, move the right hand a short distance to the right while opening into a *C hand*, ending with the fingers of the right *C hand* held by the fingers of the left *C hand*.

dilute To make thinner or less potent by mixing with another substance.

■ **mix** Beginning with the right *curved 5 hand* over the left *curved 5 hand*, palms facing each other in front of the chest, move the hands in circles moving in opposite directions.

■ **become** With the palms of both *open hands* together, right hand on top of left, twist the wrists in opposite directions in order to reverse positions.

-- [sign continues] ---→

- **weak** Beginning with the fingertips of the right *5 hand* touching the palm of the left *open hand* held in front of the chest, collapse the right hand downward with a double movement, bending the fingers each time.

---

diphtheria A contagious bacterial disease with fever in which breathing is obstructed.

- **diphtheria** Brush the fingertips of the right *D hand* downward on the throat with a double movement.

---

diplopia or **double vision** A disease of the eye in which a single object appears to be double.

- **see** Move the fingers of the right *V hand*, pointing up in front of the eyes, forward a short distance.

- **double** Twist the wrist to strike the middle finger of the right *V hand* upward on the upturned palm of the left *open hand*.

- **blur** With the palms of both *5 hands* facing forward in front of the face, move both hands in from side to side going in opposite directions.

---

dipsomaniac A person with an irresistible craving for alcoholic drink. See signs for ALCOHOLIC[1,2].

---

disability[1] Lack of fitness, power, or ability to do something.

- **disability** Tap the fingertips of the right *D hand*, palm down, on the base of the thumb of the left *B hand*, palm right.

---

disability[2] (alternate sign)

- Fingerspell abbreviation: D-A

---

discharge¹ or **release** To let go or release from the hospital after a period of time.

- **dismiss** Wipe the right *open hand*, palm down, deliberately across the upturned palm of the left *open hand* from the heel to off the fingertips.

discharge² or **issue** A flowing or issuing out of fluids or matter from the body.

- **runny** Note: Substitute the appropriate location for forming this sign. Bring the right *4 hand*, palm back and fingers pointing left, downward with a double movement from the right ear.

discoloration The state of being discolored from bruising or other internal or external injury.

- **change** With the palm side of both *A hands* together, right hand above left, twist the wrists in opposite directions in order to reverse positions.

- **color** Wiggle the fingers of the right *5 hand* in front of the mouth, fingers pointing up.

disease, disorder, ill, illness or **sick** An abnormal condition of the body or part of the body.

- **disease** Touch the bent middle finger of the right *5 hand* to the forehead while touching the bent middle finger of the left *5 hand* to the abdomen.

disinfect To cleanse of infection; free from disease germs. See sign for: **sterile¹**.

disinfectant An agent that destroys harmful disease germs but not ordinary bacteria.

- **medicine** With the bent middle finger of the right *5 hand* in the palm of the left *open hand*, palms facing each other, rock the right hand from side to side with a double movement while keeping the middle finger in place.

- **for** Beginning with the extended right finger touching the right side of the forehead, twist the hand forward, ending with the index finger pointing forward.

-- [sign continues] -->

- **clean** Slide the palm of the right *open hand* from the heel to the fingers of the upturned palm of the left *open hand*.

---

disk or **inter-vertebral disk** Cartilage connecting the adjacent vertebrae in the spinal column.

- **spine** With the extended right index finger of the right *one hand*, palm up, point to the right side of the lower back. Beginning with the right *F hand* on the thumb side of the left *F hand*, bring the right hand straight down.

- **disk** Beginning with the little-finger side of the right *O hand*, palm left, on the thumb side of the left *O hand*, palm right, bring the left hand upward over the right hand, ending with the little-finger side of the left hand on the thumb side of the right hand.

---

dislocation See sign for SPRAIN.

---

disorder, difficulty, or **problem** An abnormal physical or mental condition; an ailment. See also sign for DISEASE.

- **problem** Beginning with the knuckles of both *bent V hands*, touching in front of the chest, twist the hands in opposite directions with a deliberate movement, rubbing the knuckles against each other.

---

disordered Afflicted with a physical or mental disorder. See sign for DISORIENT.

---

disorient To cause to lose one's sense of time, place, or personal identity; confuse. Same sign used for: **disordered.** Related forms: **disorientation, disoriented.**

- **think** Touch the right side of the forehead with the extended right index finger.

- **messy** Beginning with the right *curved 5 hand* over the left *curved 5 hand*, palms facing each other, twist the hands in opposite directions to reverse their positions.

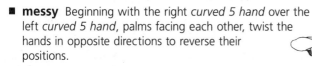

disorientation

disorientation See sign for CONFUSION.

dissection See sign for BIOPSY.

distention, enlarge, or **swollen** To expand or bulge out in all directions.

- **enlarge** Beginning with the fingertips of both *C hands* together in front of the chest, palms facing each other, pull the hands apart.

diuretic¹ Medication that forces the kidneys to excrete more urine, sodium, and potassium than normal, thereby eliminating excess body fluid.

- **medicine** With the bent middle finger of the right *5 hand* in the palm of the left *open hand*, palms facing each other, rock the right hand from side to side with a double movement while keeping the middle finger in place.

- **cause** Beginning with both *S hands* near the body, palms up and left hand nearer the body than the right hand, move the hands forward in an arc while opening into *5 hands*.

- **urine** Tap the middle finger of the right *P hand* against the nose with a double movement.

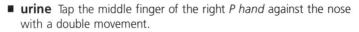

diuretic² (alternate sign)

- **medicine** With the bent middle finger of the right *5 hand* in the palm of the left *open hand*, palms facing each other, rock the right hand from side to side with a double movement while keeping the middle finger in place.

- **less** Move the right *bent hand*, palm down and fingers pointing left, from in front of the chest downward, stopping a few inches above the left *open hand*, palm up and fingers angled forward.

-- [sign continues] ---➤

■ **water** Tap the index-finger side of the right *W hand*, palm left and fingers pointing up, against the chin with a double movement.

dizzy or **vertigo** 1. Having a whirling sensation in the head. 2. Mentally confused.

■ **ears** Move the extended index fingers of both *one hands* to touch the ears.

■ **dizzy** Beginning with both *curved 5 hands* near each side of the head, palms facing the head, move the hands in alternating circular movements.

DNA See sign for DEOXYRIBONUCLEIC ACID.

doctor[1], **medical,** or **physician** A person trained and licensed to treat diseases and injuries.

■ **medical** Tap the fingertips of the right *flattened O hand* on the wrist of the upturned left *open hand* with a double movement.

doctor[2] (alternate sign)

■ **doctor** Tap the fingertips of the right *D hand* on the wrist of the upturned left *open hand* with a double movement.

donor A person who gives blood, an organ, or other biological tissue for use by another person.

■ **gift** Beginning with the right *X hand* in front of the right shoulder and the left *X hand* in front of the left side of the body, palms facing toward each other, with an alternating double movement move the right hand and then the left hand downward in an arc.

■ **person** Move both *P hands*, palms facing each other, downward along the sides of the body.

dormant

dormant See sign for LATENT.

dorsal Pertaining to the back. See signs for BACK[1,2].

dose A quantity of medicine prescribed to be taken at one time.

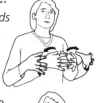

- **how-much** Beginning with the fingertips of both *curved 5 hands* touching each other in front of the body, palms facing each other, bring the hands outward to in front of each side of the chest.

- **medicine** With the bent middle finger of the right *5 hand* in the palm of the left *open hand*, palms facing each other, rock the right hand from side to side with a double movement while keeping the middle finger in place.

double vision See sign for DIPLOPIA.

douche A jet or current of water, sometimes with a dissolved medication or cleansing agent, applied to a body part, organ, or cavity for medicinal or hygienic purposes.

- **water** Tap the index-finger side of the right *W hand*, palm left and fingers pointing up, against the chin with a double movement.

- **insert** Insert the fingertips of the right *flattened O hand*, palm up and fingers pointing up, inserted up in the little-finger side of the left *O hand*, push the right hand through the left hand while opening into a *curved 5 hand*.

- **clean** Slide the palm of the right *open hand* from the heel to the fingers of the upturned palm of the left *open hand* with a double movement.

downer *Informal.* See sign for DEPRESSANT.

drainage Passage of bodily fluids through an opening or incision. Related form: **drain.**

- **drain** Beginning with the right *4 hand*, palm back and fingers pointing left, under the left *open hand* held in front of the chest, palm down, move the right hand downward slowly with a double movement.

draw blood or **give blood** To take blood for medical purposes.

- **draw-blood** Beginning with the fingers of the right *curved 5 hand*, palm up, near the crook of the extended left arm, pull the right hand to the right while closing the fingers to the thumb, forming a *flattened O hand*.

dressing See sign for BANDAGE.

drill To bore a hole in a tooth with a drill, especially to clean out decayed material before filling the tooth.

- **tooth** Touch a front tooth with the index finger of the right *one hand*.

- **drill** Point the extended index finger of the right *one hand* down near the right side of the open mouth.

drip The continuous, slow introduction of a fluid into the body, usually intravenously.

- **drip** Beginning with the right *S hand*, palm down, near the fingertips of the left *open hand*, palm down, flick the right index finger downward with a repeated movement.

drool To let saliva run from the mouth.

- **runny** Bring the right *4 hand*, palm back and fingers pointing left, downward with a double movement from the right side of the mouth.

drops or **eye drops** Liquid medicine given in a dose form from an eye dropper into the pupils of the eyes.

- **drops** Begin with the index finger and thumb of the right *F hand* in the thumb-side opening of the left *S hand* held in front of the body. Then with the extended index finger and thumb of the right *F hand*, palm down, in front of the right eye, open and close the fingers with a double movement.

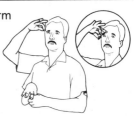

drowsy See sign for SLEEPY.

drug

drug[1]**, fix** (*slang*)**, heroin,** or **illegal drug** A habit-forming illicit substance, especially a narcotic.

- **drug** Pound the little-finger side of the right *S hand* with a double movement near the crook of the bent left arm.

drug[2] See sign for MEDICINE.

druggist, apothecary, or **pharmacist** A person who sells drugs and medicines.

- **person marker** Move both *open hands*, palms facing each other, downward along the sides of the body.

- **certify** Tap the thumbs of both *C hands* together in front of the chest with a repeated movement, palms facing each other.

- **sell** Beginning with both *flattened O hands* held in front of each side of the chest, palms down and fingers pointing down, swing the fingertips forward and back by twisting the wrists upward with a double movement.

- **medicine** With the bent middle finger of the right *5 hand* in the palm of the left *open hand*, palms facing each other, rock the right hand from side to side with a double movement while keeping the middle finger in place.

drugstore See sign for PHARMACY.

drunkenness The state of being drunk. See signs for ALCOHOLIC[1,2].

duct See sign for VESSEL.

dysfunction The malfunctioning of an organ or other body part.

- **can't** Bring the extended index finger of the right *one hand* downward hitting the extended index finger of the left *one hand* as it moves.

- **work** Tap the heel of the right *S hand*, palm forward, with a double movement on the back of the left *S hand* held in front of the body, palm down.

- **right** Bring the little-finger side of the right *one hand* down sharply on the index-finger side of the left *one hand*.

dyspepsia See sign for INDIGESTION.

dysplasia[1], deformity, or **malformation** Abnormal development of tissues, organs, or cells.

- **not** Bring the thumb of the right *10 hand* forward from under the chin with a deliberate movement.

- **right** Bring the little-finger side of the right *one hand* down sharply on the index-finger side of the left *one hand*.

- **grow** Bring the right *flattened O hand*, palm in and fingers pointing up, up through the left *C hand*, palm right, while spreading the right fingers into a *5 hand*.

dysplasia[2] See signs for ABNORMAL[1,2,3].

dyspnea Difficult or labored breathing. See sign for BREATHE.

ear¹ **1.** The organ of hearing and balance in a mammal. **2.** The external, or outer ear.

- **ear** Wiggle the right earlobe with the thumb and index finger of the closed right hand.

ear² See sign for HEAR.

ear infection An infection, usually in the middle ear.

- **ear** Touch the extended right index finger to the right ear.

- **infection** Move the right *I hand*, palm forward, from side to side with a repeated movement in front of the right shoulder.

earache A pain in the ear.

- **earache** Jab both extended index fingers toward each other with a short repeated movement near the right ear or near the ear with an earache.

earmold A device fitting into the outer ear and attached by a cord to a hearing aid receiver.

- **earmold** Twist the fingertips of the right *F hand*, palm in, near the right ear with a double movement.

earphones A set of receivers worn over or in the ears to transmit sound from a sound source.

- **earphones** Tap the fingertips of both *curved 5 hands*, palms in, on each side of the head around each ear with a double movement.

eating disorder See sign for MALNUTRITION.

EEG See signs for ELECTROENCEPHALOGRAM[1,2].

effusion The escape of a fluid, such as blood, from its natural vessels into a bodily cavity.

- **blood** While wiggling the fingers, move the right *5 hand* from the chin downward with a double movement past the back of the left *5 hand* held in front of the chest, both palms in and fingers pointing in opposite directions.

- **spread-in-body** Beginning with both *flattened O hands* in front of the chest, palms down, move the hands downward and outward while opening into *5 hands*.

ejaculate or **emission** To eject or discharge, especially semen from the penis. Related form: **ejaculation**.

- **ejaculate** While touching the wrist of the right *S hand* with the left extended index finger, palms facing in opposite directions, move the right hand forward while opening into a *4 hand*, ending with the right palm left and fingers pointing forward.

EKG See signs for ELECTROCARDIOGRAM[1,2].

elastic bandage or **Ace bandage** (*trademark*) An elasticized bandage usually in a continuous strip, used for securely binding an injured joint.

- **bandage** Move the fingers of the right *H hand*, palm in, in a circular movement completely around the left forearm.

- **elastic** Beginning with the bent index fingers of both *modified X hands* touching in front of the chest, palms in, pull the hands apart to in front of each side of the chest with a double movement.

elbow[1] The joint of the human arm, between the upper arm and the forearm.

- **elbow** Touch the bent left elbow with the extended right index finger, palm up.

elbow² (alternate sign)

- **elbow** Place the right *open hand* on the bent left elbow.

electrocardiogram¹ or **EKG** A means of studying the heart by examining sound waves created by an instrument placed on the chest.

- Fingerspell abbreviation: E-K-G

electrocardiogram² or **EKG** (alternate sign)

- **machine** With the fingers of both *curved 5 hands* loosely meshed together, palms in, move the hands up and down in front of the chest with a repeated movement.

- **show** With the extended right index finger touching the palm of the left *open hand*, palm right and fingers pointing forward, move both hands forward a short distance.

- **heartbeat** Touch the bent middle finger of the right *5 hand* on the left side of the chest. Then tap the back of the right *S hand* against the palm of the left *open hand* held in front of the chest.

electrocautery See signs for CAUTERIZE[1,2].

electroencephalogram¹ or **EEG** A means of studying the brain by measuring electric activity, also known as "brain waves," with a specific apparatus intended for that purpose.

- Fingerspell abbreviation: E-E-G

electroencephalogram² or **EEG** (alternate sign)

- **machine** With the fingers of both *curved 5 hands* loosely meshed together, palms in, move the hands up and down in front of the chest with a repeated movement.

- **show** With the extended right index finger touching the palm of the left *open hand*, palm right and fingers pointing forward, move both hands forward a short distance.

-- [sign continues] ---------------------------------->

- **mind** Touch the extended right index finger to the right side of the forehead.
- **hit** Hit the knuckle-side of the right *S hand*, palm left, against the palm of left *open hand* held in front of the head with a double movement.

---

elixir A sweetened alcoholic solution containing medicinal agents.

- **medicine** With the bent middle finger of the right *5 hand* in the palm of the left *open hand*, palms facing each other, rock the right hand from side to side with a double movement while keeping the middle finger in place.

- **sweet** Bring the fingers of the right *open hand* downward on the chin with a double movement, bending the fingers each time.

- **cocktail** Beginning with the thumb of the right *modified C hand* near the chin, palm left, tip the index finger back toward the face with a double movement.

---

embryo See sign for FETUS.

---

emergency or **medical emergency** A life-threatening illness, trauma, or other situation requiring immediate medical intervention.

- **emergency** Shake the right *E hand*, palm forward, back and forth in front of the right shoulder.

---

emergency room A hospital area equipped and staffed for the prompt treatment of acute illness, trauma, or other medical emergency.

- **emergency** Shake the right *E hand*, palm forward, back and forth in front of the right shoulder.

- **room** Beginning with both *R hands* in front of each side of the body, palms facing each other and fingers pointing forward, turn the hands sharply in opposite directions, ending with both palms in and fingers pointing in opposite directions.

emetic

emetic or **ipecac** A substance that when ingested causes vomiting.

- **medicine** With the bent middle finger of the right *5 hand* in the palm of the left *open hand*, palms facing each other, rock the right hand from side to side with a double movement while keeping the middle finger in place.

- **cause** Beginning with both *S hands* near the body, palms up and left hand nearer the body than the right hand, move the hands forward in an arc while opening into *5 hands*.

- **vomit** Beginning with the right *5 hand* near the mouth, palm left and fingers pointing forward, and the left *5 hand* forward of the right hand, palm right and fingers pointing forward, move both hands upward and forward in large arcs.

emission See sign for EJACULATE.

emotionally disturbed Having severe psychological problems.

- **emotion** Move both *E hands*, palms in and knuckles pointing toward each other, in repeated alternating circles on each side of the chest.

- **bother** Sharply tap the little-finger side of the right *open hand*, palm up at an angle, at the base of the thumb and index finger of the left *open hand* with a double movement.

empathy An insightful awareness and understanding of the feelings and behavior of another person.

- **feel** Move the bent middle finger of the right *5 hand* upward on the chest.

- **same-as** Move the right *Y hand*, palm down, from side to side with a double movement in front of the right side of the body.

emphysema A disease of the lungs resulting in enlarged air spaces.

- **lung** Rub the fingertips of both *bent hands*, palms in, up and down with a repeated movement near the center of the chest.

- **disease** Touch the bent middle finger of the right *5 hand* to the forehead while touching the bent middle finger of the left *5 hand* to the abdomen.

- **from** Beginning with the knuckle of the right *X hand*, palm in, touching the extended left index finger in front of the body, pull the right hand back toward the chest.

- **smoke** Beginning with the fingers of the right *V hand* touching the right side of the mouth, palm in and fingers pointing up, bring the hand forward with a double movement.

EMT See sign for PARAMEDIC[1,2].

endodontics The branch of dentistry dealing with the prevention, diagnosis, and treatment of diseases of the dental pulp and associated structures and tissues.

- **specialty** Slide the little-finger side of the right *B hand*, palm left and fingers pointing forward, along the index-finger side of the left *B hand* held in front of the chest, palm right and fingers pointing forward.

- **tooth** Touch a front tooth with the index finger of the right *one hand*.

-- [sign continues] --➤

- **disease** Touch the bent middle finger of the right *5 hand* to the forehead while touching the bent middle finger of the left *5 hand* to the abdomen.

endoscopy A method of diagnosing diseases by inserting an optical instrument with a lighted tip in hollow organs, such as the abdomen, pelvis, bronchial tubes or intestines. Related form: **endoscope**.

- **penis** Tap the middle finger of the right *P hand* against the nose.

- **tube** Beginning with the index-finger sides of both *F hands*, palm left, together in front of the chest, move the hands apart to in front of the sides of the chest.

- **look-inside** Point the extended fingers of the right *V hand*, palm down, toward the hole formed by the left *F hand*, palm right, held in front of the chest.

enema[1] The injection of a liquid into the rectum to clear the bowels.

- **water** tap the index finger side of the right *W hand*, palm facing left, against the chin with a double movement.

- **insert-up** Insert the extended thumb of the right *10 hand*, palm left, upward into the little- finger opening of the left *A hand*, palm right, held in front of the abdomen.

enema[2] (alternate sign)

- **enema** Insert the thumb of the right *10 hand*, palm left, upward into the little-finger opening of the left *A hand* held in front of the chest, palm right.

enlarge See sign for DISTENTION.

ENT See sign for OTORHINOLARYNGOLOGY[1].

epidemic or **plague** A disease spread from person to person and affecting many people at the same time. Same sign used for: **communicable**.

■ **disease** Touch the bent middle finger of the right *5 hand* to the forehead while touching the bent middle finger of the left *5 hand* to the abdomen.

■ **spread** Beginning with the fingers of both *flattened O hands* together in front of the chest, palms down, bring the hands forward and apart while opening into *5 hands*.

epidermis[1] or **skin** The outer layer of tissue on the body. Same sign used for: **flesh**.

■ **skin** Pinch and shake the loose skin on the back of the left *open hand* with the bent thumb and index finger of the right *5 hand*, both palms down.

epidermis[2] or **skin** (alternate sign) Same sign used for: **flesh**.

■ **skin** Pinch and shake the skin of the right cheek with the index finger and thumb of the right hand.

epidural, spinal block, or **saddle block** Insertion of an anesthetic into the lumbar part of the spine, which blocks sensation in the body from that point downward.

■ **spine** With the extended right index finger of the right *one hand*, palm up, point to the right side of the lower back. Beginning with the right *F hand* on the thumb side of the left *F hand*, bring the right hand straight up.

■ **shot** Jab the index finger of the right *L hand* to the right side of the body.

-- [sign continues] --▶

137

none Move both *O hands*, palms forward, from in front of the chest outward to each side.

■ **feel** Move the bent middle finger of the right *5 hand* upward on the chest.

■ **waist-down** Beginning with both *open hands* at the waist, right hand below the left hand, palms up and fingers pointing in opposite directions, move the right hand downward while keeping the left hand in place.

epilepsy A disorder of the nervous system characterized by a range of symptoms from sleepiness to severe convulsions. See sign for GRAND MAL. Related form: **epileptic.**

episiotomy A surgical incision to allow sufficient clearance for childbirth.

■ **vagina** Touch the index fingers and thumbs of both *L hands*, palms in and index fingers pointing down, together in front of the body.

■ **cut** Close the extended index and middle fingers of the right *V hand*, palm left and fingers pointing forward, with a double movement.

■ **sew** With the thumbs and index fingers of both *F hands* touching in front of the chest, palms facing each other, move the right hand in a double circular movement upward, meeting the fingertips of the left hand each time it passes.

epistaxis See sign for NOSEBLEED.

erection[1] The rigid state of a penis that occurs when its tissue fills with blood.

■ **penis** Tap the middle finger of the right *P hand* against the nose.

■ **erection** While holding the left *open hand* in the crook of the right elbow, bring the right *S hand*, palm left, upward from the right side of the body to in front of the right shoulder.

erection[2] (alternate sign)

■ **erect-penis** While holding the extended left index finger across the right wrist, move the extended right index finger, palm left and finger pointing forward, up with a deliberate movement.

erosion See sign for DECAY.

erythema Redness of the skin caused by inflammation.

■ **skin** Pinch the skin on the right cheek with the fingers of the right *modified X hand*.

■ **red** Brush the extended right index finger downward on the lips, bending the finger as it moves down.

erythrocyte[1], **red blood cell,** or **red blood corpuscle** Any of the cells in the blood, containing hemoglobin, that carry oxygen to the cells and tissues and carbon dioxide back to the respiratory organs.

■ **red** Brush the extended right index finger downward on the lips, bending the finger as it moves down.

-- [sign continues] ---▶

erythrocyte

- **blood** While wiggling the fingers, move the right *5 hand* from the chin downward with a double movement past the back of the left *5 hand* held in front of the chest, both palms in and fingers pointing in opposite directions.

- **cell** Move the right *F hand*, palm left, multiple places in front of the head and body.

erythrocyte², red blood cell, or red blood corpuscle
(alternate sign)

- **part** Slide the little-finger side of the right *open hand*, palm left and fingers pointing forward, across the palm of the left *open hand*, palm up.

- **blood** While wiggling the fingers, move the right *5 hand* from the chin downward with a double movement past the back of the left *5 hand* held in front of the chest, both palms in and fingers pointing in opposite directions.

- **exchange** Beginning with both *modified X hands* in front of the body, right hand somewhat forward of the left hand, move the right hand back toward the body in an upward arch while moving the left hand forward with a downward arc.

- **oxygen** Shake the right *O hand* in front of the right shoulder.

esophagus The muscular tube connecting the throat and stomach through which food passes.

- **tube** Beginning with the right *F hand* on the throat and the left *F hand* over the right hand, slide the right hand down the chest.

-- [sign continues] --→

- **for** Beginning with the extended right finger touching the right side of the forehead, twist the hand forward, ending with the index finger pointing forward.

- **food** Bring the fingertips of the right *flattened O hand* to the lips with a double movement.

euthanasia or **mercy killing** The act of killing a suffering person painlessly, or allowing the person to die by withholding treatment; usually reserved for a person having an incurable, painful disease or condition.

- **allow** Beginning with both *open hands* in front of the waist, palms facing each other and fingers pointing down, bring the fingers forward and upward by bending the wrists.

- **die** Beginning with both *open hands* in front of the body, right palm down and left palm up, flip the hands to the right, turning the right palm up and the left palm down.

evaluation[1] The diagnostic study of a physical or mental condition.

- **evaluation** Move both *E hands*, palms forward, up and down with a repeated alternating movement in front of each side of the body.

evaluation[2] (alternate sign)

- **examine** Beginning with the fingertips of the right *9 hand* touching the palm of the upturned left *open hand* held in front of the chest, turn the right hand over, ending with the right palm up.

-- [sign continues]

- **decide** Move the extended right index finger from the right side of the forehead, palm left, down in front of the chest while changing into an *F hand*, ending with both *F hands* moving forward in front of the body.

---

examination[1], check up, or **physical examination** An examination of a person's body by a doctor in order to determine the person's state of health or physical fitness.

- **body** Pat the palm side of both *open hands* first on each side of the chest and then on each side of the abdomen.

- **inspect** Move the extended right index finger from near the right eye down to move from the heel to the fingers of the upturned palm of the left *open hand*.

---

examination[2], check up, or **physical examination** (alternate sign)

- **look-for** Move both *C hands*, palms facing each other, with repeated alternating movements beginning in front of the face and moving down to in front of the chest with each movement.

---

examine, check, or **inspect** To observe, test, or investigate a person's body, especially in order to evaluate general health or determine the cause of illness.

- **inspect** Move the extended right index finger from near the right eye down to move from the heel to the fingers of the upturned palm of the left *open hand*.

---

excise[1] or **remove** To remove by surgically cutting out. Related form: **excision.**

- **operate** Move the thumb of the right *A hand*, palm down, across the upturned palm of the left *open hand* held in front of the chest.

-- [sign continues] -->

- **remove** Bring the palm side of the right *curved hand* down on the palm of the left *open hand* while changing to an *A hand*. Then move the right hand downward to the right while opening into a *5 hand*.

excise[2] or **remove** (alternate sign) Related form: **excision**.

- **eliminate** Beginning with the knuckles of both *modified X hands* touching in front of the body, palms in, bring the right hand upward and outward to the right while flicking the thumb upward.

excrement Waste matter discharged from the intestines through the anus; feces. See signs for BOWEL MOVEMENT[1,2].

exhale To breathe out. See sign for BREATHE.

exhaustion, fatigue, or **prostration** Extreme weariness, usually caused by exertion. Same sign used for: **tired**.

- **lie** Bring the right *V hand* from in front of the chest, palm up, down to land on palm of the left *open hand*. Then pull the right hand across the left palm back toward the body.

expel To breathe out. See sign for BREATHE.

expire[1] To breathe out. See sign for BREATHE.

expire[2] See sign for DIE.

exposure See sign for CONTACT. Related form: **expose**.

extended care Generalized health or nursing care, as for convalescents, the disabled, or the elderly, when hospitalization is not required. See signs for NURSING HOME[1,2,3].

external See sign for SUPERFICIAL.

extract[1] or **pull-a-tooth** The act of removing a tooth. Related form: **extraction**.

- **extract-tooth** Beginning with the knuckles of the right *bent V hand*, palm down, near the right side of the mouth, pull the hand forward with a short movement.

extract² or **pull-a-tooth** (alternate form)

- **pull-a-tooth** Beginning with the right *S hand* near the right corner of the mouth, palm forward, pull the hand deliberately forward and outward a short distance.

extremities See sign for LIMBS.

eye An organ of sight, one of a pair located in the skull. Same sign used for: **ocular, optic, optical.**

- **eye** Tap the extended right index finger at the outward side of the right eye with a double movement. For the plural, point the right index finger to the right eye and the left index finger to the left eye.

eye chart A chart for testing vision, usually containing letters in rows of decreasing size that are to be read at a fixed distance.

- **eye** Tap the extended right index finger at the outward side of the right eye with a double movement.

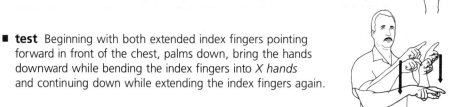

- **test** Beginning with both extended index fingers pointing forward in front of the chest, palms down, bring the hands downward while bending the index fingers into *X hands* and continuing down while extending the index fingers again.

- **square** With both extended index fingers, palms down, trace a square in the air, beginning together in front of the chest, moving apart to each side, moving straight down, and then together again at the bottom.

eye patch See sign for PATCH².

eyeglasses, eye wear, glasses, or **spectacles** Corrective eyewear consisting of two glass or plastic lenses set in a frame, usually with earpieces. Same sign used for: **goggles.**

- **glasses** Tap the thumbs of both *modified C hands*, palms facing each other, near the outside corner of each eye.

eyewear See sign for EYEGLASSES.

face The front part of the head. Related form: **facial.**

■ **face** Move the extended index finger of the right *one hand* in a circle around the face.

face-lift Plastic surgery for removal of facial defects, such as wrinkles or sagging.

■ **operate** Bring the thumbs of both *10 hands* downward on each cheek.

■ **push-up** With the fingertips of both *open hands*, palms down, push up on each cheek.

faint To suffer a temporary loss of consciousness, typically caused by a lack of sufficient oxygen to the brain. See sign for COMA.

Fallopian tubes Organs in the female reproductive tract through which an egg passes from the ovary to the uterus.

■ **tube** Beginning with the fingertips of both *G hands* near each other in front of the abdomen, palms facing each other, bring the hands outward to each side.

■ **ovary** Place the index-finger side of both *F hands*, palms down, against each side of the abdomen.

145

false negative or false positive Test results that incorrectly
indicate having or not having a condition.

- **test** Beginning with both extended index fingers pointing forward in front of the chest, palms down, bring the hands downward while bending the index fingers into *X hands* and continuing down while extending the index fingers again.

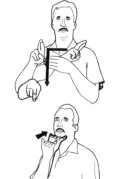

- **result** Move the fingertips of the right *R hand*, palm down, along the length of the index finger of the left *B hand*, palm in, and then down off the fingertips.

- **wrong** Bring the knuckles of the right *Y hand* back against the chin.

false teeth See signs for DENTURES[1,2].

family medicine See sign for FAMILY PRACTICE.

family practice, family medicine, or general practice
Medical specialization in general medicine that requires additional training and leads to board certification.

- **family** Beginning with the fingertips of both *F hands* touching in front of the chest, palms facing forward, bring the hands away from each other in outward arcs while turning the palms in, ending with the little fingers touching.

- **doctor** Tap the fingertips of the right *D hand* on the wrist of the upturned left *open hand* with a double movement.

fantasy See sign for HALLUCINATION.

farsightedness or hypermetropia Seeing distant objects
clearly while nearby objects appear blurred.
Related form: **farsighted.**

- **can** Move both *S hands*, palms down, downward simultaneously with a short double movement in front of each side of the body.

-- [sign continues] --->

- **see** Move the fingers of the right *V hand,* pointing up in front of the eyes, forward a short distance.

- **far** Beginning with the palm sides of both *A hands* together in front of the eyes, move the right hand forward.

- **can't** Bring the extended index finger of the right *one hand* downward hitting the extended index finger of the left *one hand* as it moves.

- **see** Move with the fingers of the right *V hand,* pointing up in front of the eyes, forward a short distance.

- **near** Bring the back of the right *open hand* from the chest forward toward the left *open hand*, both palms in and fingers pointing in opposite directions.

fast¹ or **abstain** To do without food voluntarily.

- **fast** Move the fingertips of the right *F hand*, palm in, from left to right across the mouth.

fast² or **abstain** (alternate sign)

- **food** Bring the fingertips of the right *flattened O hand* to the lips.

- **none** Move both *O hands*, palms forward, from in front of the chest outward to each side.

fat, corpulent, obese, or **overweight** Having body weight that is 20 percent or more than the accepted standard for a person's height, weight, sex, and physical condition. Same sign used for: **obesity.**

- **fat** Move both *curved 5 hands* from in front of each side of the chest, palms in and fingers pointing toward each other, outward in large arcs to each side of the body.

fatal Causing or capable of causing death.

- **happen** Beginning with the extended index fingers of both *one hands* pointing forward in front of the body, palms up, flip the hands over toward each other, ending with palms down.

- **cause** Beginning with both *S hands* near the body, palms up and left hand nearer the body than the right hand, move the hands forward in an arc while opening into *5 hands*.

- **die** Beginning with both *open hands* in front of the body, right palm down and left palm up, flip the hands to the right, turning the right palm up and the left palm down.

fatality or **casualty** Death resulting from an accident or disaster.

- **himself** Bring the knuckles of the right *10 hand*, palm left, firmly against the side of the extended left index finger pointing up in front of the chest, palm right.

- **die** Beginning with both *open hands* in front of the body, right palm down and left palm up, flip the hands to the right, turning the right palm up and the left palm down.

fatigue See sign for EXHAUSTION.

fear A distressing feeling of anxiety and worry, as over impending danger.
- **fear** Move both *5 hands* toward each other with a short double movement in front of the chest, fingers pointing toward each other.

febrile Of, marked by, or having a fever. See sign for FEVER.

feces Waste matter discharged from the intestines through the anus; excrement. See signs for BOWEL MOVEMENT[1,2].

feeble See sign for DEBILITY.

feeble-minded See signs for MENTALLY RETARDED[1,2].

feed To give food to. See sign for ADMINISTER.

feel To experience sensations, such as sound, light, or pain. See sign for SENSATION.

female or **woman** Being of the sex that normally is able to conceive and bear young.
- **female** Beginning with the thumb of the right *10 hand* on the right side of the chin, bring the hand downward while opening into a *5 hand*, ending with the thumb touching the chest.

fester To become painful and inflamed, often forming pus.
- **cut** Slide the side of the extended right index finger, palm in, across the back of the left *open hand*, palm down.

- **infection** Move the right *I hand*, palm forward, from side to side with a repeated movement in front of the right shoulder.

fetid Having an offensive odor.
- **smell** Move the palm side of the right *open hand* upward in front of the nose with a double movement.

-- [sign continues] --➤

fetus

- **bad** Move the fingers of the right *open hand* from the mouth, palm in and fingers pointing up, downward while flipping the palm quickly down as the hand moves.

---

fetus or **embryo** The young in the womb after the second month of gestation. Related form: **fetal.**

- **baby** With the right bent arm resting on the left bent arm, swing the arms from side to side with a double movement.

- **grow** Bring the right *flattened O hand*, palm in and fingers pointing up, up through the left *C hand*, palm right, while spreading the right fingers into a *5 hand*.

- **inside** Move the fingers of the right *flattened O hand* downward with a short double movement into the thumb side of the left *O hand* held in front of the chest.

- **abdomen** Pat the abdomen with the right *open hand*.

---

fever Above-normal body temperature. Normal mouth temperature is 98.6°, and normal rectal temperature is 99.6°. Same sign used for: **febrile.**

- **temperature** Slide the back of the extended right index finger, palm in and fingers pointing left, up the extended left index finger, palm right and finger pointing up, stopping at the top.

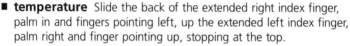

- **high** Move the right *H hand*, palm in and fingers pointing left, from in front of the right side of the chest upward to near the right side of the head.

---

field See sign for SPECIALTY.

field of vision See sign for VISUAL FIELD.

fill-a-prescription To take or send the doctor's written prescription to a pharmacy and buy the prescribed medicine.

- **doctor** Tap the fingertips of the right *D hand* on the wrist of the upturned left *open hand* with a double movement.

- **write** With the right index finger and thumb pinched together, slide the palm side of the right hand from the heel to the fingers of the upturned left *open hand*.

- **buy** Beginning with the back of the right *flattened O hand* in the palm of the left *open hand*, both palms up, move the right hand forward in an arc.

- **medicine** With the bent middle finger of the right *5 hand* in the palm of the left *open hand*, palms facing each other, rock the right hand from side to side with a double movement while keeping the middle finger in place.

filling A substance such as cement, amalgam, gold, or the like, used to fill a cavity caused by decay in a tooth.

- **tooth** Touch a front tooth with the index finger of the right *one hand*.

- **inside** Move the fingers of the right *flattened O* hand downward with a short double movement in the palm side of the left *O hand* held near the left side of the mouth.

- **closed** Bring the index fingers of both *B hands* sharply together in front of the right side of the face, palms forward.

fit

fit See sign for CONVULSION.

fix *Slang.* See sign for DRUG.

fixation See sign for OBSESSION.

flatulence or **gas** A chronic accumulation of gas in the intestinal tract. Same sign used for: **pass gas.** Related form: **flatus.**

- **flatulence** Beginning with the wrists of both *S hands* crossed in front of the body, palms down, right hand under the left hand, push the right hand forward while opening into a *5 hand*.

flesh The muscular and fatty tissue on the body that is covered by skin. See signs for EPIDERMIS[1,2].

flu See sign for INFLUENZA.

fluids, beverages, or **liquids** Any drinkable liquids.

- **any** Beginning with the right *10 hand* in front of the chest, palm up, twist the wrist down to the right, ending with the palm down.

- **drink** Beginning with the thumb of the right *C hand* near the chin, palm left, tip the hand up toward the face.

flush or **blush** To redden, especially in the face, as from embarrassment.

- **flush** Beginning with both *flattened O hands* near each cheek, palms facing each other, spread the fingers slowly upward, forming *5 hands*.

follow directions or **follow doctor's orders** To obey instruction or guidance.

- **explain** Beginning with the fingers of both *F hands* in front of the chest, palms facing each other and finger pointing forward, move the hands forward and back with an alternating movement.

-- [sign continues] --->

- **follow** With the knuckles of the right *10 hand*, palm left, near the wrist of the left *10 hand*, palm right, move both hands forward a short distance.

- **directions** Beginning with both *D hands* in front of the chest, palms facing each other and index fingers pointing forward, move the hands forward and back with an alternating movement.

follow doctor's orders See sign for FOLLOW DIRECTIONS.

fontanel (or **fontanelle**) or **soft spot** A space between the skull bone of a fetus or an infant that is covered by a membrane.

- **baby** With the right bent arm resting on the left bent arm, swing the arms from side to side with a double movement.

- **top-of-head** With elbows extended, place the fingers of both *open hands* on top of each side of the head.

- **soft** Beginning with both *curved 5 hands* in front of each side of the chest, palms up, bring the hands down with a double movement while closing the fingers to the thumbs each time.

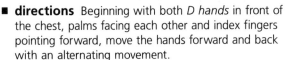

food poisoning An acute condition of the stomach and intestines characterized by headache, fever, chills, pain, nausea, and diarrhea. See sign for BOTULISM.

foot The end part of the leg, below the ankle joint, that is stood upon or is moved for walking.

- **foot** Move the bent middle finger of the right *5 hand* up and down the length of the left *open hand* with a repeated movement, both palms down.

foreskin A fold of skin that covers the head of a penis.

- **penis** Tap the middle finger of the right *P hand* against the nose.

- **skin** Pinch and shake the loose skin on the back of the left *open hand* with the bent thumb and index finger of the right *5 hand*.

- **peel** Move the index finger and thumb of the right *F hand* downward with a double movement from the tip to the base of the extended left index finger of the left *one hand*, palm right and finger pointing up.

fracture or **break** 1. The breaking of a bone 2. The injury caused by a broken bone. See also GREENSTICK, SIMPLE FRACTURE, COMPLETE FRACTURE, OPEN FRACTURE.

- **break** Beginning with both *S hands* in front of the body, index fingers touching and palms down, move the hands away from each other while twisting the wrists with a deliberate movement, ending with the palms facing each other.

- **bone** With a double movement, tap the back of the right *bent V hand*, palm up, on the back of the left *S hand*, palm down.

full term[1] The entire time of a normal pregnancy.

- **baby** With the right bent arm resting on the left bent arm, swing the arms from side to side with a double movement.

- **full** Slide the palm of the right *open hand*, palm down, from right to left across the index-finger side of the left *S hand*, palm right.

-- [sign continues] --->

- **develop** Move the fingertips of the right *D hand*, palm left, upward from the heel to the fingers of the left *open hand*, palm right and fingers pointing up.

full term² (alternate sign)

- **nine-month** Move the fingertips of the right *9 hand*, palm left, downward from the fingertip to the base of the extended index finger of the left *one hand*, palm right and finger pointing up.

functional Able to perform in a regular manner.

- **work** Tap the heel of the right *S hand*, palm forward, with a double movement on the back of the left *S hand* held in front of the body, palm down.

funny bone A place at the back of the elbow that when struck produces a tingling sensation.

- **hit** Hit the bent left elbow with the palm side of the right *A hand*, palm up.

- **nerve** Move the extended right index finger from the bent left elbow held across the chest, up the back of the left arm to the wrist.

fusion¹ or **repair** The restoration of a tear to sound condition.

- **fusion** Beginning with both *H hands* apart in front of the chest, palms in and fingers pointing toward each other, bring the hands together to touch fingertips.

fusion² (alternate sign) See sign for ARTICULATION.

gain weight To acquire an increased number of pounds.

- **increase** Beginning with the right *H hand*, palm up, slightly lower than the left *H hand*, palm down, flip the right hand over, ending with the extended right fingers across the extended left fingers. Repeat at a higher level.

- **weight** With the middle-finger side of the right *H hand* across the index-finger side of the left *H hand*, palms angled toward each other, tip the right hand up and down with a repeated movement.

gas See sign for FLATULENCE.

gastritis An inflammation of the stomach lining.

- **lining** Move the right extended finger from the index finger to the thumb of the left *C hand* held in front of the chest, palm right.

- **infection** Shake the right *I hand* in front of the right side of the chest, palm forward.

gastrointestinal Pertaining to or affecting the stomach and intestines.

- **abdomen** Pat the abdomen with the right *open hand*.

-- [sign continues] --->

- **disease** Touch the bent middle finger of the right *5 hand* to the forehead while touching the bent middle finger of the left *5 hand* to the abdomen.

gay See sign for HOMOSEXUAL.

gender[1] or **sex** The classification of people by sex.

- **male** Beginning with the thumb of the right *10 hand* on the right side of the forehead, bring the hand downward while opening into a *5 hand*, ending with the thumb touching the chest.

- **female** Beginning with the thumb of the right *A hand* on the chin, bring the hand downward while opening into a *5 hand*, ending with the thumb touching the chest.

- **which** Beginning with both *10 hands* in front of each side of the chest, palms in, move the hands up and down with an alternating movement.

gender[2] or **sex** (alternate sign)

- **sex** Touch the index-finger side of the right *X hand*, first near the right eye and then to the right side of the chin.

general anesthesia See signs for ANESTHESIA[1,2,3].

general practice See sign for FAMILY PRACTICE.

genetic

genetic, biological, or **hereditary** Pertaining to the role that genes contribute to origin or development. Same sign used for: **heredity.**

- **ancestor** Beginning with both *5 hands* in front of the right shoulder, left hand somewhat forward of the right hand, palms facing in and fingers pointing toward each other, move the hands backward in alternating repeated arcs over the right shoulder.

---

genital herpes, herpes, or **herpes simplex virus** A sexually-transmitted viral disease characterized by blisters around the genitals.

- **sex** Touch the index-finger side of the right *X hand*, first near the right eye and then to the right side of the chin.

- **spot** Place the palm side of the right *F hand* on the lower abdomen.

- **swell** With the fingertips of the right *flattened O hand* on the lower abdomen, raise the right hand a short distance while opening the fingers to a *curved 5 hand*.

- **water** Tap the index-finger side of the right *W hand*, palm left and fingers pointing up, against the chin with a double movement.

---

genital warts or **condyloma** Wart-like growths on the skin around the anus or genitals that are spread by sexual contact.

- **penis** Tap the middle finger of the right *P hand* against the nose.

-- [sign continues] -->

■ **vagina** Touch the index fingers and thumbs of both *L hands*, palms in and index fingers pointing down, together in front of the body.

■ **anus** Point the extended right index finger first to the thumb side of the left *F hand*, palm facing forward, and then to behind the right hip.

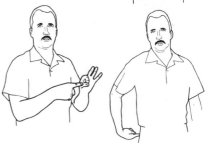

■ **bump** Beginning with the side of the extended right index finger, palm down on the left wrist, bring the right finger upward in a small arc, ending with the back of the right index finger on the back of the left *open hand*.

geriatrics A branch of medicine dealing with the diseases, debilities, and care of older people.

■ **specialty** Slide the little-finger side of the right *B hand*, palm left and fingers pointing forward, along the index-finger side of the left *B hand* held in front of the chest, palm right and fingers pointing forward.

■ **people** Move both *P hands*, palms down, in alternating forward circles in front of each side of the body.

■ **old** Move the right *C hand* from near the chin, palm left, downward a short distance while closing into an *S hand*.

---

germ A disease-producing microorganism.

- Fingerspell: G-E-R-M

German measles See sign for RUBELLA.

---

gestation The period of time that a fetus is in the mother's womb, which is an average of 39 weeks from conception until delivery.

- **pregnant** Beginning with both *5 hands* entwined in front of the abdomen, bring the hands forward.

- **nine-month** Move the fingertips of the right *9 hand*, palm left, upward from the fingertip to the base of the extended index finger of the left *one hand*, palm right and finger pointing up.

---

gingiva See sign for GUMS.

---

gingivitis See sign for PYORRHEA.

---

give blood See sign for DRAW-BLOOD.

---

glasses See sign for EYEGLASSES.

---

glaucoma An eye disease characterized by abnormally high pressure in the eyeball causing a loss of vision.

- **exceed** Beginning with the fingers of the right *bent hand* on the back of the left *bent hand*, both palms down, bring the right hand upward.

- **water** Tap the index-finger side of the right *W hand*, palm left and fingers pointing up, against the chin with a double movement.

- **pressure** Push the palm of the right *5 hand*, palm down, on the index-finger side of the left *S hand*, palm right, forcing the left hand downward.

-- [sign continues] ---→

■ **eye** Tap the extended right index finger at the outward side of the right eye with a double movement.

gluteus maximus See signs for BUTTOCKS[1,2].

goggles Protective eyeglasses typically with shields on the sides. See sign for EYE-GLASSES.

goiter An abnormal enlargement of the thyroid gland visible as a swelling at the front of the neck.

■ **goiter** Beginning with the palm side of the right *S hand* on front of the neck, pull the hand forward while changing into a *curved 5 hand*.

gonad A part of the reproductive system that produces and releases female eggs or male sperm; an ovary or testicle.

■ **testicles** Shake both *C hands* near each other in front of the abdomen, palms up.

■ **ovary** Place the palm side of both *F hands*, fingers pointing down, against each side of the abdomen.

gonorrhea See signs for SEXUALLY TRANSMITTED DISEASE[1,2].

graft A portion of living tissue surgically transplanted from one part of an individual to another, or from one individual to another, for its adhesion and growth.

■ **skin** Pinch and shake the loose skin on the back of the left *open hand* with the bent thumb and index finger of the right *5 hand*.

-- [sign continues]

grand mal

- **exchange** Beginning with both *modified X hands* in front of the body, right hand somewhat forward of the left hand, move the right hand back toward the body in an upward arc while moving the left hand forward with a downward arc.

grand mal A disorder characterized by severe convulsions with loss of consciousness experienced by people with this form of epilepsy. Same sign used for: **epilepsy, epileptic, seizure.**

- **seizure** Wiggle the right *bent V hand*, palm up, around on the palm of the left *open hand*, while repeatedly bending the right index and middle fingers.

greenstick An incomplete bone fracture, in which one side is broken and the other side is intact. See also COMPLETE FRACTURE, FRACTURE, OPEN FRACTURE, SIMPLE FRACTURE.

- **bone** With a double movement, tap the back of the right *bent V hand*, palm up, on the back of the left *S hand*, palm down.

- **not** Bring the thumb of the right *10 hand* forward from under the chin with a deliberate movement.

- **full** Slide the palm of the right *open hand*, palm down, from right to left across the index-finger side of the left *S hand*, palm right.

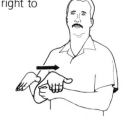

- **break** Beginning with both *S hands* in front of the body, index fingers touching and palms down, move the hands away from each other while twisting the wrists with a deliberate movement, ending with the palms facing each other.

groin The part of the body where the thigh meets the lower abdomen.

- **groin** With the extended right index finger, point to the groin area.

---

growth See sign for TUMOR.

---

guard See sign for PROTECT.

---

gum or **gingiva** The firm, fleshy tissue along the jaws that surrounds the necks of the teeth. Note: Add the person marker before this sign to form the medical professional: **periodontist.**

- **gums** Touch the upper gums with the extended right index finger.

---

gynecologist See sign for GYNECOLOGY.

---

gynecology The field of medicine dealing with health maintenance and the diseases of women, especially concerning the reproductive organs. Note: Add the person marker before this sign to form the medical professional: **gynecologist.**

- **medical** Touch the fingertips of the right *flattened O hand* on the wrist of the upturned left *open hand*.

- **specialty** Slide the little-finger side of the right *B hand*, palm left and fingers pointing forward, along the index-finger side of the left *B hand* held in front of the chest, palm right and fingers pointing forward.

- **female** Beginning with the thumb of the right *A hand* on the chin, bring the hand downward while opening into a *5 hand*, ending with the thumb touching the chest.

hair
Fine threadlike strands growing from the scalp, which, when growing together, provide a coating for the human head.

- **hair** Hold a strand of hair with the thumb and index finger of the right *F hand*, palm left, and shake it with a repeated movement.

hallucination, delusion, or fantasy
The sensation of encountering apparent sights, sounds, or other experiences that in actuality do not exist.

- **hallucination** Beginning with the fingertips of both *5 hands* touching each side of the head, palms down, bring the hands forward while wiggling the fingers.

hallucinogen
A substance that produces hallucinations.

- **pill** Beginning with the index finger of the right *A hand* tucked under the right thumb, palm in, flick the index finger toward the mouth with a double movement.

- **hallucination** Beginning with the fingertips of both *5 hands* touching each side of the head, palms down, bring the hands forward while wiggling the fingers.

hand
The free end of the arm, consisting of the wrist, the thumb and fingers, and the area between, used for touching, grasping, seizing, manipulating, etc.

- **hand** Pat the fingers of the left *curved hand* with a double movement on the back of the right *open hand*, both palms down.

handicap
A physical or mental disability that makes the ordinary activities of daily life difficult.
- Fingerspell abbreviation: H-C

hangover
The disagreeable aftereffects of drinking too much alcohol.

- **alcoholic** Move the thumb of the right *10 hand* in an arc from right to left past the chin.

-- [sign continues] --→

- **tomorrow** Move the palm side of the right *10 hand*, palm left, from the right side of the chin forward while twisting the wrist forward.

- **headache** With both extended index fingers pointing toward each other in front of the forehead, palms down, jab the fingers toward each other with a short double movement.

hard-of-hearing Having a reduced ability to hear.

- **hear** Touch the extended right index finger to near the right ear.
- Fingerspell abbreviation: H-H

hay fever An allergic reaction affecting the eyes and respiratory tract caused by pollen or other plants. See signs for ALLERGY[1, 2, 3].

head or **cranium** The upper part of the body, joined to the trunk by the neck, containing the skull, the brain, and the face. Same sign used for: **cerebral, cephalic.**

- **head** Touch the fingertips of the right *bent hand* first to the right side of the chin and then to the right side of the forehead.

head cold See sign for COLD.

headache or **migraine** A pain located in the head, as at the temples.

- **pain** With both extended index fingers pointing toward each other in front of the forehead, palms down, jab the fingers toward each other with a short double movement.

health The general condition of one's body with regard to soundness, vigor, etc. Same sign used for: **human, hygiene.**

- **health** Touch the fingertips of both *H hands*, palms in, first to each side of the chest and then to each side of the waist.

health food Natural food popularly believed to promote or sustain good health through its nutrients.

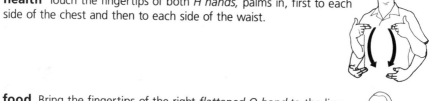

- **health** Touch the fingertips of both *H hands,* palms in, first to each side of the chest and then to each side of the waist.

- **food** Bring the fingertips of the right *flattened O hand* to the lips with a double movement.

health insurance Insurance that compensates a person for medical expenses, including hospitalization.

- **health** Touch the fingertips of both *H hands,* palms in, first to each side of the chest and then to each side of the waist.

- **insurance** Move the right *I hand*, palm forward, from side to side with a repeated movement in front of the right shoulder.

health maintenance organization or **HMO** An insurance program that provides prepaid comprehensive health services, including preventive care, treatment, and hospitalization.

- Fingerspell abbreviation: H-M-O

healthy or **well** Possessing good health.

- **healthy** Beginning with the fingertips of both *curved 5 hands* touching near each shoulder, bring the hands downward and forward with a deliberate movement while closing into *S hands.*

hear To take in sound by the ear. Same sign used for: **auditory, aural, ear, hearing, sound.**

- **hear** Touch the extended right index finger to near the right ear.

hearing 1. The sense of perceiving sound. 2. The act of perceiving sound. See sign for HEAR.

hearing aid An electronic device, worn by a person, used to amplify sound.

- **hearing-aid** Twist the right *modified X hand* forward near the right ear.

hearing-impaired Having reduced hearing.

- **hearing-impaired** Beginning with the extended fingers of the right *H hand* pointing to the right ear, palm down, move the hand forward while changing into an *I hand*.

heart The muscular organ of the body that acts as a pump to circulate the blood. Same sign used for: **cardiac, coronary.**

- **heart** Tap the bent middle finger of the right *5 hand*, palm in, with a repeated movement on the left side of the chest.

heart attack See sign for CARDIAC ARREST.

heart burn A burning discomfort coming from the stomach through the lower esophagus, seeming to be localized about the heart.

- **heart** Touch the bent middle finger of the right *5 hand* on the left side of the chest.

- **feel** Move the bent middle finger of the right *5 hand* upward on the chest.

- **burn** Move the right *flattened O hand*, fingers pointing up, upward from the abdomen to the chest while opening the fingers slightly.

heart disease An abnormal condition of the heart that impairs its functioning.

- **heart** Touch the bent middle finger of the right *5 hand* on the left side of the chest.

-- [sign continues] --➤

heart failure

■ **disease** Touch the bent middle finger of the right *5 hand* to the forehead while touching the bent middle finger of the left *5 hand* to the abdomen.

heart failure **1.** A fatal condition in which the heart ceases to function. **2.** A condition in which the heart pumps inadequate amounts of blood.

■ **heart** Touch the bent middle finger of the right *5 hand* on the left side of the chest.

■ **stop** Hit the little-finger side of the right *open hand* on the palm of the left *open hand*.

heartbeat The pulsing rhythm of the heart.

■ **heartbeat** Touch the bent middle finger of the right *5 hand* on the left side of the chest. Then tap the palm side of the right *A hand* against the chest with a double movement.

heat exhaustion or **heat prostration** A reaction to intense heat, characterized by weakness, nausea, dizziness, and profuse sweating.

■ **sun** Beginning with the right *flattened O hand* above the right shoulder, palm down, bring the right hand downward toward the face while opening into a *curved 5 hand*.

■ **body** Pat the palm side of both *open hands* first on each side of the chest and then on each side of the abdomen.

■ **weak** Beginning with the fingertips of the right *5 hand* touching the palm of the left *open hand* held in front of the chest, collapse the right hand downward with a double movement, bending the fingers each time.

heat prostration See sign for HEAT EXHAUSTION.

heat stroke See sign for SUNSTROKE.

help See signs for AID[1,2].

hematology The study of the nature, function, and disease of the blood and of blood-forming organs.

- **medical** Touch the fingertips of the right *flattened O hand* on the wrist of the upturned left *open hand*.

- **specialty** Slide the little-finger side of the right *B hand*, palm left and fingers pointing forward, along the index-finger side of the left *B hand* held in front of the chest, palm right and fingers pointing forward.

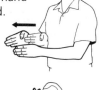

- **disease** Touch the bent middle finger of the right *5 hand* to the forehead while touching the bent middle finger of the left *5 hand* to the abdomen.

- **blood** While wiggling the fingers, move the right *5 hand* from the chin downward with a double movement past the back of the left *open hand* held in front of the chest, both palms in and fingers pointing in opposite directions.

hematoma A blood-filled swelling of tissue or an organ caused by a break in a blood vessel.

- **hit-arm** Bring the knuckles of the right *S hand* sharply against the left upper arm.

- **inside** Move the fingers of the right *flattened O hand* downward with a short double movement in the thumb side of the left *O hand* held in front of the chest.

-- [sign continues] --➤

hemophilia

- **blood** While wiggling the fingers, move the right *5 hand* downward with a double movement past the back of the left *open hand* held in front of the chest, both palms in and fingers pointing in opposite directions.

- **break** Beginning with both *S hands* in front of the body, index fingers touching and palms down, move the hands away from each other while twisting the wrists with a deliberate movement, ending with the palms facing each other.

- **runny-arm** Move the fingers of the right *4 hand* downward on the left upper arm with a double movement.

- **spread** Beginning with the fingertips of both *flattened O hands* together in front of the chest, palms in and fingers pointing down, move the hands downward and apart while opening into *5 hands*.

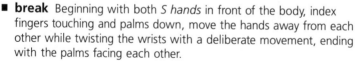

- **swell** With the fingertips of the right *flattened O hand* on the back of the bent left arm, raise the right hand a short distance.

---

hemophilia A hereditary tendency to having uncontrollable bleeding, even from minor wounds, due to the absence of the clotting factor in the blood. Same sign used for: **bleeder.**

- **blood** While wiggling the fingers, move the right *5 hand* from the chin downward with a double movement past the back of the left *5 hand* held in front of the chest, both palms in and fingers pointing in opposite directions.

-- [sign continues] --->

- **disease** Touch the bent middle finger of the right *5 hand* to the forehead while touching the bent middle finger of the left *5 hand* to the abdomen.

- **cut** Slide the side of the extended right index finger, palm in, across the back of the left *open hand*, palm down.

- **can't** Bring the extended index finger of the right *one hand* downward hitting the extended index finger of the left *one hand* as it moves.

- **stop** Hit the little-finger side of the right *open hand* on the palm of the left *open hand*.

hemorrhage To bleed profusely.

- **blood** While wiggling the fingers, move the right *5 hand* from the chin downward with a double movement past the back of the left *open hand* held in front of the chest, both palms in and fingers pointing in opposite directions.

- **not** Bring the thumb of the right *10 hand* forward from under the chin with a deliberate movement.

- **stop** Hit the little-finger side of the right *open hand* on the palm of the left *open hand*.

hemorrhoid

hemorrhoid or **pile** A swollen mass of dilated veins located near the anus, sometimes painful and bleeding.

- **buttocks** Touch the extended right index finger to the right buttock.

- **blood** While wiggling the fingers, move the right *5 hand* from the chin downward with a double movement past the back of the left *5 hand* held in front of the chest, both palms in and fingers pointing in opposite directions.

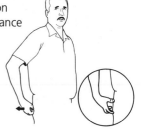

- **swell** With the fingertips of the right *flattened O hand* on the back of the right hip, move the right hand a short distance to the right while opening the fingers to a *curved 5 hand*.

---

hereditary See sign for GENETIC.

---

heredity The transmission of genetic characteristics from parents to offspring. See sign for GENETIC.

---

hernia See sign for RUPTURE.

---

heroin See sign for DRUG.

---

herpes See sign for GENITAL HERPES.

---

herpes simplex virus See sign for GENITAL HERPES.

---

hiccup An involuntary, spasmodic inhalation, producing a short, sharp sound.

- **hiccup** Beginning with the bent index finger of the right hand tucked under the right thumb, palm in and finger pointing up, flick the index finger upward with a double movement in front of the chest.

---

high blood pressure See sign for HYPERTENSION.

hip The part of the body that curves outward on either side below the waist and at the top of the thigh.

- **hip** Tap the fingertips of the right *bent hand*, palm up, against the right hip with a double movement.

HIV[1] (*Human Immunodeficiency Virus*) or **AIDS virus** A retrovirus that causes AIDS.

- Fingerspell abbreviation: H-I-V

HIV[2] (*Human Immunodeficiency Virus*) or **Aids virus** (alternate sign)

- **person marker** Move both *open hands*, palms facing each other, downward along the sides of the body.

- **body** Pat the palm side of both *open hands* first on each side of the chest and then on each side of the abdomen.

- **protect** With the wrists of both *S hands* crossed in front of the chest, palms facing in opposite directions, move the hands forward a short distance.

- **disease** Touch the bent middle finger of the right *5 hand* to the forehead while touching the bent middle finger of the left *5 hand* to the abdomen.

- **fail** Slide the back of the right *V hand*, palm up, from the heel to off the fingers of the upturned left *open hand*.

HMO

HMO See sign for HEALTH MAINTENANCE ORGANIZATION.

holistic medicine See sign for ALTERNATIVE MEDICINE.

home delivery The act of giving birth at home, as compared to the more usual practice of giving birth in a birthing center or hospital.

- **baby** With the right bent arm resting on the left bent arm, swing the arms from side to side with a double movement.

- **birth** Beginning with the back of the right *open hand* against the palm of the left *open hand*, both palms in and fingers pointing in opposite directions, move the right hand down under the little-finger side of the left hand, ending with the right palm facing down.

- **where** Move the extended right index finger, palm forward, from side to side in front of the right shoulder.

- **home** Touch the fingertips of the right *flattened O hand* first to the right side of the chin and then to the right cheek.

homosexual or **gay** **1.** A person who is sexually attracted to persons of the same sex. **2.** Of or pertaining to homosexuals or homosexuality. Related form: **homosexuality**.

- **gay** Bring the fingertips of the right *G hand*, palm in, back to touch the chin with a double movement.

hooked *Slang.* Addicted to drugs. See sign for ADDICTION¹.

hordeolum See sign for STY.

hospice A health care facility, or a system of professional home visits and supervision, for supportive care of the terminally ill.

- **home** Touch the fingertips of the right *flattened O hand* first to the right side of the chin and then to the right cheek.

- **take-care-of** With the little-finger side of the right *K hand* across the index-finger side of the left *K hand*, move the hands in a repeated flat circle in front of the body.

- **will** Move the right *open hand*, palm left and fingers pointing up, from the right side of the chin forward while tipping the fingers forward.

- **die** Beginning with both *open hands* in front of the body, right palm down and left palm up, flip the hands to the right, turning the right palm up and the left palm down.

hospital An institution, staffed with doctors and nurses, in which sick and injured people are treated and cared for.

- **hospital** Bring the fingertips of the right *H hand*, palm right, first downward a short distance on the upper left arm and then across from back to front.

hot flash or **hot flush** A sudden, temporary sensation of heat experienced by some women during menopause.

- **hot** Beginning with the right *curved 5 hand* in front of the mouth, palm in, twist the wrist forward with a deliberate movement while turning the hand down.

- **flush** Beginning with both *flattened O hands* near each cheek, palms facing each other, spread the fingers slowly upward, forming *5 hands*.

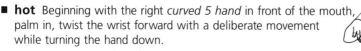

hot flush

hot flush See sign for HOT FLASH.

---

human Being a person or being characteristic of people. See sign for HEALTH.

---

hurt¹, bear, sore, or **wound** 1. To cause pain or injury.
  2. To feel pain.
  - **hurt** Beginning with the thumb of the right *A hand* touching the chin, palm left, twist the wrist back, ending with the palm facing in.

---

hurt² See signs for PAIN¹,².

---

hydrotherapy The use of water in the treatment of disease or injury, as with soothing baths or sprays for wounds or heated pools for stiffened joints.
  - **water** Tap the index-finger side of the right *W hand*, palm left and fingers pointing up, against the chin with a double movement.

  - **therapy** Beginning with the little-finger side of the right *T hand*, palm in, on the upturned palm of the left *open hand*, move both hands upward in front of the chest.

---

hygiene Practices, such as cleanliness, that are conducive to health. See sign for HEALTH.

---

hyperactive See sign for NERVOUS.

---

hyperactivity Excessive activity in children, sometimes associated with neurological or psychological causes. Same sign used for: **hyperkinesia.**
  - **person** Move both *P hands*, palms facing each other, downward along the sides of the body.

  - **can't** Bring the extended index finger of the right *one hand* downward hitting the extended index finger of the left *one hand* as it moves.

-- [sign continues] --➤

- **control** Beginning with both *modified X hands* in front of each side of the body, right hand forward of the left hand and palms facing each other, move the hands forward and back with a repeated movement.

- **frantic** With the heel of the right *X hand* on the back of the left *open hand*, palm down, twist the right hand around with a random movement.

hyperglycemia An abnormally high level of glucose in the blood.

- **sugar** Bring the fingers of the right *U hand* downward on the chin with a double movement, bending the fingers each time.

- **inside** Move the fingers of the right *flattened O hand* downward with a short double movement in the thumb side of the left *O hand* held in front of the chest.

- **blood** While wiggling the fingers, move the right *5 hand* from the chin downward with a double movement past the back of the left *5 hand* held in front of the chest, both palms in and fingers pointing in opposite directions.

- **exceed** Beginning with the fingers of the right *bent hand* on the back of the left *bent hand*, both palms down, bring the right hand upward.

hyperkinesia An abnormal amount of uncontrolled muscular action. See sign for HYPERACTIVITY.

hypermetropia See sign for FARSIGHTED.

hyperphagia See sign for BULIMIA NERVOSA.

hypertension or **high blood pressure** A condition of abnormally elevated blood pressure.

- **high** Move the right *H hand*, palm in and fingers pointing left, from in front of the right side of the chest upward to near the right side of the head.

- **blood-pressure** While wiggling the fingers, move the right *5 hand* downward with a double movement past the back of the left *open hand* held in front of the chest, both palms in and fingers pointing in opposite directions. With the right *C hand* grasp the upper left arm.

hyperthermia An usually high fever.

- **body** Pat the palm side of both *open hands* first on each side of the chest and then on each side of the abdomen.

- **temperature** Slide the back of the extended right index finger, palm in and fingers pointing left, up the extended index finger of the left hand, palm right and finger pointing up, stopping at the top.

hypertrophy Excessive growth of a body part due to an increase in the size of its cells.

- With the extended index finger of the right *one hand*, palm down, point to the back of the downturned left hand.

- **enlarge** Beginning with the fingertips of both *C hands* together in front of the chest, palms facing each other, pull the hands apart.

hyperventilation Fast or deep respiration resulting in abnormally low levels of carbon dioxide in the blood.

- **breathe** With the right *5 hand* in front of the chest above the left *5 hand*, fingers pointing in opposite directions and palms in, move both hands forward and back toward the chest with a double movement.

-- [sign continues] ---➤

■ **fast** Beginning with the extended index fingers of both *one hands* pointing forward in front of the chest, pull the hands back toward the chest while changing to *S hands*.

■ **not** Bring the thumb of the right *10 hand* forward from under the chin with a deliberate movement.

■ **enough** Push the palm side of the right *open hand*, palm down, forward across the thumb side of the left *S hand*.

■ **oxygen** Shake the right *O hand* in front of the right shoulder.

hypnosis **1.** To put into a trance or trance-like state; make vulnerable to control. **2.** To hold spellbound; transfix; fascinate. Related form: **hypnotize.**

■ **hypnosis** Slowly wiggle the fingers of both *5 hands*, palms down and fingers pointing forward.

■ **hypnosis** Swing the right index finger, palm in and finger pointing down in front of the eyes, slowly from side to side with a repeated movement.

hypodermic[1], **injection, vaccine,** or **syringe** **1.** Of or characterized by the injection of drugs under the skin. **2.** A hypodermic syringe. **3.** A dose of medicine administered by syringe.

■ **hypodermic** Move the index finger of the right *3 hand* from in front of the right shoulder, palm right, back against the right upper arm while closing the middle finger to the thumb.

hypodermic[2] See sign for SHOT.

hypoglycemia

hypoglycemia An abnormally low level of glucose in the blood.

- **sugar** Bring the fingers of the right *U hand* downward on the chin with a double movement, bending the fingers each time.

- **inside** Move the fingers of the right *flattened O hand* downward with a short double movement in the thumb side of the left *O hand* held in front of the chest.

- **blood** While wiggling the fingers, move the right *5 hand* from the chin downward with a double movement past the back of the left *5 hand* held in front of the chest, both palms in and fingers pointing in opposite directions.

- **not** Bring the thumb of the right *10 hand* forward from under the chin with a deliberate movement.

- **enough** Push the palm side of the right *open hand*, palm down, forward across the thumb side of the left *S hand*.

---

hypotension or **low blood pressure** A condition of abnormally lowered blood pressure.

- **less** Move the right *open hand*, palm down and fingers pointing left, from in front of the chest downward, stopping a few inches above the left *open hand*, palm up and fingers angled forward.

- **blood-pressure** While wiggling the fingers, move the right *5 hand* downward with a double movement past the back of the left *open hand* held in front of the chest, both palms in and fingers pointing in opposite directions. With the right *C hand* grasp the upper left arm.

hypothermia Subnormal body temperature.

- **body** Pat the palm side of both *open hands* first on each side of the chest and then on each side of the abdomen.

- **temperature** Slide the back of the extended right index finger, palm in and fingers pointing left, up the extended index finger of the left hand, palm right and finger pointing up, stopping at the bottom.

hysterectomy[1] An operation in which the uterus is removed.

- **female** Beginning with the thumb of the right *10 hand* on the right side of the chin, bring the hand downward while opening into a *5 hand*, ending with the thumb touching the chest.

- **operate** Move the extended thumb of the right *10 hand*, palm down, from left to right across the abdomen.

- **remove** Move the right *curved hand* in to the abdomen. Change the right hand to an *A hand* and move it forward to the right while opening to a *5 hand*, palm facing down.

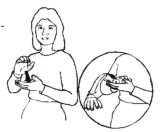

hysterectomy[2] (alternate sign)

- **uterus** Beginning with the fingertips of both *U hands* touching in front of the body, palms down, move the hands outward away from each other and downward to again touch fingertips in front of the abdomen.

-- [sign continues] --->

hysterectomy

- **operate-abdomen** Move the extended thumb of the right *10 hand*, palm down, from left to right across the abdomen.

- **remove-from-abdomen** Move the right *curved hand* in to the abdomen. Change the right hand to an *A hand* and move it forward to the right while opening to a *5 hand*, palm facing down.

ibuprofen See sign for ASPIRIN.

ICU See sign for INTENSIVE CARE UNIT.

identical twin One of two children born at the same time from the same fertilized egg.

- **twin** Touch the index-finger side of the right *T hand*, palm left, first to the right side of the chin and then to the left side of the chin.

- **looks** Move the extended index finger of the right *one hand* in a circle around the face.

- **same-as** Move the right *Y hand*, palm down, from side to side with a double movement in front of the right side of the body.

ill See sign for DISEASE. Related form: **illness.**

illegal drug See sign for DRUG.

immobilize To prevent or restrict normal movement by use of a splint, cast, or prescribed bed rest.

- **can't** Bring the extended index finger of the right *one hand* downward hitting the extended index finger of the left *one hand* as it moves.

- **move** Beginning with both *flattened O hands* apart in front of the right side of the body, palms down, move the hands simultaneously in an arc to the left.

immune

immune[1] Resistance against infection by the body's natural defenses.

- **protect** With the wrists of both *S hands* crossed in front of the chest, palms facing in opposite directions, move the hands forward a short distance.

- **from** Beginning with the knuckle of the right *X hand*, palm in, touching the extended left index finger in front of the body, pull the right hand back toward the chest.

- **disease** Touch the bent middle finger of the right *5 hand* to the forehead while touching the bent middle finger of the left *5 hand* to the abdomen.

immune[2] (alternate sign)

- **can't** Bring the extended index finger of the right *one hand* downward hitting the extended index finger of the left *one hand* as it moves.

- **get** Beginning with the little-finger side of the right *curved 5 hand*, palm left, on the index-finger side of the left *curved 5 hand*, palm right, bring the hands back toward the chest while closing into *S hands*.

- **disease** Touch the bent middle finger of the right *5 hand* to the forehead while touching the bent middle finger of the left *5 hand* to the abdomen.

immunization Producing immunity by giving a vaccine, either orally or by injection, of modified forms of the germs that cause a disease, causing the body to produce antibodies that create an immunity.

- **shot** Bend the thumb of the right *L hand* down while touching the left upper arm with the index finger.

- **pill** Beginning with the index finger of the right *A hand* tucked under the right thumb, palm in, flick the index finger toward the mouth with a double movement.

- **prevent** With the little-finger side of the right *B hand* against the index-finger side of the left *B hand*, palms facing in opposite directions, move the hands forward a short distance.

- **disease** Touch the bent middle finger of the right *5 hand* to the forehead while touching the bent middle finger of the left *5 hand* to the abdomen.

implant To insert or graft tissue, an organ, or an inert substance into the body.

- **operate** Move the thumb of the right *A hand*, palm down, across the left side of the chest.

- **insert** Move the fingers of the right *flattened O hand* with a downward movement in the thumb side of the left *O hand* held close to the chest.

impotent An inability for a male to achieve or sustain an erection or to ejaculate during intercourse.

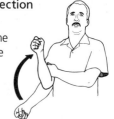

- **erection** While holding the left *open hand* in the crook of the right elbow, bring the right *S hand*, palm left, upward from the right side of the body to in front of the right shoulder.

- **can't** Bring the extended index finger of the right *one hand* downward hitting the extended index finger of the left *one hand* as it moves.

impregnate To make pregnant. See signs for CONCEIVE[1,2].

improve or **better** To become better.

- **improve** Touch the little-finger side of the right *open hand*, palm back, first to the wrist and then near the crook of the extended right arm.

incapacitate To deprive of ability or strength.

- **become** With the palms of both *open hands* together, right hand on top of left, twist the wrists in opposite directions in order to reverse positions.

- **weak** Beginning with the fingertips of the right *5 hand* touching the palm of the left *open hand* held in front of the chest, collapse the right hand downward with a double movement, bending the fingers each time.

incision or **cut** A surgical cut into a tissue or an organ.

- **knife** Slide the side of the extended right index finger, palm in, with a double movement at an angle down the length of the extended left index finger, palm right, turning the right palm down each time as it moves off the end of the left index finger.

-- [sign continues] ------------------------->

- **cut** Slide the side of the extended right index finger, palm in, across the back of the left *open hand*, palm down.

incoherent Lacking logical or meaningful connection.

- **blur** With the palms of both *5 hands* facing forward in front of the face, move both hands in from side to side going in opposite directions.

- **mind** Touch the index finger of the right *one hand* against the right side of the forehead.

- **talk** Beginning with the index-finger side of the right *4 hand* in front of the mouth, palm left and fingers pointing up, move the hand forward with a double movement.

- **can't** Bring the extended index finger of the right *one hand* downward hitting the extended index finger of the left *one hand* as it moves.

incurable Of or designating an illness that cannot be cured.

- **can't** Bring the extended index finger of the right *one hand* downward hitting the extended index finger of the left *one hand* as it moves.

- **healthy** Beginning with the fingertips of both *curved 5 hands* touching near each shoulder, bring the hands downward and forward with a deliberate movement while closing into *S hands*.

indigestion

indigestion or **dyspepsia** A feeling of discomfort after eating, such as heartburn, nausea, or bloating.

- **eat** Bring the fingertips of the right *flattened O hand* to the lips.

- **wrong** Bring the knuckles of the right *Y hand* back against the chin.

- **chew** With the palm sides of both *A hands* together, right hand on top of the left hand, move the right hand in small repeated circles in opposite directions, causing the knuckles of the two hands to rub together.

- **nausea** Move the fingertips of the right *curved 5 hand* in a repeated circle on the stomach.

induce[1] To bring about or cause.

- **cause** Beginning with both *S hands* near the body, palms up and left hand nearer the body than the right hand, move the hands forward in an arc while opening into *5 hands*.

- **happen** Beginning with the extended index fingers of both *one hands* pointing forward in front of the body, palms up, flip the hands over toward each other, ending with palms down.

induce[2] (alternate sign)

- **force** Beginning with the right *C hand* in front of the right shoulder, palm forward, and the left arm bent across the body, move the right hand downward and forward, ending with the right wrist across the left wrist, both palms down.

inebriation The state of being drunk. See signs for ALCOHOLIC[1,2].

infant A child in the earliest period of life. See signs for NEWBORN[1,2].

infection[1] Same sign used for: **insurance**.

- **infection** Move the right *I hand*, palm forward, from side to side with a repeated movement in front of the right shoulder.

infection[2] (alternate sign)

- **disease** Touch the bent middle finger of the right *5 hand* to the forehead while touching the bent middle finger of the left *5 hand* to the abdomen.

- **inside** Move the fingers of the right *flattened O hand* downward with a short double movement in the thumb side of the left *O hand* held in front of the chest.

- **body** Pat the palm side of both *open hands* first on each side of the chest and then on each side of the abdomen.

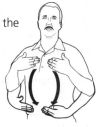

- **spread** Beginning with the fingers of both *flattened O hands* together in front of the chest, palms in and fingers pointing down, move the hands downward and apart while opening into *5 hands*.

infectious See sign for CONTAGIOUS.

infertile See signs for STERILE[2,3].

infiltrate To enter gradually through pores or small openings. See sign for PENETRATE.

inflammation

inflammation Redness, swelling, and fever in a local area of the body, often with pain.

- **hurt** Note: Form sign near the location of the inflammation. Beginning with both extended index fingers pointing toward each other in front of the chest, palms in, jab the fingers toward each other with a short repeated movement.

- **red** Brush the extended right index finger downward on the lips, bending the finger as it moves down.

- **swell** With the fingertips of the right *curved 5 hand* on the back of the bent left arm, raise the right hand a short distance.

- **pain** Beginning with the extended index fingers of both *one hands* pointing toward each other in front of the chest, both palms in, jab the fingers toward each other with a double movement.

influenza or **flu** An acute and contagious viral disease characterized by fever, exhaustion, severe aches, and inflammation of the respiratory system, often affecting the body as a whole.

- Fingerspell: F-L-U

informed consent A patient's agreement to a medical procedure or to participation in a clinical study after being informed of the medical facts and possible risks.

- **sign** Place the extended fingers of the right *H hand*, palm down, firmly down on the upturned palm of the left *open hand* held in front of the chest.

- **paper** Brush the heel of the right *open hand*, with a double movement on the heel of the left *open hand*, palms facing each other.

-- [sign continues] ------------------->

■ **before** Beginning with the back of the right *open hand*, palm in and fingers pointing left, touching the back of the left *open hand*, palm forward, move the right hand in toward the chest.

ingest To take into the body, as food or liquid. Related form: **ingestion.**

■ **eat** Bring the fingertips of the right *flattened O hand* to the lips.

■ **drink** Beginning with the thumb of the right *C hand* near the chin, palm left, tip the hand up toward the face.

■ **swallow** Move the extended right index finger from the chin, palm left and finger pointing up, downward the length of the neck.

inhalant Something, such as a medicated spray, that is inhaled for the effect of its vapor.

■ **medicine** With the bent middle finger of the right *5 hand* in the palm of the left *open hand*, palms facing each other, rock the right hand from side to side with a double movement while keeping the middle finger in place.

■ **inhale** Move the back of the right *5 hand*, palm down and fingers pointing forward, back toward the nose while closing into a *flattened O hand*.

inhale To breathe in.

■ **inhale** Move the back of the right *5 hand*, palm down and fingers pointing forward, back toward the nose while closing into a *flattened O hand*.

inject

inject, innoculate, shoot, or **vaccinate** To cause a liquid to enter the body through a needle piercing the skin.

- **inject** Move the extended index finger of the right *L hand*, palm right, against the left upper arm.

---

injection See signs for HYPODERMIC, SHOT.

---

injury See signs for PAIN[1,2].

---

innoculate See sign for INJECT.

---

inoculation[1] See sign for SHOT.

---

inoculation[2] See sign for VACCINATION.

---

inoperable Not suitable for surgery.

- **can't** Bring the extended index finger of the right *one hand* downward hitting the extended index finger of the left *one hand* as it moves.

- **operate** Move the thumb of the right *A hand*, palm down, across the upturned palm of the left *open hand* held in front of the chest.

---

inquest The official inquiry into the cause of an unnatural death. See sign for CORONER.

---

insane[1] See sign for MENTALLY ILL.

---

insane[2] Suffering from a mental disorder. See sign for PSYCHOPATH.

---

insemination To impregnate a female by the injection of semen into her reproductive organs.

- **false** Brush the extended right index finger across the tip of the nose from right to left by bending the wrist.

-- [sign continues] ---→

- **insert-up** Beginning with the fingertips of the right *flattened O hand*, palm up and fingers pointing up, inserted up in the little-finger side of the left *O hand*, push the right hand up through the left hand.

- **cause** Beginning with both *S hands* near the body, palms up and left hand nearer the body than the right hand, move the hands forward in an arc while opening into *5 hands*.

- **pregnant** Beginning with both *5 hands* entwined in front of the abdomen, bring the hands forward.

---

insomnia[1] Chronic difficulty in falling or staying asleep. Same sign used for: **alert, awake.**

- **insomnia** Place both *C hands* around the wide-open eyes with the thumbs on each cheek, palms forward.

---

insomnia[2] (alternate sign) Same sign used for: **alert, awake.**

- **can't** Bring the extended index finger of the right *one hand* downward hitting the extended index finger of the left *one hand* as it moves.

- **sleep** Lay the right cheek against the right *open hand*.

---

inspect See sign for EXAMINE.

insulin 1. A hormone produced by the pancreas that helps regulate sugar in the blood and helps produce energy. **2.** A commercial preparation taken for treatment of diabetes.

- **sugar** Bring the fingers of the right *U hand* downward on the chin with a double movement, bending the fingers each time.

- **shot** Bend the thumb of the right *L hand* down while touching the left upper arm, with the index finger.

insurance 1. Coverage by contract with a business offering monetary reimbursement as protection for loss in return for payment of a premium. **2.** The premium paid for this coverage. See sign for INFECTION[1].

intensive care unit or **ICU** An area of a hospital where patients who are seriously ill are given more care than is available in other hospital units.

- Fingerspell abbreviation: I-C-U

inter-vertebral disk See sign for DISK.

intercourse[1], coitus, sex, sexual intercourse, or **sexual relations**
Sexual relations. Same sign used for: **copulate.**

- Fingerspell abbreviation: I-C

intercourse[2], coitus, sex, sexual intercourse, or **sexual relations** (alternate sign) Same sign used for: **copulate.**

- **intercourse** Bring the right *V hand* downward in front of the chest to tap against the heel of the left *V hand* with a double movement, palms facing each other.

intermittent See sign for IRREGULAR.

intern A person serving a period of supervised experience on the staff of a hospital, especially a recent graduate of medical school. Related form: **internship.**

- **intern** Slide the little-finger side of the right *I hand*, palm left, back and forth with a double movement on the back of the left *open hand*, palm down and fingers pointing right.

internal Within the body.

- **inside** Move the fingers of the right *flattened O hand* downward with a short double movement in the thumb side of the left *O hand* held in front of the chest.

- **body** Pat the palm side of both *open hands* first on each side of the chest and then on each side of the abdomen.

internal bleeding Blood spreading in the body, outside the vessels and normal paths of blood circulation.

- **bleed** Brush the extended right index finger downward on the lips, bending the fingers as it moves down. While wiggling the fingers, move the right *5 hand* downward with a double movement past the back of the left *5 hand* held in front of the chest, both palms in and fingers pointing in opposite directions.

- **inside** Move the fingers of the right *flattened O hand* downward with a short double movement into the thumb side of the left *O hand* held in front of the chest.

- **body** Pat the palm side of both *open hands* first on each side of the chest and then on each side of the abdomen.

internal medicine A branch of medicine dealing with the diagnosis and non-surgical treatment of diseases, especially of internal organ systems.

- **medical** Touch the fingertips of the right *flattened O hand* on the wrist of the upturned left *open hand*.

-- [sign continues] --➤

- **specialty** Slide the little-finger side of the right *B hand*, palm left and fingers pointing forward, along the index-finger side of the left *B hand* held in front of the chest, palm right and fingers pointing forward.

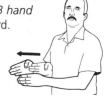

- **inside** Move the fingers of the right *flattened O hand* downward with a short double movement in the thumb side of the left *O hand* held in front of the chest.

- **body** Pat the palm side of both *open hands* first on each side of the chest and then on each side of the abdomen.

---

intestine The tubular canal that extends from the stomach to the anus, which helps to digest food, absorb nutrients, and carry waste matter to be discharged.

- **intestine** Move with the right *F hand*, palm in, in a wavy movement from the middle of the abdomen to the right side.

---

intoxicated See signs for ALCOHOLIC[1,2].

---

intrauterine device or **IUD** Any of a variety of devices inserted into the uterus to prevent the growth of fertilized eggs as a means of birth control.

- Fingerspell abbreviation: I-U-D

---

intravenous injection or **IV** An injection through the veins used to administer medications or feeding.

- Fingerspell abbreviation: I-V

---

invalid A person suffering from disease or disability. Related form: invalidism.

- **person** Move both *P hands*, palms facing each other, downward along the sides of the body.

-- [sign continues] --->

- **weak** Beginning with the fingertips of the right *5 hand* touching the palm of the left *open hand* held in front of the chest, collapse the right hand downward with a double movement, bending the fingers each time.

- **can't** Bring the extended index finger of the right *one hand* downward hitting the extended index finger of the left *one hand* as it moves.

- **walk** Beginning with both *3 hands* in front of each side of the body, palms down and fingers pointing forward, move the hands forward and back with an alternating double movement.

---

ipecac See sign for EMETIC.

---

iris The colored part of the eye containing the pupil in the center.
- **eye** Tap the extended right index finger at the outward side of the right eye with a double movement.

- **color** Wiggle the fingers of the right *5 hand* in front of the mouth, fingers pointing up.

---

irregularity Happening only occasionally or under certain conditions. Same sign used for: **intermittent**. Related form: **irregular**.
- **not** Bring the thumb of the right *10 hand* forward from under the chin with a deliberate movement.

- **regular** Brush the little-finger side of the right *one hand* across the index-finger side of the left *one hand*, as the right hand moves in a double circular movement toward the chest.

irrigate To flood with water or other liquid to clean wounds or areas of the body that undergo surgery.

- **water** Tap the index-finger side of the right *W hand*, palm left and fingers pointing up, against the chin with a double movement.

- **for** Beginning with the extended right finger touching the right side of the forehead, twist the hand forward, ending with the index finger pointing forward.

- **clean** Slide the palm of the right *open hand* from the heel to the fingers of the upturned palm of the left *open hand*.

- **less** Move the right *open hand*, palm down and fingers pointing left, from in front of the chest downward, stopping a few inches above the left *open hand*, palm up and fingers angled forward.

- **pain** Beginning with the extended index fingers of both *one hands* pointing toward each other in front of the chest, both palms in, jab the fingers toward each other with a double movement.

---

irritate See sign for ITCH.

---

issue See sign for DISCHARGE².

---

itch, irritate, or scratch An uneasy irritating sensation in the skin.

- **scratch** Move the fingertips of the right *curved 5 hand* up and down with a double movement on the back of the left *open hand*, both palms in.

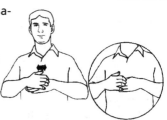

IUD See sign for INTRAUTERINE DEVICE.

IV See sign for INTRAVENOUS INJECTION.

---

jaundice Yellow skin and whites of the eyes, dark urine and light stools: symptoms of disease of the liver and blood.

- **yellow** Move the right *Y hand* with a twisting double movement in front of the right shoulder.

- **skin** Pinch and shake the loose skin on the back of the left *open hand* with the bent thumb and index finger of the right *5 hand*.

---

jaw[1] The bony structure of the lower part of the face, supporting the mouth and teeth.

- **jaw** Move the fingertips of both *curved hands* from the outside of each cheek downward toward the chin.

---

jaw[2] (alternate sign)

- **jaw** Move the extended index fingers of both *one hands* from the outside of each cheek downward toward the chin.

---

joint[1] or **socket** Structure made up of ligaments and cartilage that holds bones together and enables them to move easily in relation to each other.

- **joint** Cup the right *curved hand* over the thumb side of the left *S hand*.

---

joint[2] or **socket** (alternate sign)

- **elbow** Note: Substitute other parts of the body where joints are located. Touch the bent left elbow with the palm of the right *open hand*.

- **joint** Cup the right *curved hand* over the thumb side of the left *S hand*.

---

kidney One of a pair of organs in the abdominal cavity that filter waste matter from the blood.

■ **kidney** Place the palm side of the right *F hand* against the right side.

---

kidney stone A stony accumulation of minerals abnormally formed in the kidneys.

■ **kidney** Place the palm side of the right *F hand* against the right side.

■ **kidney-stone** Move the right *F hand,* palm left, downward in front of the chest while changing into an *A hand.* Then tap the knuckles of the right *A hand* on the back of the left *S hand* held in front of the chest, both palms down.

---

knee The joint between the thigh and the lower leg.

■ **knee** Tap the extended right index finger on the bent right knee with a double movement. Note: A right *open hand* or *F hand* may be used instead.

---

kyphosis See sign for SCOLIOSIS.

---

labor¹ The physical efforts and pain of childbirth.

■ Fingerspell: L-A-B-O-R

---

labor² (alternate sign)

■ **baby** With the right bent arm resting on the left bent arm, swing the arms from side to side with a double movement.

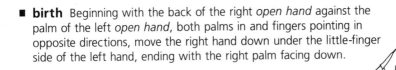

■ **ready** Move both *R hands* from in front of the right side of the body, palms down and fingers pointing forward, in a smooth movement to in front of the left side of the body.

■ **birth** Beginning with the back of the right *open hand* against the palm of the left *open hand*, both palms in and fingers pointing in opposite directions, move the right hand down under the little-finger side of the left hand, ending with the right palm facing down.

■ **dilate** Beginning with the left *C hand* around the right *S hand*, palms facing each other in front of the abdomen, move the right hand a short distance to the right while opening into a *C hand*, ending with the fingers of the right *C hand* held by the fingers of the left *C hand*.

■ **pain** Beginning with the extended index fingers of both *one hands* pointing toward each other in front of the chest, both palms in, jab the fingers toward each other with a double movement.

lactation **1.** The secretion of milk. **2.** The period of time that a mother produces milk.

- **breast** Touch the fingertips of the right *bent hand* first on the left side of the chest and then on the right side of the chest.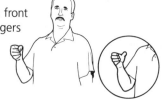

- **milk** Beginning with the right *S hand*, palm left, in front of the right side of the body, open and close the fingers with a double movement, forming a *C hand* each time.

Lamaze method A method of childbirth in which the mother is prepared physically and psychologically to give birth without using drugs.

- **practice** Rub the knuckles of the right *A hand*, palm down, back and forth with a double movement on the extended left index finger held in front of the chest, palm in and finger pointing right.

- **breathe** With the right *5 hand* in front of the chest above the left *5 hand*, fingers pointing in opposite directions and palms in, move both hands forward and back toward the chest with a double movement.

- **for** Beginning with the extended right finger touching the right side of the forehead, twist the hand forward, ending with the index finger pointing forward.

- **birth** Beginning with the back of the right *open hand* against the palm of the left *open hand*, both palms in and fingers pointing in opposite directions, move the right hand down under the little-finger side of the left hand, ending with the right palm facing down.

lame See sign for CRIPPLED.

laminectomy Surgical procedure to remove a portion of the lower vertebra.

- **spine** With the extended right index finger of the right *one hand*, palm up, point to the right side of the lower back. Beginning with the right *F hand* on the thumb side of the left *F hand*, bring the right hand straight up.

- **operate** Move the thumb of the right *A hand*, palm down, across the upturned palm of the left *open hand* held in front of the chest.

lance To make a clean cut with a surgical knife, often to drain off fluids. See sign for LACERATION.

lancet See sign for SCALPEL.

laryngectomy Surgical procedure to remove all or part of the larynx.

- **operate-throat** Drag the thumb of the right *A hand*, downward on the neck.

- **remove-from-neck** Beginning with the fingers of the *curved 5 hand* on the throat, move the hand forward while changing to an *S hand*. Then turn the right wrist forward while changing into an *5 hand*, palm down and fingers pointing forward.

laryngitis Inflammation of the larynx, often accompanied by a sore throat, hoarseness or loss of voice, and a dry cough.

- **can't** Bring the extended index finger of the right *one hand* downward hitting the extended index finger of the left *one hand* as it moves.

- **talk** Beginning with the index-finger side of the right *4 hand* in front of the mouth, palm left and fingers pointing up, move the hand forward with a double movement.

larynx See sign for THROAT.

latent or **dormant** Of, pertaining to, or representing a disease that is present but not active; something that exists in an undeveloped form. Same sign used for: **latent period.**

- **not-yet** Bend the wrist of the right *open hand*, palm back and fingers pointing down, back with a double movement near the right side of the waist.

- **hit** Strike the knuckles of the right *S hand* against the extended index finger of the left *one hand* pointing up in front of the chest.

latent period The interval between exposure to a disease and its development. See sign for LATENT.

lateral or **side** Situated on, directed toward, or coming from the side.

- **side** Bring the right *open hand*, palm facing left and fingers pointing forward, downward in front of the right side of the body.

laughing gas See sign for NITROUS OXIDE.

laxative Medication used to relieve constipation by loosening the feces.

- **medicine** With the bent middle finger of the right *5 hand* in the palm of the left *open hand*, palms facing each other, rock the right hand from side to side with a double movement while keeping the middle finger in place.

- **help** With the little-finger side of the left *A hand* in the palm of the right *open hand*, move both hands upward in front of the chest.

- **cause** Beginning with both *S hands* near the body, palms up and left hand nearer the body than the right hand, move the hands forward in an arc while opening into *5 hands*.

-- [sign continues] --->

■ **bowel movement** Beginning with the thumb of the right *10 hand* inserted in the little-finger side of the left *A hand*, palms facing in opposite directions, bring the right hand deliberately downward.

learning disability[1] Difficulty in reading and writing experienced by school-age children, caused by an impaired central nervous system. Related form: **learning disabled.**

■ Fingerspell abbreviation: L-D

learning disability[2] (alternate sign) Related form: **learning disabled.**

■ **learn** Beginning with the fingertips of the right *curved 5 hand* on the upturned left *open hand*, bring the right hand up while closing the fingers and thumb into a *flattened O hand* near the forehead.

■ **disability** Tap the fingertips of the right *D hand*, palm down, on the base of the thumb of the left *B hand*, palm right.

leg One of a pair of parts of the body extending from the thigh to the ankle; used to support the body and for walking, running, etc.

■ **leg** Beginning with the left *open hand* on the upper leg, bend the leg, sliding the left hand downward toward the knee.

lessen See signs for DECREASE[1,2,3].

lethal Capable of causing death.

■ **cause** Beginning with both *S hands* near the body, palms up and left hand nearer the body than the right hand, move the hands forward in an arc while opening into *5 hands*.

-- [sign continues] ---▶

- **die** Beginning with both *open hands* in front of the body, right palm down and left palm up, flip the hands to the right, turning the right palm up and the left palm down.

lethargy Fatigue; weariness. See sign for TIRED[1].

leukemia A cancerous disease in which leukocytes increase abnormally in the tissues and often in the blood.

- **white** Beginning with the fingertips of the right *curved 5 hand* on the chest, pull the hand forward while closing the fingers into a *flattened O hand*.

- **blood** While wiggling the fingers, move the right *5 hand* from the chin downward with a double movement past the back of the left *5 hand* held in front of the chest, both palms in and fingers pointing in opposite directions.

- **cell** Move the right *F hand*, palm left, to multiple places in front of the head and body.

- **disease** Touch the bent middle finger of the right *5 hand* to the forehead while touching the bent middle finger of the left *5 hand* to the abdomen.

leukocyte[1] or **white blood cell** A white or colorless blood cell of the immune system having a nucleus.

- **white** Beginning with the fingertips of the right *curved 5 hand* on the chest, pull the hand forward while closing the fingers into a *flattened O hand*.

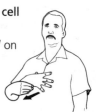

-- [sign continues] --->

- **blood** While wiggling the fingers, move the right *5 hand* from the chin downward with a double movement past the back of the left *5 hand* held in front of the chest, both palms in and fingers pointing in opposite directions.

- **cell** Move the right *F hand*, palm left, to multiple places in front of the head and body.

leukocyte[2] or **white blood cell** (alternate sign)

- **part** Slide the little-finger side of the right *open hand*, palm left and fingers pointing forward, across the palm of the left *open hand*, palm up.

- **blood** While wiggling the fingers, move the right *5 hand* from the chin downward with a double movement past the back of the left *5 hand* held in front of the chest, both palms in and fingers pointing in opposite directions.

- **against** Hit the fingertips of the right *bent hand* into the left *open hand*, palm right and fingers pointing forward.

- **disease** Touch the bent middle finger of the right *5 hand* to the forehead while touching the bent middle finger of the left *5 hand* to the abdomen.

lice See signs for PEDICULOSIS[1,2].

licensed practical nurse or **LPN** A nurse who is licensed to provide basic nursing care under the supervision of a Registered Nurse or a doctor.

- Fingerspell abbreviation: L-P-N

lie down

lie down or **recline** To be in or stay in a horizontal position. Same sign used for: **supine.**

- **lie-down** Beginning with the back of the right *V hand* on the palm of the left *open hand*, both palms up, pull the right hand in toward the body.

life expectancy The expected number of years of life based on statistical estimates that take into account occupation, physical condition, sex, etc.

- **life** Move both *L hands* upward from each side of the body to each side of the chest.

- **extend** Beginning with the thumb side of the right *S hand* against the little-finger side of the left *S hand*, move the right hand forward and downward with a wavy movement.

life-support Equipment or other measures that are used to sustain or artificially substitute for essential body functions, such as breathing.

- **life** Move both *L hands* upward from each side of the body to each side of the chest.

- **depend** With the extended right index finger across the extended left index finger, palms down, move both fingers down.

- **machine** With the fingers of both *curved 5 hands* loosely meshed together, palms in, move the hands up and down in front of the chest with a repeated movement.

limbs or extremities Arms and legs.

- **arm** Slide the palm of the right *curved hand* up the length of the extended left arm beginning at the wrist.

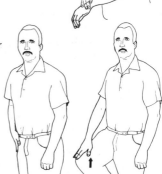

- **leg** Beginning with the left *open hand* on the upper leg, bend the leg sliding the left hand downward toward the knee.

limp See sign for CRIPPLED.

liniment See sign for OINTMENT.

lip One of two fleshy folds that surround the mouth.

- **lip** Draw a rectangle around the edge of the mouth with the extended right index finger, palm down.

liposuction Surgical removal of excess fat from under the skin by means of a small incision and vacuum suctioning.

- Fingerspell: F-A-T
- **suck-body** Beginning with the fingertips of the right *5 hand* on the abdomen, bring the hand forward with a double movement, closing into a *flattened O hand* each time.

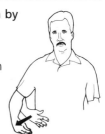

liquid diet[1] A diet that restricts someone to the consumption of substances that need no chewing.

- **eat** Bring the fingertips of the right *flattened O hand* to the lips.

-- [sign continues] ---➤

liquid diet

- **soft** Beginning with both *curved 5 hands* in front of each side of the chest, palms up, bring the hands down with a double movement while closing the fingers to the thumbs each time.

- **none** Move both *O hands*, palms forward, from in front of the chest outward to each side.

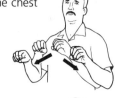

- **hard** Strike the little-finger side of the right *bent V hand* sharply against the index-finger side of the left *bent V hand*, palms facing in opposite directions.

liquid diet² (alternate sign)

- **liquid-diet** Beginning with the right *L hand*, palm down, in front of the right side of the chest, move the right hand in an arc to the left, while raising the elbow, to insert the thumb in the thumb-side opening of the left *S hand*.

liquids See sign for FLUIDS.

live or survive To exist or dwell. Related form: life.

- **life** Move both *L hands* upward from each side of the body to each side of the chest.

living will See signs for ADVANCE DIRECTIVE[1,2].

lockjaw[1] or tetanus A spasm of the jaw muscles causing an inability to open the jaws.

- **jaw** Move the extended index fingers of both *one hands* from the outside of each cheek downward toward the chin.

-- [sign continues] -->

- **freeze** Beginning with both *5 hands* in front of each side of the body, palms down and fingers pointing forward, pull the hands back toward the body while constricting the fingers.

lockjaw[2] or **tetanus** (alternate sign)

- **hurt** Beginning with both extended index fingers pointing toward each other in front near the right jaw, palms in, jab the fingers toward each other with a short repeated movement.

- **jaw** Move the extended index fingers of both *one hands* from the outside of each cheek downward toward the chin.

- **freeze** Beginning with both *5 hands* in front of each side of the body, palms down and fingers pointing forward, pull the hands back toward the body while constricting the fingers.

---

lordosis See sign for SCOLIOSIS.

---

lotion See sign for OINTMENT.

---

low blood pressure See sign for HYPOTENSION.

LPN See sign for LICENSED PRACTICAL NURSE.

---

lumbago See sign for BACKACHE.

---

lumbar Pertaining to the back. See signs for BACK[1,2].

---

lump[1], bump, or **node** A small swelling, as one caused by a blow or an infection.

- **bump** Beginning with the extended right index finger, on the back of the left wrist, palm down, bring the right finger upward in a small arc, ending with the back of the right index finger on the back of the left *open hand*, palm down.

---

lump

lump², bump, or node (alternate sign)

- **bump** Note: Form this sign near the location of the lump being discussed. Beginning with the finger-tips of the right *curved 5 hand* on the right side of the head, move the hand upward a short distance.

lump³, bump, or node (alternate sign)

- **bump** Note: Form this sign near the location of the lump being discussed. Beginning with the index-finger side of the right *B hand* touching the right side of the head, twist the wrist to bring the little-finger side against the right side of the forehead.

lumpectomy Surgical removal of a cyst or tumor from the breast.

- **bump** Note: Form this sign near the location of the lump being discussed. Beginning with the extended right index finger on the back of the left wrist, palm down, bring the right finger upward in a small arc, ending with the back of the right index finger on the left *open hand*, palm down.

- **operate** Note: Form this sign near the location of the lump to be removed. Move the thumb of the right *A hand*, palm down, downward on the right side of the chest.

- **remove** Bring the palm side of the right *curved hand* down on the palm of the left *open hand* while changing to an *A hand*. Then move the right hand downward to the right while opening in to a *5 hand*.

lung One of the two organs in the chest that form a special breathing apparatus. Same sign used for: **pulmonary**.

- **lung** Rub the fingertips of both *bent hands*, palms in, up and down with a repeated movement near the center of the chest.

magnet See sign for ABSORB.

magnetic resonance imaging[1] or **MRI** A diagnostic method that uses a strong magnetic field to study the body's internal structures and a computer to produce detailed pictures. Same sign used for: **magnetic resonance scanner.**
- Fingerspell abbreviation: M-R-I

magnetic resonance imaging[2] or **MRI** (alternate sign) Same sign used for: **magnetic resonance scanner.**

- **lie-down** Insert the extended fingers of the right *H hand*, palm down, under the left *C hand* held in front of the chest, palm down.

- **picture** Move the right *C hand*, palm forward, from near the right side of the face downward, ending with the index-finger side of the right *C hand* against the palm of the left *open hand* held in front of the chest, palm right.

- **head** Touch the fingertips of the right *bent hand* first to the right side of the chin and then to the right side of the forehead.

magnetic resonance scanner A diagnostic scanner used in magnetic resonance imaging. See signs for MAGNETIC RESONANCE IMAGING[1,2]

male or **man** A person of the sex that fathers babies.

- **male** Beginning with the thumb of the right *10 hand* on the right side of the forehead, bring the hand downward while opening into a *5 hand*, ending with the thumb touching the chest.

213

malformation

malformation[1] See sign for DYSPLASIA.

malformation[2] See signs for ABNORMAL[1,2,3].

malignant (of a tumor) Characterized by uncontrolled growth; cancerous and invasive. See sign for CANCER[2].

mammary Of or pertaining to the breast. See sign for BREAST.

mammillary or **nipple** The small projection on a breast that, in females, contains the conduit for the milk glands.

- **nipple** Place the thumb side of the right *F hand*, palm left, first on the left side of the chest and then the right side.

mammogram A type of diagnostic x-ray of the female breast that reveals cancerous growths while they are still treatable.

- **breast** Touch the fingertips of the right *bent hand* first on the left side of the chest and then on the right side of the chest.

- **press** With the right *open hand*, palm down and fingers pointing left, over the left *open hand*, palm up and fingers pointing right in front of the chest, move the hands toward each other with a deliberate short movement.

- **take-picture** With the left *open hand*, palm up and fingers pointing right, in front of the chest, and the right *flattened O hand* above the left hand, palm in and fingers pointing in, open the right hand into a *5 hand* and close to a *flattened O hand* again.

man See sign for MALE.

manage See sign for CONTROL.

manipulation To examine or treat by skillful use of the hands, as in palpation, reduction of dislocations, or changing the position of a fetus.

- **skill** Grasp the little-finger side of the left *open hand* with the curved right fingers. Then pull the right hand forward and downward while closing the fingers into the palm.

-- [sign continues] ---➤

- **massage** With both *open hands* apart in front of the body, palms down, move the hands down at an angle with a repeated movement closing the fingers to *A hands* each time.

---

marker or **tumor marker** A chemical found in elevated quantities in the blood or other body fluid that suggests that cancer is present.

- **analyze** With both *V hands* pointing toward each other in front of the chest, palms down, move the fingers down and apart with a double movement, bending the fingers each time.

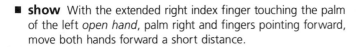

- **blood** While wiggling the fingers, move the right *5 hand* from the chin downward with a double movement past the back of the left *5 hand* held in front of the chest, both palms in and fingers pointing in opposite directions.

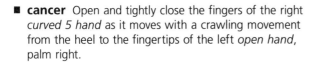

- **show** With the extended right index finger touching the palm of the left *open hand*, palm right and fingers pointing forward, move both hands forward a short distance.

- **cancer** Open and tightly close the fingers of the right *curved 5 hand* as it moves with a crawling movement from the heel to the fingertips of the left *open hand*, palm right.

---

marrow¹ The soft center of bones that is a major site of cell production.

- **skeleton** With the hands crossed at the wrists, tap the fingers of both *bent V hands* on the opposite side of the chest.

- **hole** Move the extended right index finger, palm in and finger pointing left, in a circular movement around the opening of the thumb side of the left *O hand*.

marrow² (alternate sign)

- **bone** With a double movement, tap the back of the right *bent V hand*, palm up, on the back of the left *S hand*, palm down.

- **hole** Move the extended right index finger, palm in and finger pointing left, in a circular movement around the opening of the thumb side of the left *O hand*.

mastectomy The surgical removal of all or part of a woman's breast, usually to prevent the spread of cancer.

- **breast** Touch the fingertips of the right *bent hand* first on the left side of the chest and then on the right side of the chest.

- **operate** Move the extended thumb of the right *10 hand*, palm down, downward on the right side of the chest.

- **remove** Beginning with the fingers of the *curved 5 hand* on the right side of the chest, move the hand forward while changing to an *S hand*. Then turn the wrist forward and move the hand down while changing into an *S hand*, palm down and fingers pointing forward.

masturbation¹ Manipulation of one's genitals in order to stimulate an orgasm.

- **male-masturbation** Move the right *S hand*, palm up, forward and back at an angle with a repeated movement in front of the chest.

masturbation² (alternate sign used for female masturbation)

- **female-masturbation** Insert the bent middle finger of the right *5 hand*, palm down, up and down with a double movement in the thumb-side opening of the left *S hand* held in front of the chest, palm in.

maternity The state of being a mother.

- **female** Beginning with the thumb of the right *A hand* on the chin, bring the hand downward while opening into a *5 hand*, ending with the thumb touching the chest.

- **pregnant** Beginning with both *5 hands* entwined in front of the abdomen, bring the hands forward.

matter See sign for PUS.

measles A contagious viral disease marked by fever and red spots on the skin.

- **measles** Beginning with the fingertips of both *curved 5 hands* on each lower cheek, touch the fingers several places on the cheeks as the hands move upward.

medical Related to the science or practice of medicine.

- **medical** Tap the fingertips of the right *flattened O hand* on the wrist of the upturned left *open hand* with a double movement.

medical chart or **chart** A sheet giving an itemized patient history of dates and times for data such as temperature, medicines, and doses.

- **paper** Brush the heel of the right *open hand*, with a double movement on the heel of the left *open hand*, palms facing each other.

- **list** Touch the little-finger side of the right *bent hand* palm in, several times on the palm of the left *open hand*, palm right and fingers pointing up, as it moves from the fingers downward to the heel.

medical emergency See sign for EMERGENCY.

medical examiner

medical examiner See sign for CORONER.

Medicare A government sponsored insurance program for elderly or disabled people.

- **insurance** Move the right *I hand*, palm forward, from side to side with a repeated movement in front of the right shoulder.

- **program** Move the middle finger of the right *P hand*, palm left, from the heel, over the fingertips, and wrist of the left *open hand*, palm in and fingers pointing up.

- **for** Beginning with the extended right finger touching the right side of the forehead, twist the hand forward, ending with the index finger pointing forward.

- **old** Move the right *C hand* from near the chin, palm left, downward a short distance while closing into an *S hand*.

- **people** Move both *P hands*, palms down, in alternating forward circles in front of each side of the body.

medicate To treat with medicine. See sign for MEDICINE. Related form: **medication**.

medicine, drug or **medication** A drug or preparation used in treating disease. Same sign used for: **medicate**. Related form: **medicinal**.

- **medicine** With the bent middle finger of the right *5 hand* in the palm of the left *open hand*, palms facing each other, rock the right hand from side to side with a double movement while keeping the middle finger in place.

menarche The first menstrual period.

- **first** Beginning with the extended right index finger pointing up in front of the right side of the chest, palm forward, twist the hand, ending with the palm in.

- **menstruation** Tap the palm side of the right *A hand* against the right cheek with a double movement.

---

meningitis A bacterial infection causing an inflammation of the membrane of the brain or spinal cord.

- **serious** With the fingertip of the extended right index finger on the right side of the chin, twist the hand back and forth with a small double movement.

- **disease** Touch the bent middle finger of the right *5 hand* to the forehead while touching the bent middle finger of the left *5 hand* to the abdomen.

- **sometimes** Bring the extended right index finger, palm in, downward against the upturned palm of the left *open hand* and up again in a rhythmic double circular movement.

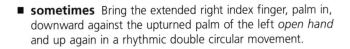

- **cause** Beginning with both *S hands* near the body, palms up and left hand nearer the body than the right hand, move the hands forward in an arc while opening into *5 hands*.

- **deaf** Touch the tip or side of the extended right index finger first to near the right ear and then to near the right side of the mouth.

menopause or **change of life** The period in midlife during which menstruation naturally ceases.

- **old** Move the right *C hand* from near the chin, palm left, downward a short distance while closing into an *S hand*.

- **menstruation** Tap the palm side of the right *A hand* against the right cheek with a double movement.

- **stop** Hit the little-finger side of the right *open hand* on the palm of the left *open hand*.

---

menses See sign for MENSTRUATION.

---

menstrual cramps The involuntary, painful spasms of the abdomen that can occur during menstruation.

- **menstruation** Tap the palm side of the right *A hand* against the right cheek with a double movement.

- **cramp** Beginning with the thumb side of both *A hands* touching in front of the body, both palms down, twist the right hand downward, ending with palm in.

---

menstruation, menses, or **period** A discharging of blood and tissue from the uterus at monthly intervals, between puberty and menopause, by a nonpregnant female.

- **menstruation** Tap the palm side of the right *A hand* against the right cheek with a double movement.

---

mental or **mind** Related to the mind; the mind itself.

- **mind** Touch the fingers of the right *M hand* against the right side of the forehead.

mental health Psychological well-being and satisfactory adjustment to society.

- **mental** Touch the fingers of the right *M hand* against the right side of the forehead.

- **health** Touch the fingertips of both *H hands*, palms in, first to each side of the chest and then to each side of the waist.

mentally ill or **insane** Having any of various forms of psychosis or severe neurosis. Related form: **mental illness.**

- **mental** Touch the fingers of the right *M hand* against the right side of the forehead.

- **disease** Touch the bent middle finger of the right *5 hand* to the forehead while touching the bent middle finger of the left *5 hand* to the abdomen.

mentally retarded[1], developmentally disabled, or feeble-minded
Having a developmental disorder characterized by a limited ability to learn. Related form: **mental retardation.**

- **mind** Touch the index finger of the right *one hand* against the right side of the forehead.

- **slow** Pull the fingers of the right *5 hand* from the fingers to the wrist of the left *open hand,* both palms down.

mentally retarded[2], developmentally disabled, or feeble-minded
(alternate sign) Related form: **mental retardation.**

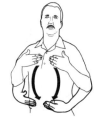

- **weak-mind** Keeping the fingertips of the right *curved hand* on the right side of the forehead, palm down, collapse the fingers with a double movement, bringing the palm close to the forehead each time.

mercy killing See sign for EUTHANASIA.

metastasis The spread of cancerous cells or infectious germs from their original location to other parts of the body. Related form: **metastasize.**

- **body** Pat the palm side of both *open hands* first on each side of the chest and then on each side of the abdomen.

- **disease** Touch the bent middle finger of the right *5 hand* to the forehead while touching the bent middle finger of the left *5 hand* to the abdomen.

- **spread-in-body** Beginning with both *flattened O hands* in front of each side of the chest, fingers pointing down, move the hands downward and outward, while opening into *5 hands.*

midwife A nurse with special training and experience with childbirth.

- **female** Beginning with the thumb of the right *A hand* on the chin, bring the hand downward while opening into a *5 hand*, ending with the thumb touching the chest.

- **specialty** Slide the little-finger side of the right *B hand*, palm left and fingers pointing forward, along the index-finger side of the left *B hand* held in front of the chest, palm right and fingers pointing forward.

- **baby** With the right bent arm resting on the left bent arm, swing the arms from side to side with a double movement.

- **birth** Beginning with the back of the right *open hand* against the palm of the left *open hand*, both palms in and fingers pointing in opposite directions, move the right hand down under the little-finger side of the left hand, ending with the right palm facing down.

migraine[1] A severe, recurrent headache characterized by pressure or throbbing beginning on one side of the head and accompanied by nausea and other disturbances.

- **migraine** Beginning with the thumb side of the right *modified C hand* against the forehead, bring the hand forward a short distance.

migraine[2] See sign for HEADACHE.

milk tooth, deciduous tooth, or **baby tooth** One of the first 20 temporary teeth.

- **baby** With the right bent arm resting on the left bent arm, swing the arms from side to side with a double movement.

-- [sign continues] --➤

mind

tooth Touch a front tooth with the index finger of the right *one hand*.

---

mind¹, cerebrum, or **brain** The part of a person with the capacity to think, reason, perceive, etc.

■ **mind** Tap the index finger of the right *X hand* against the right side of the forehead with a double movement.

---

mind², cerebrum, or **brain** (alternate sign)

■ **mind** Touch the index finger of the right *one hand* against the right side of the forehead.

---

mind³ See sign for MENTAL.

---

mole A small, often dark, raised spot on the skin.

■ **brown** Slide the index-finger side of the right *B hand*, palm left, down the right cheek with a double movement.

■ **spot** Place the index-finger side of the right *F hand*, palm forward, against the right cheek.

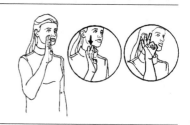

---

monitor, care for, or **take care of** To observe for a special purpose.

■ **take-care-of** With the little-finger side of the right *K hand* across the index-finger side of the left *K hand*, move the hands in a repeated flat circle in front of the body.

---

morning sickness Nausea occurring in the early part of the day during the first months of pregnancy.

■ **pregnant** Beginning with both *5 hands* entwined in front of the abdomen, bring the hands forward.

-- [sign continues] ---▶

- **every-morning** With the left *open hand* in the crook of the bent right arm and the right *open hand* held up in front of the left side of the chest, palm in and fingers pointing up, swing the right hand from left to right in front of the chest.

- **sick** Touch the bent middle finger of the right *5 hand* to the forehead while touching the bent middle finger of the left *5 hand* to the abdomen.

---

morphine A narcotic derived from opium and used in medicine as a pain reliever and sedative.

- **strong** Move both *S hands* forward with a deliberate movement from each shoulder.

- **shot** Move the index finger of the right *L hand* sharply against the left upper arm.

- **stop** Hit the little-finger side of the right *open hand* on the palm of the left *open hand*.

- **pain** Beginning with the extended index fingers of both *one hands* pointing toward each other in front of the chest, both palms in, jab the fingers toward each other with a deliberate movement while turning the palms up.

-- [sign continues]

motion sickness

- **easy** Brush the fingertips of the right *curved hand* upward on the back of the fingertips of the left *curved hand* with a double movement, both palms up.

- **addiction** Hook the index finger of the right *X hand* in the right corner of the mouth and pull outward a short distance.

motion sickness Nausea and dizziness resulting from the effects of movement in travel.

- **boat** With the little-finger sides of both *curved hands* together, palms up, move the hands forward in a bouncing double arc.

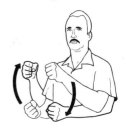

- **car** Beginning with both *S hands* in front of the chest, palms in and left hand higher than the right hand, move the hands in an up-and-down arc with a repeated alternating movement.

- **airplane** Move the right hand with the thumb, index finger, and little finger extended, palm down, upward to the left in an arc, beginning in front of the right shoulder.

- **nausea** Move the fingertips of the right *curved 5 hand* in a repeated circle on the stomach.

-- [sign continues] -->

- **sick** Touch the bent middle finger of the right *5 hand* to the forehead while touching the bent middle finger of the left *5 hand* to the abdomen.

mouth or **oral** The opening and cavity in the head through which food passes, containing the tongue, gums, and teeth.

- **mouth** Draw a circle around the edge of the mouth with the extended right index finger, palm down.

mouth-to-mouth resuscitation[1]**, cardiopulmonary resuscitation,** or **CPR** a method of artificial respiration in which a person rhythmically blows air into the victim's lungs.

- Fingerspell abbreviation: C-P-R

mouth-to-mouth resuscitation[2]**, cardiopulmonary resuscitation,** or **CPR** (alternate sign)

- **lie-down** Lay the back of the right *V hand* on the palm of the left *open hand*, both palms up.

- **mouth** Move the extended right index finger from right to left across the lips, palm in and finger pointing up.

- **blow** With the fingers of the right *flattened C hand* on the fingers of the *flattened C hand* in front of the mouth, palms facing each other, mime blowing.

227

MRI

MRI See signs for MAGNETIC RESONANCE IMAGING[1,2].

MS See sign for MULTIPLE SCLEROSIS.

mucus Slippery liquid produced by the lining of internal cavities and tubular systems, which serves to moisten and protect. Related form: **mucous**.

- **white** Beginning with the fingertips of the right *curved 5 hand* on the chest, pull the hand forward while closing the fingers into a *flattened O hand*.

- **thick** With the thumb and index finger of the right *S hand* extended and curved in front of the mouth, palm in, move the hand forward in an arc.

- **runny** Bring the right *4 hand*, palm back and fingers pointing left, downward with a double movement from the nose.

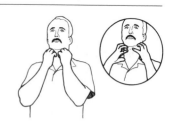

multiple sclerosis or **MS** A disease marked by patches of hardened tissue in the brain or spinal cord resulting in partial or complete paralysis and muscular twitching.

- Fingerspell abbreviation: M-S

mumps A contagious viral disease marked by swollen glands.

- **mumps** Beginning with both *curved 5 hands* on each side of the neck, palms facing in, bring the hands outward a short distance while spreading the fingers slightly.

muscle[1] A special bundle of tissue in the body composed of long cells that contract to produce movement.

- **muscle** Tap the fingertips of the right *M hand* against the upper part of the bent left arm with a double movement.

muscle² (alternate sign)

- **muscle** Beginning with the index-finger side of the right *M hand*, palm down and fingers pointing left, against the upper bent left arm, bring the right hand downward while twisting the palm up, ending with the little-finger side of the right hand on the left forearm.

---

myopic or nearsighted (alternate sign) Related form: myopia.

- **can** Move both *S Hands*, palms down, downward simultaneously with a short double movement in front of each side of the body.

- **see** Move with the fingers of the right *V hand*, pointing up in front of the eyes, forward a short distance.

- **near** With both open hands, palms in and fingers pointing up, held up in front of the face, left hand nearer the face than the right hand, move the right hand in toward the back of the left hand.

- **can't** Bring the extended index finger of the right *one hand* downward hitting the extended index finger of the left *one hand* as it moves.

- **see** Move with the fingers of the right *V hand*, pointing up in front of the eyes, forward a short distance.

-- [sign continues] -->

myopic

■ **far** Beginning with the palm sides of both *A hands* together in front of the chest, move the right hand forward in an arc.

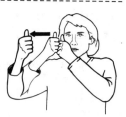

---

narcolepsy A disorder characterized by frequent episodes of deep sleep.

- **sleep** Bring the right *open hand*, palm left and fingers pointing up, in against the right cheek.

- **can't** Bring the extended index finger of the right *one hand* downward hitting the extended index finger of the left *one hand* as it moves.

- **control** Beginning with both *modified X hands* in front of each side of the body, right hand forward of the left hand and palms facing each other, move the hands forward and back with a repeated movement.

---

narcotic Medication used to control severe pain, which can become addictive and cause reduced breathing, nausea, vomiting, low blood pressure, and constipation.

- **medicine** With the bent middle finger of the right *5 hand* in the palm of the left *open hand*, palms facing each other, rock the right hand from side to side with a double movement while keeping the middle finger in place.

- **stop** Hit the little-finger side of the right *open hand* on the palm of the left *open hand*.

- **pain** Beginning with the extended index fingers of both *one hands* pointing toward each other in front of the chest, both palms in, jab the fingers toward each other with a double movement.

-- [sign continues] -->

- **can** Move both *S hands*, palms down, downward simultaneously with a short double movement in front of each side of the body.

- **habit** With the heel of the right *C hand* on the back of the left *S hand*, move both hands downward while changing the right hand to an *S hand*.

nasal passage The cavity above the roof of the mouth that divides into two halves which open onto the face through the nostrils. See sign for NOSTRIL.

nasal See sign for NOSE.

natural childbirth Childbirth involving little or no use of drugs or anesthesia. Usually natural childbirth is preceded by a program preparing the mother for the childbirth process.

- **natural** Move the right *N hand* in a small circle and then straight down to land on the back of the left *open hand*.

- **baby** With the right bent arm resting on the left bent arm, swing the arms from side to side with a double movement.

- **birth** Beginning with the back of the right *open hand* against the palm of the left *open hand*, both palms in and fingers pointing in opposite directions, move the right hand down under the little-finger side of the left hand, ending with the right palm facing down.

natural Having undergone little or no processing and containing no chemical additives. See sign for NORMAL.

naturopathy A method of treating disease without surgery or synthetic drugs, but using fasting, special diets, massage, etc., to assist the natural healing process.

- **specialty** Slide the little-finger side of the right *B hand*, palm left and fingers pointing forward, along the index-finger side of the left *B hand* held in front of the chest, palm right and fingers pointing forward.

- **natural** Move the right *N hand* in a small circle and then straight down to land on the back of the left *open hand*.

- **medicine** With the bent middle finger of the right *5 hand* in the palm of the left *open hand*, palms facing each other, rock the right hand from side to side with a double movement while keeping the middle finger in place.

nausea¹ or upset stomach Sickness at the stomach accompanied by a distaste for food and an urge to vomit.

- **nausea** Move the fingertips of the right *curved 5 hand* in a repeated circle on the stomach.

nausea² or upset stomach (alternate sign)

- **feel** Move the bent middle finger of the right *5 hand* upward on the chest.

- **same-as** Move the right *Y hand*, palm down, from side to side with a double movement in front of the right side of the body.

-- [sign continues] -->

navel

- **want** Beginning with both *curved 5 hands* in front of the body, both palms up and fingers pointing forward, bring the hands back toward the chest while constricting the fingers toward the palms.

- **vomit** Beginning with the right *5 hand* near the mouth, palm left and fingers pointing forward, and the left *5 hand* forward of the right hand, palm right and fingers pointing forward, move both hands upward and forward in large arcs.

---

navel See sign for UMBILICUS.

---

nearsighted See signs for MYOPIC[1,2].

---

neck The part of the body that connects the head and the shoulders.

- **neck** Tap the fingertips of the right *bent hand*, palm down, against the neck with a double movement. Note: a right extended index finger may be used instead.

---

necropsy See sign for AUTOPSY.

---

negative[1] Failing to show a positive result in a diagnostic test.

- **test** Beginning with both extended index fingers pointing forward in front of the chest, palms down, bring the hands downward while bending the index fingers into *X hands* and continuing down while extending the index fingers again.

- **answer** Beginning with both extended index fingers pointing up in front of the mouth, right hand nearer the mouth than the left and palms forward, bend the wrists down simultaneously, ending with the fingers pointing forward and the palms down.

- **negative** Bring the thumb side of the extended right index finger, palm down and finger pointing forward, against the palm of the left *open hand*, palm right and fingers pointing up.

negative[2] (alternate sign)

- **no** Snap the extended right index and middle fingers closed to the extended right thumb, palm down, while moving the hand down slightly.

- **not** Bring the thumb of the right *10 hand* forward from under the chin with a deliberate movement.

- **have** Bring the fingertips of both *bent hands* in to touch each side of the chest.

---

neonate See signs for NEWBORN[1,2].

---

neoplasm See sign for TUMOR.

---

nerve[1] One or more bundles of fibers that, as part of a system, convey impulses of sensation, motion, etc., between the brain or spinal cord and other parts of the body.

- Fingerspell: N-E-R-V-E

---

nerve[2] (alternate sign)

- **nerve** Move the fingertips of the right *N hand*, palm down, from the wrist to the crook of the back of the bent left arm.

---

nervous or **hyperactive** Easily excited or irritated; jumpy.

---

nervous breakdown A non-technical term for any disabling mental or emotional disorder requiring treatment.

- **nervous** Shake both *5 hands* with a loose, repeated movement in front of each side of the body, palms in, and fingers pointing in.

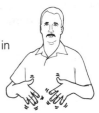

-- [sign continues] --➤

- **get** Beginning with the little-finger side of the right *curved 5 hand*, palm left, on the index-finger side of the left *curved 5 hand*, palm right, bring the hands back toward the chest while closing into *S hands*.

- **breakdown** Beginning with the fingertips of both *curved 5 hands* touching in front of the chest, palms facing each other, allow the fingers to loosely drop, ending with the palms down.

- **nervous** Shake both *5 hands* with a loose, repeated movement in front of each side of the body, palms facing in and fingers pointing down.

nervous system A mechanism in the body that coordinates internal functions and responses to stimuli.

- **nervous** Shake both *5 hands* with a loose, repeated movement in front of each side of the body, palms facing in and fingers pointing down.

- **system** Beginning with the index-finger sides of both *S hands* touching in front of the chest, palms down, move the hands outward to in front of each shoulder and then straight down a short distance.

newborn[1] or **neonate** A child in its first 28 days of life. Same sign used for: **baby, infant.**

- **new** Slide the back of the right *curved hand*, palm up, from the fingertips to the heel of the upturned left *open hand*.

-- [sign continues] ---➤

- **baby** With the right bent arm resting on the left bent arm, swing the arms from side to side with a double movement.

newborn[2] or **neonate** (alternate sign) Same sign used for: **baby, infant.**

- **recent** With the little-finger side of the right *X hand* against the right cheek, palm back, bend the right index finger down with a small repeated movement.

- **birth** Beginning with the back of the right *open hand* against the palm of the left *open hand*, both palms in and fingers pointing in opposite directions, move the right hand down under the little-finger side of the left hand, ending with the right palm facing down.

nipple See sign for MAMMILLARY.

nitrous oxide or **laughing gas** A colorless, odorless gas used as an anesthetic.

- **mask** Bring the right *curved hand*, palm in, toward the face with a deliberate movement to cover the nose and mouth.

- **feel** Move the bent middle finger of the right *5 hand* upward on the chest.

- **none** Move both *O hands*, palms forward, from in front of the chest outward to each side.

- **pain** Beginning with the extended index fingers of both *one hands* pointing toward each other in front of the chest, both palms in, jab the fingers toward each other with a double movement.

nocturnal emission An involuntary ejaculation of semen during sleep.

- **wet** Tap the index-finger side of the right *W hand*, palm left, against the chin. Then, beginning with both *5 hands* in front of the body, palms up, bring the hands downward while closing the fingers into *O hands* with a double movement.

- **dream** Move the extended right index finger from touching the right side of the forehead, palm down, outward to the right while bending the finger up and down.

node See signs for LUMP[1,2,3].

normal The usual condition. Same sign used for: **natural, organic.**

- **natural** Move the right *N hand* in a small circle and then straight down to land on the back of the left *open hand.*

nose The part of the face protruding above the lips and having openings for breathing and smelling. Related form: **nasal.**

- **nose** Touch the nose with the extended index finger of the right *one hand.*

nose job (*informal*) or **rhinoplasty** Plastic surgery of the nose.

- **nose** Touch the nose with the extended index finger of the right *one hand.*

- **fix** Brush the fingertips of both *flattened O hands* across each other repeatedly as the hands move up and down in opposite directions in a double movement.

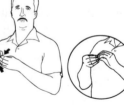

nosebleed or **epistaxis** Bleeding from the nostrils.

- **blood** While wiggling the fingers, move the right *5 hand* from the chin downward with a double movement past the back of the left *open hand* held in front of the chest, both palms in and fingers pointing in opposite directions.

- **drip** Beginning with the back of right *S hand*, palm down, near the nose, flick the right index finger downward with a repeated movement.

nostril Either of two external openings in the nose. Same sign used for: **nasal passage**.

- **nostril** Move the extended right index finger in a small circle near the bottom of the nose.

Novocaine *Trademark*. See signs for PROCAINE[1,2].

noxious Harmful or injurious to health.

- **danger** Move the thumb of the right *10 hand*, palm left, upward on the back of the left *A hand*, palm in, with a double movement.

numb[1] Stripped of the power of feeling.

- **feel** Move the bent middle finger of the right *5 hand* upward on the chest.

- **none** Move both *O hands*, palms forward, from in front of the chest outward to each side.

numb

numb[2] (alternate sign)

- **freeze** Beginning with both *5 hands* in front of each side of the body, palms down and fingers pointing forward, pull the hands back toward the body while constricting the fingers.

- **can't** Bring the extended index finger of the right *one hand* downward hitting the extended index finger of the left *one hand* as it moves.

- **feel** Move the bent middle finger of the right *5 hand* upward on the chest.

nurse[1] A person trained to care for ill people.

- **nurse** Tap the extended fingers of the right *N hand*, palm down, with a double movement on the wrist of the left *open hand* held in front of the body, palm up.

nurse[2] See signs for BREAST FEED[1,2].

nurse practitioner A registered nurse with additional training; qualified to diagnose and treat common or minor ailments.

- Fingerspell abbreviation: N-P

nursing home[1], convalescent home, or **rest home** A residential facility providing care for people needing care, including the elderly, the ill, etc. Same sign used for: **extended care.**

- **home** Touch the fingertips of the right flattened O hand first to the right side of the chin and then to the right cheek.

- **take-care-of** With the little-finger side of the right *K hand* across the index-finger side of the left *K hand*, move the hands in a repeated flat circle in front of the body.

- **old** Move the right *C hand* from near the chin, palm left, downward a short distance while closing into an *S hand*.

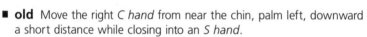

-- [sign continues] --→

- **people** Move both *P hands*, palms down, in alternating forward circles in front of each side of the body.

---

nursing home², convalescent home, or rest home (alternate sign) Same sign used for: **extended care.**

- **place** Beginning with the middle fingers of both *P hands* touching in front of the body, palms facing each other, move the hands apart in a circular movement back until they touch again near the chest.

- **stay** With the thumb of the right *10 hand* on the thumbnail of the left *10 hand*, both palms down in front of the chest, move the hands forward and downward a short distance.

- **nurse** Tap the extended fingers of the right *N hand* on the wrist of the left *open hand* held in front of the body, palm up.

- **take-care-of** With the little-finger side of the right *K hand* across the index-finger side of the left *K hand*, move the hands in a repeated flat circle in front of the body.

---

nursing home³, convalescent home, or rest home
(alternate sign) Same sign used for: **extended care.**

- **nurse** Tap the extended fingers of the right *N hand* on the wrist of the left *open hand* held in front of the body, palm up.

- **home** Touch the fingertips of the right *flattened O hand* first to the right side of the chin and then to the right cheek.

obese See sign for FAT. Related form: **obesity.**

obsession or **fixation** The domination of one's thoughts by a persistent idea, desire, etc. Same sign used for: **obsessive-compulsive.**

■ **obsession** With the bent middle finger of the right *5 hand* on the back of the left *open hand*, both palms down, move the hands forward in a repeated circular movement in front of the body.

obsessive-compulsive 1. Characterized by the symptoms of obsessive-compulsive disorder. 2. A person with obsessive-compulsive disorder. See sign for OBSESSION.

obsessive-compulsive disorder An anxiety disorder involving persistent and disturbing thoughts, impulses, or images plus repetitive driven behaviors that interfere with normal life and relationships.

■ **obsession** With the bent middle finger of the right *5 hand* on the back of the left *open hand*, both palms down, move the hands forward in a repeated circular movement in front of the body.

■ **behavior** Move both *B hands*, palms forward, simultaneously from side to side in front of the body with a repeated swinging movement.

obstetrician[1] A doctor specially trained to provide health care for pregnant mothers. See signs for OBSTETRICS[1,2]

obstetrics[1] A branch of medicine concerned with childbirth and the care and treatment of women before and during childbirth. Same sign used for: **obstetrician.**

■ Fingerspell: O-B

obstetrics² (alternate sign) Note: add the person marker before this sign to form the medical professional: **obstetrician.**

- **specialty** Slide the little-finger side of the right *B hand*, palm left and fingers pointing forward, along the index-finger side of the left *B hand* held in front of the chest, palm right and fingers pointing forward.

- **pregnant** Beginning with both *5 hands* entwined in front of the abdomen, bring the hands forward.

---

obstruction Something that is in the way and prevents normal function. See sign for PREVENT.

---

occipital Related to the back part of the skull.

- **point to location** With the extended right index finger point to the back of the head.

---

occurrence¹ Something that appears or happens.

- **happen** With the extended index fingers of both *one hands* pointing forward in front of the body, palms up, flip the hands over toward each other, ending with palms down.

---

occurrence² (alternate sign)

- **show-up** Push the extended right index finger, palm left, upward between the index finger and middle finger of the left *open hand*, palm down.

---

ocular

ocular Of, pertaining to, or for the eyes. See sign for EYE.

oculist A doctor specially trained to diagnose and treat diseases of the eyes. See sign for OPHTHALMOLOGY.

OD See signs for OVERDOSE[1,2,3].

odor A quality that affects the sense of smell. See sign for OLFACTORY.

ointment, liniment, lotion, or **salve** A soft, usually greasy and medicated, preparation for application to the skin.

- **medicine** With the bent middle finger of the right *5 hand* in the palm of the left *open hand*, palms facing each other, rock the right hand from side to side with a double movement while keeping the middle finger in place.

- **rub** Rub the fingers of the right *open hand* with a quick repeated movement on the back of the left *open hand*, both palms down.

olfactory Related to the sense of smell. Same sign used for: **odor, smell.**

- **smell** Move the palm side of the right *open hand* upward in front of the nose with a double movement.

oncologist A doctor specially trained to diagnose and treat cancer. See sign for ONCOLOGY.

oncology The branch of medical science dealing with tumors, including the origin, development, diagnosis, and treatment of cancer. Note: add the person marker before this sign to form the medical professional: **oncologist.**

- **medical** Touch the fingertips of the right *flattened O hand* on the wrist of the upturned left *open hand*.

- **specialty** Slide the little-finger side of the right *B hand*, palm left and fingers pointing forward, along the index-finger side of the left *B hand* held in front of the chest, palm right and fingers pointing forward.

-- [sign continues] -->

■ **cancer** Open and tightly close the fingers of the right *curved 5 hand* as it moves with a crawling movement from the heel to the fingertips of the left *open hand*, palm right.

---

oophorectomy, ovariectomy, or **ovariotomy** The surgical removal of the ovary.

■ **female** Beginning with the thumb of the right *A hand* on the chin, bring the hand downward while opening into a *5 hand*, ending with the thumb touching the chest.

■ **operate-abdomen** Move the extended thumbs of both *10 hands*, outward on each side of the abdomen.

■ **ovary** Place the palm side of both *F hands*, fingers pointing down, against each side of the abdomen.

■ **eliminate** Beginning with the thumbs of both *A hands* tucked in near each side of the abdomen, palms in, move the hands outward while flicking the thumbs out.

---

open fracture A broken bone accompanied by a break in the skin covering the area. Formerly known as: **compound fracture**. See also COMPLETE FRACTURE, FRACTURE, GREENSTICK, SIMPLE FRACTURE.

■ **bone** With a double movement, tap the back of the right *bent V hand*, palm up, on the back of the left *S hand*, palm down.

-- [sign continues] --➤

- **break** Beginning with both *S hands* in front of the body, index fingers touching and palms down, move the hands away from each other while twisting the wrists with a deliberate movement, ending with the palms facing each other.

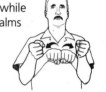

- **bone-pop-up** Beginning with the palm side of right *S hand* on the forearm of the bent left arm, flick the right index finger up.

- **through** Slide the little-finger side of the right *open hand* between the middle finger and ring finger of the left *open hand* held up in front of the chest, palm right and fingers pointing up.

- **skin** Pinch and shake the loose skin on the back of the left *open hand* with the bent thumb and index finger of the right *5 hand*.

open-heart surgery Surgery performed on the exposed heart with the aid of a heart-lung machine.

- **open-heart** Beginning with the index-finger side of both *B hands* touching in front of the left side of the chest, palms down, twist both wrists up while bringing the hands apart to in front of each side of the chest, ending with the palms facing each other.

- **heart** Touch the bent middle finger of the right *5 hand* on the left side of the chest.

- **operate** Move the extended thumb of the right *10 hand*, palm down, downward on the left side of the chest.

operable Of or describing a condition that can be treated by surgery.

■ **can** Move both *S hands*, palms down, downward simultaneously with a short double movement in front of each side of the body.

■ **operate** Move the thumb of the right *A hand*, palm down, across the upturned palm of the left *open hand* held in front of the chest.

operate To perform a surgical procedure for remedying an injury or dysfunction in the body. Note: Add the person marker before this sign to form the medical professional: **surgeon.** Same sign used for: **surgery, surgical.** Related form: **operation.**

■ **operate** Move the thumb of the right *A hand*, palm down, across the upturned palm of the left *open hand* held in front of the chest.

ophthalmologist A doctor specially trained to diagnose and treat diseases of the eye. See sign for OPHTHALMOLOGY.

ophthalmology The branch of medicine dealing with the anatomy, functions, and disease of the eye. Note: add the person marker before this sign to form the medical professionals: **oculist, ophthalmologist.**

■ **medical** Touch the fingertips if the right *flattened O hand* on the wrist of the upturned left *open hand*.

■ **specialty** Slide the little-finger side of the right *B hand*, palm left and fingers pointing forward, along the index-finger side of the left *B hand* held in front of the chest, palm right and fingers pointing forward.

■ **eyes** With the extended index fingers of both *one hands* point to the bottom of each eye.

-- [sign continues] ---→

ophthalmoscope

- **disease** Touch the bent middle finger of the right *5 hand* to the forehead while touching the bent middle finger of the left *5 hand* to the abdomen.

ophthalmoscope An instrument used for viewing the interior of the eye, especially the retina.

- **eye** Tap the extended right index finger at the outward side of the right eye with a double movement.

- **otoscope** Move the thumb of the right *modified X hand*, palm left, in and out with a short double movement from the nose while watching the hand move.

optic or **optical** Of or pertaining to the eye or to sight. See sign for EYE.

optic Pertaining to the eyes. Related form: **optical**.

- **connect** Beginning with both *curved 5 hands* apart in front of the body, bring the hands together to intersect with each other by closing the thumb to the index finger of each hand.

- **eye** Tap the extended right index finger at the outward side of the right eye with a double movement.

optician A person who makes or sells eyeglasses and contact lens.

- **person marker** Move both *open hands*, palms facing each other, downward along the sides of the body.

- **make** Beginning with the little-finger side of the right *S hand* on the index-finger side of the left *S hand*, separate the hands slightly, twist the wrists in opposite directions, and touch the hands together again.

-- [sign continues]

- **glasses** Tap the thumbs of both *modified C hands*, palms facing each other, near the outside corner of each eye.

optometrist A licensed specialist who examines eyes for defects and prescribes corrective lenses.

- **medical** Tap the fingertips of the right *flattened O hand* on the wrist of the upturned left *open hand* with a double movement.

- **specialty** Slide the little-finger side of the right *B hand*, palm left and fingers pointing forward, along the index-finger side of the left *B hand* held in front of the chest, palm right and fingers pointing forward.

- **eyes** With the extended index fingers of both *one hands* point to the bottom of each eye.

- **test** Beginning with both extended index fingers pointing forward in front of the chest, palms down, bring the hands downward while bending the index fingers into *X hands* and continuing down while extending the index fingers again.

oral See sign for MOUTH.

organic Derived from living organisms without chemical additives. See sign for NORMAL.

orgasm See signs for CLIMAX[1,2].

osteoarthritis See sign for ARTHRITIS.

osteopathy A system of treating diseases that places emphasis on massage and manipulation, but does not exclude other treatment. See signs for CHIROPRACTIC[1,2]. Related form: **osteopathic**.

osteoporosis A disease in which bones become increasingly porous and brittle, occurring especially in women after menopause.

- **bone** With a double movement, tap the back of the right *bent V hand*, palm up, on the back of the left *S hand*, palm down.

- **soft** Beginning with both *curved 5 hands* in front of each side of the chest, palms up, bring the hands down with a double movement while closing the fingers to the thumbs each time.

- **weak** Beginning with the fingertips of the right *5 hand* touching the palm of the left *open hand* held in front of the chest, collapse the right hand downward with a double movement, bending the fingers each time.

otitis media Inflammation of the middle ear, characterized by pain, dizziness, and impaired hearing.

- **ear** Touch the right ear with the extended right index finger.

- **infection** Move the right *I hand*, palm forward, from side to side with a repeated movement in front of the right shoulder.

otologist A doctor whose specialty is the treatment of diseases of the ear. See sign for OTOLOGY.

otology The study and treatment of diseases of the ear. Note: Add the person marker before this sign to form the medical professional: otologist.

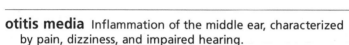

- **specialty** Slide the little-finger side of the right *B hand*, palm left and fingers pointing forward, along the index-finger side of the left *B hand* held in front of the chest, palm right and fingers pointing forward.

- **ear** Touch the right ear with the extended right index finger.

-- [sign continues] -->

- **disease** Touch the bent middle finger of the right *5 hand* to the forehead while touching the bent middle finger of the left *5 hand* to the abdomen.

otorhinolaryngology[1] or **ENT** The study and treatment of diseases of the ear, nose, and throat. Note: add the person marker before this sign to form the medical professional: **otorhinolaryngologist.**

- Fingerspell abbreviation: E-N-T

otorhinolaryngology[2] (alternate sign) Note: add the person marker before this sign to form the medical professional: **otorhinolaryngologist.**

- **medical** Touch the fingertips of the right *flattened O hand* on the wrist of the upturned left *open hand*.

- **specialty** Slide the little-finger side of the right *B hand*, palm left and fingers pointing forward, along the index-finger side of the left *B hand* held in front of the chest, palm right and fingers pointing forward.

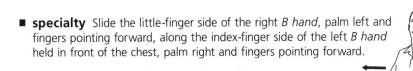

- **disease** Touch the bent middle finger of the right *5 hand* to the forehead while touching the bent middle finger of the left *5 hand* to the abdomen.

- **ear** Touch the right ear with the extended right index finger.

- **nose** Touch the nose with the extended index finger of the right *one hand*.

-- [sign continues] --->

otorhinolarynogologist

- **throat** Brush the extended fingertips of the right *G hand* downward along the length of the neck.

otorhinolarynogologist A doctor whose specialty is the treatment of the ear, nose, and throat. See signs for OTORHINOLARYNGOLOGY[1,2].

otoscope An instrument used for viewing the interior of the ear

- **ear** Touch the right ear with the extended right index finger.

- **otoscope** Move the thumb of the right *modified X hand*, palm left, in and out with a short double movement from the nose while watching the hand move.

outpatient A person who receives treatment at a hospital without residing there.

- **outside** Beginning with the right *flattened O hand* inserted in the palm side of the left *C hand*, bring the right hand upward.

- **patient** Move the extended middle finger of the right *p hand* first down and then forward on the left upper arm.

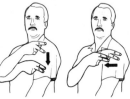

- **not** Bring the thumb of the right *10 hand* forward from under the chin with a deliberate movement.

- **stay** With the thumb of the right *10 hand* on the thumbnail of the left *10 hand*, both palms down in front of the chest, move the hands forward and downward a short distance.

ovariectomy See sign for OOPHORECTOMY.

ovariotomy See sign for OOPHORECTOMY.

ovary The female sexual gland where eggs mature and ripen for fertilization.
■ **ovary** Place the palm side of both *F hands*, fingers pointing down, against each side of the abdomen.

over-the-counter drug A drug sold legally without a prescription.
■ **can** Move both *S hands*, palms down, downward simultaneously with a short double movement in front of each side of the body.

■ **buy** Beginning with the back of the right *flattened O hand* in the palm of the left *open hand*, both palms up, move the right hand forward in an arc.

■ **medicine** With the bent middle finger of the right *5 hand* in the palm of the left *open hand*, palms facing each other, rock the right hand from side to side with a double movement while keeping the middle finger in place.

■ **store** Beginning with both *flattened O hands* held in front of each side of the chest, palms down and fingers pointing down, swing the fingertips forward and back by twisting the wrists up and down with a double movement.

overdose[1] or **OD** **1.** Too large a dose of a drug. **2.** To take an excessive, harmful, or fatal amount of a drug.
■ Fingerspell abbreviation: O-D

253

overdose

overdose[2] or OD (alternate sign used for an overdose of over-the-counter or prescription drugs)

- **exceed** Beginning with the fingers of the right *bent hand* on the back of the left *bent hand*, both palms down, bring the right hand upward.

- **medicine** With the bent middle finger of the right *5 hand* in the palm of the left *open hand*, palms facing each other, rock the right hand from side to side with a double movement while keeping the middle finger in place.

overdose[3] or OD (alternate sign used for an overdose with illegal drugs)

- **exceed** Beginning with the fingers of the right *bent hand* on the back of the left *bent hand*, both palms down, bring the right hand upward.

- **drug** Pound the little-finger side of the right *S hand* with a double movement near the crook of the bent left arm.

overweight See sign for FAT.

ovulation The monthly process in which an egg leaves the ovary for possible fertilization by sperm. Related form: **ovulate**.

- **menstruation** Tap the palm side of the right *A hand* against the right cheek with a double movement.

- **monthly** Move the extended right index finger, palm in and finger pointing left, from the tip to the base of the extended left index finger, palm right and finger pointing up in front of the chest, with a double movement.

oxygen[1] A gas without color or odor that forms part of the breathable atmosphere.

- **oxygen** Shake the right *O hand*, palm forward, in front of the right shoulder.

oxygen² (alternate sign)

- **nose** Touch the nose with the extended index finger of the right *one hand*.

- **mask** Bring the right *curved 5 hand*, palm in, toward the face with a deliberate movement to cover the nose and mouth.

pacemaker An electronic device surgically implanted beneath the skin to provide a normal heartbeat by electrical stimulation of the heart muscle.

■ **machine** With the fingers of both *curved 5 hands* loosely meshed together, palms in, move the hands up and down in front of the chest with a repeated movement.

■ **control** Beginning with both *modified X hands* in front of each side of the body, right hand forward of the left hand and palms facing each other, move the hands forward and back with a repeated movement.

■ **false** Brush the extended right index finger across the tip of the nose from right to left by bending the wrist.

■ **heartbeat** Touch the bent middle finger of the right *5 hand* on the left side of the chest. Then tap the back of the right *S hand* against the palm of the left *open hand* held in front of the chest.

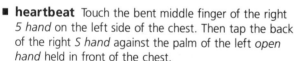

---

pain¹, ache, hurt, injury, sore, or **tender** Unpleasant sensation arising from stimulation of sensory nerves located throughout the body.

■ **pain** Beginning with the extended index fingers of both *one hands* pointing toward each other in front of the chest, both palms in, jab the fingers toward each other with a double movement.

---

pain², ache, hurt, injury, sore, or **tender** (alternate sign)

■ **pain** Beginning with both extended index fingers pointing toward each other in front of the chest, right palm down and left palm up, twist the wrists in opposite directions, ending with the right palm up and the left palm down.

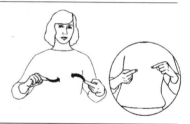

painkiller A drug or treatment that relieves pain, especially an analgesic.

- **medicine** With the bent middle finger of the right *5 hand* in the palm of the left *open hand*, palms facing each other, rock the right hand from side to side with a double movement while keeping the middle finger in place.

- **stop** Hit the little-finger side of the right *open hand* on the palm of the left *open hand*.

- **pain** Beginning with the extended index fingers of both *one hands* pointing toward each other in front of the chest, both palms in, jab the fingers toward each other with a double movement.

pale Lacking warm or intense skin color. See signs for PALLOR[1,2].

palliative Medication that relieves pain without contributing to the healing process.

- **medicine** With the bent middle finger of the right *5 hand* in the palm of the left *open hand*, palms facing each other, rock the right hand from side to side with a double movement while keeping the middle finger in place.

- **suffer** With the thumbnail of the right *A hand* on the chin, twist the hand down with a double movement.

- **reduce** Move the right *bent hand* from in front of the chest downward to a few inches above the left *bent hand*, palms facing each other.

pallor

pallor¹ A condition of extreme paleness, as from illness. Same sign used for: **pale.**

- **skin** Pinch and shake the loose skin on the back of the left *open hand* with the bent thumb and index finger of the right *5 hand*.

- **white-face** Beginning with the fingertips of the right *5 hand* on the chest, pull the hand forward while closing into a *flattened O hand*. Then move the hand upward toward the face while changing into a *5 hand*.

pallor² (alternate sign) Same sign used for: **pale.**

- **skin** Pinch and shake the skin of the right cheek with the index finger and thumb of the right *modified X hand*.

- **pale** Bring the palm side of the right *open hand*, fingers pointing up, downward on the right cheek.

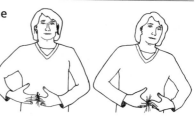

palpate To examine by touch, especially for the purpose of diagnosing an illness or condition.

- **palpate** In a number of locations, push the fingers of both *open hands* on the stomach, both palms in and fingers near each other.

palpitate To beat rapidly, as the heart does. See sign for PULSATION.

Pap smear, Papanicolaou test, or **Pap test** A test routinely done to screen for cancer of the cervix and uterus in an early and treatable stage.

- **vagina** Touch the index fingers and thumbs of both *L hands*, palms in and index fingers pointing down, together in front of the body.

- **scratch** With the extended index finger of the right *X hand* scratch in the pelvic area.

Pap test See sign for Pap smear.

Papanicolaou test See sign for Pap smear.

paraldehyde See sign for tranquilizer.

paralysis A condition in which all or part of the body has lost the ability to move or feel sensation.
- **freeze** Beginning with both *5 hands* in front of each side of the body, palms down and fingers pointing forward, pull the hands back toward the body while constricting the fingers.

paramedic[1] **or EMT** A person who is trained to provide emergency medical treatment or to assist a physician.
- Fingerspell abbreviation: E-M-T

paramedic[2] **or EMT** (alternate sign)
- **emergency** Shake the right *e hand*, palm forward, back and forth in front of the right shoulder.

- **medical** Touch the fingertips of the right *flattened O hand* on the wrist of the upturned left *open hand*.

- **technical** Tap the bent middle finger of the right *5 hand*, palm up, upward on the little-finger side of the left *open hand*, palm right and fingers pointing forward, with a double movement.

- **person marker** Move both *open hands*, palms facing each other, downward along the sides of the body.

paranoia

paranoia[1] Mental illness in which a person believes that he or she is being talked about or plotted against. Related form: **paranoid**.

- **suspicious** Beginning with the extended right index finger touching the right side of the forehead, palm down, bring the hand forward a short distance with a double movement, bending the index finger into an *X hand* each time.

- **people** Move both *P hands*, palms down, in alternating forward circles in front of each side of the body.

- **against-me** Hit the fingertips of the right *bent hand* against the palm of the left *open hand*, palm forward and fingers pointing up, pushing both hands back toward the chest.

---

paranoia[2] (alternate sign) Related form: **paranoid**.

- **paranoid** Beginning with the extended middle finger of the right *P hand* touching the right side of the forehead, palm left, move the right hand quickly forward with a double movement while bending the middle finger down.

---

paraplegic A person who has paralysis of the lower limbs due to spinal disease or injury.

- **waist-down** Beginning with both *open hands* at the waist, right hand below the left hand, palms up and fingers pointing in opposite directions, move the right hand downward while keeping the left hand in place.

- **freeze** Beginning with both *5 hands* in front of each side of the body, palms down and fingers pointing forward, pull the hands back toward the body while constricting the fingers.

paregoric A drug derived from opium used as a mild sedative and to treat diarrhea.

- **medicine** With the bent middle finger of the right *5 hand* in the palm of the left *open hand*, palms facing each other, rock the right hand from side to side with a double movement while keeping the middle finger in place.

- **less** Move the right *bent hand*, palm down and fingers pointing left, from in front of the chest downward, stopping a few inches above the left *open hand*, palm up and fingers angled forward.

- **bowel movement** Beginning with the thumb of the right *10 hand* inserted in the little-finger side of the left *A hand*, palms facing in opposite directions, bring the right hand deliberately downward.

Parkinson's disease See sign for TREMOR.

parturition See sign for CHILDBIRTH.

pass gas To experience flatulence. See sign for FLATULENCE.

pass out[1] or **black out** To lose consciousness. Same sign used for: **stupor.**

- Fingerspell abbreviation: Place the thumb side of the right *P hand*, and then the right *O hand*, against the forehead, palm left.

pass out[2] or **black out** (alternate sign) Same sign used for: **stupor.**

- **pass out** Beginning with the right *P hand* in front of the right shoulder, palm left, move the hand down while changing to an *O hand*, ending with the little-finger side of the right *O hand* on the palm of the left *open hand* held in front of the chest, palm up.

passive smoking The inhaling of the cigarette, cigar, or pipe smoke of others by a nonsmoker in close proximity.

- **inhale** Move the back of the right *5 hand*, palm down and fingers pointing forward, back toward the nose while closing into a *flattened O hand*.

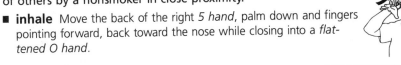

-- [sign continues] -->

patch

■ **other** Beginning with the right *10 hand* in front of the chest, palm down, flip the hand over to the right, ending with palm up.

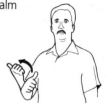

■ **person** Move both *P hands*, palms facing each other, downward along the sides of the body.

■ **smoke** Beginning with the fingers of the right *V hand* touching the right side of the mouth, palm in and fingers pointing up, bring the hand forward with a double movement.

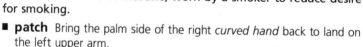

patch¹ or **The patch** A medicated dressing, usually with a slow-released, low dose of nicotine, worn by a smoker to reduce desire for smoking.

■ **patch** Bring the palm side of the right *curved hand* back to land on the left upper arm.

patch² or **eye patch** A pad worn to protect an injured eye.

■ **eye-patch** Place the fingers of the right *open hand* on the right eye, palm in and fingers pointing left.

paternity test A blood test in which genetic markers are compared to assess the relationship, if any, between a man and an offspring.

■ **baby** With the right bent arm resting on the left bent arm, swing the arms from side to side with a double movement.

-- [sign continues] --➤

262

- **blood** While wiggling the fingers, move the right *5 hand* from the chin downward with a double movement past the back of the left *open hand* held in front of the chest, both palms in and fingers pointing in opposite directions.

- **test** Beginning with both extended index fingers pointing forward in front of the chest, palms down, bring the hands downward while bending the index fingers into *X hands* and continuing down while extending the index fingers again.

- **match** Beginning with both *curved 5 hands* in front of each side of the chest, palms in, bring the hands together, ending with the bent fingers of both hands meshed together in front of the chest.

- **father** Tap the thumb of the right *5 hand*, palm right and fingers pointing up, against the forehead.

pathologist A doctor whose specialty is the analysis of blood, cells, etc., to determine abnormalities in structure and function that may characterize a particular disease. See sign for PATHOLOGY.

pathology The study of diseases and especially the changes in structure and function that constitute disease. Note: Add the person marker before this sign to form the medical professional: **pathologist.**

- **specialty** Slide the little-finger side of the right *b hand*, palm left and fingers pointing forward, along the index-finger side of the left *b hand* held in front of the chest, palm right and fingers pointing forward.

- **analyze** With both *V hands* pointing toward each other in front of the chest, palms down, move the fingers down and apart with a double movement, bending the fingers each time.

-- [sign continues]

patient

- **disease** Touch the bent middle finger of the right *5 hand* to the forehead while touching the bent middle finger of the left *5 hand* to the abdomen.

patient A person under medical care or treatment.

- **patient** Move the extended middle finger of the right *P hand* first down and then forward on the left upper arm.

pectoral Of or pertaining to the chest. See sign for CHEST.

pediatrician A doctor specializing in working with children, their development and diseases. See sign for PEDIATRICS.

pediatrics The medical branch concerned with the development, care, and diseases of babies and children. Note: Add the person marker before this sign to form the medical professional: **pediatrician.**

- **medical** Tap the fingertips of the right *flattened O hand* on the wrist of the upturned left *open hand* with a double movement.

- **specialty** Slide the little-finger side of the right *B hand*, palm left and fingers pointing forward, along the index-finger side of the left *B hand* held in front of the chest, palm right and fingers pointing forward.

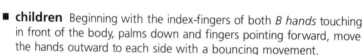

- **children** Beginning with the index-fingers of both *B hands* touching in front of the body, palms down and fingers pointing forward, move the hands outward to each side with a bouncing movement.

pediculosis¹ or **lice** An infestation of lice, especially in hairy parts of the body. Same sign used for: **crab louse**.

■ **bug** With the extended thumb of the right *3 hand* on the nose, palm left, bend the extended index and middle fingers with a double movement.

■ **scratch** Move the fingertips of the right *curved 5 hand* up and down with a double movement near the pelvic area.

pediculosis² or **lice** (alternate sign used for head lice) Same sign used for: **crab louse**.

■ **bug** With the extended thumb of the right *3 hand* on the nose, palm left, bend the extended index and middle fingers with a double movement.

■ **scratch** Move the fingertips of the right *bent 3 hand* up and down with a double movement on the right side of the head.

pelvic exam Examination of a woman's reproductive organs to diagnose pregnancy or detect diseases.

■ **vagina** Touch the index fingers and thumbs of both *L hands*, palms in and index fingers pointing down, together in front of the body.

■ **inspect** Move the extended right index finger from the nose down to strike sharply off the upturned palm of the left *open hand*, and then upward again.

penetrate¹ or **puncture** To enter by piercing. Same sign used for: **infiltrate**. Related form: **penetration**.

■ **penetrate** Insert the extended right index finger, palm in and finger pointing downward, with a deliberate movement between the middle and ring fingers of the left *open hand* held in front of the chest, palm down and fingers pointing right.

penetrate[2] or **puncture** (alternate sign) Same sign used for: infiltrate. Related form: **penetration**.

- **insert** Push the extended index finger of the right *one hand*, palm down, into the thumb-side opening of the left *S hand* held in front of the chest, palm down.

penicillin Any of several antibiotics produced naturally and used widely to prevent and treat bacterial infections and other diseases.

- **medicine** With the bent middle finger of the right *5 hand* in the palm of the left *open hand*, palms facing each other, rock the right hand from side to side with a double movement while keeping the middle finger in place.

- **infection** Move the right *I hand*, palm forward, from side to side with a repeated movement in front of the right shoulder.

- **dissolve** Beginning with both *flattened O hands* in front of the body, palms up, move the thumb of each hand smoothly across each fingertip, starting with the little fingers and ending as *10 hands* while moving the hands outward to each side.

penis or **phallus** The male organ used for sexual intercourse and urination.

- **penis** Touch the middle finger of the right *P hand* against the nose.

pep pills See sign for AMPHETAMINE.

peptic See sign for DIGESTION.

period See sign for MENSTRUATION.

periodontist See sign for GUM.

periodontitis See sign for PYORRHEA.

peripheral vision See sign for VISUAL FIELD.

perish See sign for DIE.

---

peristalsis Successive waves of involuntary muscle contractions that move food through hollow tubes in the body, such as the alimentary canal.

- **peristalsis** With the fingertips of both *C hands* on the chest, right hand above the left hand, bring the hands downward while changing into *S hands*. Repeat several times.

---

permanent teeth The second set of teeth, following milk teeth, that last until old age and consist of 32 teeth.

- **full** Slide the palm of the right *open hand*, palm down, from right to left across the index-finger side of the left *S hand*, palm right.

- **continue** Beginning with the thumb of the right *10 hand* on the thumbnail of the left *10 hand*, both palms down in front of the chest, move the hands forward.

- **teeth** Move the curved index finger of the right *X hand* from right to left across the top front teeth.

---

phallus See sign for PENIS.

---

pharmacist See sign for DRUGGIST.

---

pharmacy, apothecary, or **drugstore** A store that sells drugs and medicines and often toiletries, stationery, and other items; drugstore.

- **store** Beginning with both *flattened O hands* held in front of each side of the chest, palms down and fingers pointing down, swing the fingertips forward and back by twisting the wrists upward with a double movement.

- **buy** Beginning with the back of the right *flattened O hand* in the palm of the left *open hand*, both palms up, move the right hand forward in an arc.

-- [sign continues] -->

- **medicine** With the bent middle finger of the right *5 hand* in the palm of the left *open hand*, palms facing each other, rock the right hand from side to side with a double movement while keeping the middle finger in place.

pharyngitis or **sore throat** Inflammation of the linings of the throat.

- **pain** With both extended index fingers pointing toward each other near the throat, palms down, jab the fingers toward each other with a short double movement.

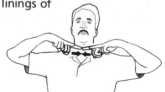

phlegm The thick mucus secreted in the respiratory passages, as during a cold.

- **phlegm** Move the right *curved 5 hand*, palm in, upward in front of the chest to in front of the mouth. Then turn the hand over, bringing the palm side of the right *curved 5 hand* down into the palm of the left *open hand* held in front of the body, palm up.

physical examination See signs for EXAMINATION[1,2].

physical Of or pertaining to the body. See sign for BODY.

physical therapy Treatment of diseases by physical or mechanical means of treating the bone, muscular, and nervous systems to help restore normal function after disease or injury.

- **body** Pat the palm side of both *open hands* first on each side of the chest and then on each side of the abdomen.

- **therapy** Beginning with the little-finger side of the right *T hand*, palm in, on the upturned palm of the left *open hand*, move both hands upward in front of the chest.

physician See sign for DOCTOR[1].

physician's directive See signs for ADVANCE DIRECTIVE[1,2].

pigment The natural substance that produces color in skin.

- **skin** Pinch and shake the loose skin on the back of the left *open hand* with the bent thumb and index finger of the right *5 hand*.

- **color** Wiggle the fingers of the right *5 hand* in front of the mouth, fingers pointing up.

pile See sign for HEMORRHOID.

pill[1], capsule, caplet, or **tablet** Medicine formed in a small rounded mass to be swallowed whole.

- **pill** Beginning with the thumb of the right *A hand* tucked under the right index finger, palm left, flick the thumb upward toward the mouth with a double movement.

pill[2], capsule, caplet, or **tablet** (alternate sign)

- **pill** Beginning with the index finger of the right *A hand* tucked under the thumb, flick the right index finger open toward the mouth with a double movement.

pimple One of the small inflamed swellings of acne. See signs for ACNE[1,2].

pinkeye See signs for CONJUNCTIVITIS[1,2].

placebo or **placebo effect** A treatment that alters a person's condition or behavior because he or she expects a change to occur.

- **compare** With both *curved hands* in front of each side of the chest, alternately turn one hand and then the other toward the face while turning the other hand in the opposite direction, keeping the palms facing each other and the fingers pointing up.

- **group-group** Beginning with both *C hands* in front of the right side of the chest, palms facing each other, bring the hands away from each other in outward arcs while turning the palms in, ending with the little fingers near each other. Repeat in front of the left shoulder.

-- [sign continues] -->

placenta

- **false** Brush the extended right index finger across the tip of the nose from right to left by bending the wrist.

- **medicine** With the bent middle finger of the right *5 hand* in the palm of the left *open hand*, palms facing each other, rock the right hand from side to side with a double movement while keeping the middle finger in place.

- **real** Beginning with the thumb side of the right *one hand* in front of the mouth, palm left, push the extended index finger upward and forward in an arc.

- **medicine** With the bent middle finger of the right *5 hand* in the palm of the left *open hand*, palms facing each other, rock the right hand from side to side with a double movement while keeping the middle finger in place.

---

placenta An organ that attaches and grows inside the uterus during pregnancy, providing nutrients to the fetus from the mother's bloodstream through the umbilical cord. Same sign used for: **afterbirth**.

- **birth** Beginning with the back of the right *open hand* against the palm of the left *open hand*, both palms in and fingers pointing in opposite directions, move the right hand down under the little-finger side of the left hand, ending with the right palm facing down.

- **sac** Beginning with the little fingers of both *C hands* touching in front of the abdomen, palms up, bring the hands apart and upward a short distance, ending with the palms facing each other.

---

plague See sign for EPIDEMIC.

plasma The liquid part of the blood that remains after the blood cells are removed. See sign for BLOOD.

plastic surgery See sign for COSMETIC SURGERY.

plate See signs for DENTURES[1,2].

platelet Blood cells that assist in the blood-clotting process.

- **part** Slide the little-finger side of the right *open hand*, palm left and fingers pointing forward, across the palm of the left *open hand*, palm up.

- **blood** While wiggling the fingers, move the right *5 hand* from the chin downward with a double movement past the back of the left *5 hand* held in front of the chest, both palms in and fingers pointing in opposite directions.

- **cause** Beginning with both *S hands* near the body, palms up and left hand nearer the body than the right hand, move the hands forward in an arc while opening into *5 hands*.

- **become** With the palms of both *open hands* together, right hand on top of left, twists the wrists in opposite directions in order to reverse positions.

- **hard** Strike the little-finger side of the right *bent V hand* sharply against the index-finger side of the left *bent V hand*, palms facing in opposite directions.

pneumonia An infection of the lungs characterized by inflammation and congestion.

- **pneumonia** Rub the middle fingers of both *P hands*, palm in and fingers pointing toward each other, up and down on each side of the chest with a double movement.

podiatrist A health-care professional trained in medical and surgical treatment of foot disorders. See sign for PODIATRY.

---

podiatry or **chiropody** The care of the foot, especially the diagnosis and treatment of foot disorders. Note: Add the person marker before this sign to form the medical professional: **podiatrist**.

- **medical** Touch the fingertips of the right *flattened O hand* on the wrist of the upturned left *open hand*.

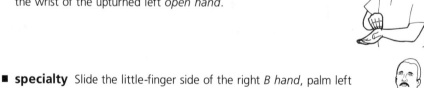

- **specialty** Slide the little-finger side of the right *B hand*, palm left and fingers pointing forward, along the index-finger side of the left *B hand* held in front of the chest, palm right and fingers pointing forward.

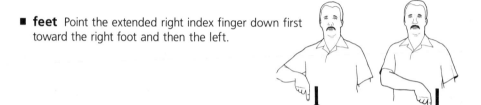

- **feet** Point the extended right index finger down first toward the right foot and then the left.

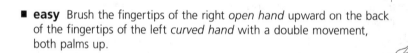

---

polyp A growth, arising from dry mucous membranes, such as in the nose, cervix, or colon.

- **bump** Beginning with the extended right index finger on the back of the left wrist, palm down, bring the right finger upward in a small arc, ending with the right index finger on the left *open hand*, palm down.

- **blood** While wiggling the fingers, move the right *5 hand* from the chin downward with a double movement past the back of the left *5 hand* held in front of the chest, both palms in and fingers pointing in opposite directions.

- **easy** Brush the fingertips of the right *open hand* upward on the back of the fingertips of the left *curved hand* with a double movement, both palms up.

positive¹ Showing the presence of disease.

- **test** Beginning with both extended index fingers pointing forward in front of the chest, palms down, bring the hands downward while bending the index fingers into *X hands* and continuing down while extending the index fingers again.

- **answer** Beginning with both extended index fingers pointing up in front of the mouth, right hand nearer the mouth than the left and palms forward, bend the wrists down simultaneously, ending with the fingers pointing forward and the palms down.

- **positive** Bring the side of the of the extended right index finger with a double movement against the thumb side of the extended left index finger, ending with the fingers pointing at angles in opposite directions in front of the chest.

positive² (alternate sign)

- **yes** Move the right *S hand*, palm forward, up and down in front of the right shoulder by bending the wrist with a double movement.

- **have** Bring the fingertips of both *bent hands* in to touch each side of the chest.

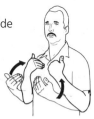

post-partum The period of time following childbirth.

- **after** Push the little-finger side of the right *B hand* over the index-finger side of the left *B hand* held in front of the chest, palm in and fingers pointing right.

-- [sign continues] ------>

postoperative

- **birth** Beginning with the back of the right *open hand* against the palm of the left *open hand*, both palms in and fingers pointing in opposite directions, move the right hand down under the little-finger side of the left hand, ending with the right palm facing down.

postoperative The period of recuperation and return to normal health after surgery.

- **after** Push the little-finger side of the right *B hand* over the index-finger side of the left *B hand* held in front of the chest, palm in and fingers pointing right.

- **operate** Move the thumb of the right *A hand*, palm down, across the upturned palm of the left *open hand* held in front of the chest.

potency The quality of having power to bring about a certain result.

- **strong** Move both *S hands* forward with a deliberate movement from each shoulder.

- **medicine** With the bent middle finger of the right *5 hand* in the palm of the left *open hand*, palms facing each other, rock the right hand from side to side with a double movement while keeping the middle finger in place.

potentiate To increase the efficiency or potency of a drug by administering a second drug at the same time.

- **strong** Move both *S hands* forward with a deliberate movement from each shoulder.

-- [sign continues] --

■ **increase** Beginning with the right *H hand*, palm up, slightly lower than the left *H hand*, palm down, flip the right hand over, ending with the extended right fingers across the extended left fingers. Repeat several times moving the hands upward each time.

potion A dose of a liquid medicine.

■ **medicine** With the bent middle finger of the right *5 hand* in the palm of the left *open hand*, palms facing each other, rock the right hand from side to side with a double movement while keeping the middle finger in place.

■ **cocktail** Beginning with the thumb of the right *modified C hand* near the mouth, palm left, tip the index finger back toward the face with a double movement.

practical nurse A professional nurse who is licensed to provide routine care for the sick, and who does not have the qualifications of a registered nurse.

■ Fingerspell abbreviation: P-N

preemie *Slang.* See sign for PREMATURE.

pregnant¹ Having a baby developing in the womb.

■ **pregnant** Beginning with the right *5 hand,* on the abdomen, palm in and fingers pointing down, bring the hand forward while curving the fingers.

pregnant² (alternate sign)

■ **pregnant** Beginning with both *5 hands* entwined in front of the abdomen, bring the hands forward.

premature, pre-term, or **preemie** (*slang*). Born after a gestation period of less than 37 weeks.

- **baby** With the right bent arm resting on the left bent arm, swing
  the arms from side to side with a double movement.

- **birth** Beginning with the back of the right *open hand* against the
  palm of the left *open hand*, both palms in and fingers pointing in
  opposite directions, move the right hand down under the little-finger
  side of the left hand, ending with the right palm facing down.

- **early** Push the bent middle finger of the right *5 hand*
  across the back of the left *open hand*, both palms down.

- **not-yet** Bend the wrist of the right *open hand*, palm back and fingers
  pointing down, back with a double movement near the right side of
  the waist.

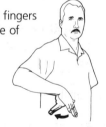

- **develop** Move the fingertips of the right *D hand*, palm left, upward
  from the heel to the fingers of the left *open hand*, palm right and
  fingers pointing up.

prenatal care Treatment of the mother during pregnancy to insure
uncomplicated childbirth and a healthy baby.

- **pregnant** Beginning with both *5 hands* entwined in front of the
  abdomen, bring the hands forward.

-- [sign continues] -->

- **before** Beginning with the back of the right *open hand*, palm in and fingers pointing left, touching the back of the left *open hand*, palm forward, move the right hand in toward the chest.

- **birth** Beginning with the back of the right *open hand* against the palm of the left *open hand*, both palms in and fingers pointing in opposite directions, move the right hand down under the little-finger side of the left hand, ending with the right palm facing down.

- **take-care-of** With the little-finger side of the right *K hand* across the index-finger side of the left *K hand*, move the hands in a repeated flat circle in front of the body.

prenatal Occurring before or existing at birth.

- **during** Beginning with both extended index fingers in front of each side of the body, palms down, move the fingers forward and upward in parallel arcs.

- **pregnant** Beginning with both *5 hands* entwined in front of the abdomen, bring the hands forward.

preoperative See sign for PREP.

preoperative sedation Medication given by injection prior to surgery to relax and calm the patient.

- **before** Beginning with the back of the right *open hand*, palm in and fingers pointing left, touching the back of the left *open hand*, palm forward, move the right hand in toward the chest.

-- [sign continues] --➤

- **operate** Move the thumb of the right *A hand*, palm down, across the upturned palm of the left *open hand* held in front of the chest.

- **help** With the little-finger side of the left *A hand* in the palm of the right *open hand*, move both hands upward in front of the chest.

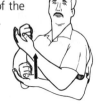

- **rest** With the arms crossed at the wrists, lay the palm of each *open hand* near the opposite shoulder.

prep, preoperative, or **preparation** The preparation of a patient for a surgical procedure.

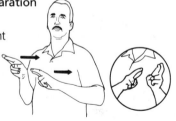

- **ready** Move both *R hands* from in front of the right side of the body, palms down and fingers pointing forward, in a smooth movement to in front of the left side of the body.

- **for** Beginning with the extended right finger touching the right side of the forehead, twist the hand forward, ending with the index finger pointing forward.

- **operate** Move the thumb of the right *A hand*, palm down, across the upturned palm of the left *open hand* held in front of the chest.

preparation See sign for PREP.

presbycusis A form of hearing loss that normally accompanies aging and may also be caused by earwax build-up, medications, exposure to loud noises, or some combination of these.

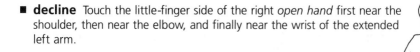

- **hear** Bring the extended right index finger to touch the right ear.

- **decline** Touch the little-finger side of the right *open hand* first near the shoulder, then near the elbow, and finally near the wrist of the extended left arm.

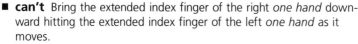

- **can't** Bring the extended index finger of the right *one hand* downward hitting the extended index finger of the left *one hand* as it moves.

- **hear** Bring the extended right index finger to touch the right ear.

presbyopia Form of farsightedness that normally accompanies aging.

- **eye** Tap the extended right index finger at the outward side of the right eye with a double movement.

- **decline** Touch the little-finger side of the right *open hand* several places down the length of the extended left arm beginning near the shoulder and ending near the wrist.

- **can't** Bring the extended index finger of the right *one hand* downward hitting the extended index finger of the left *one hand* as it moves.

-- [sign continues] ------->

prescribe

- **see** Move with the fingers of the right *V hand,* pointing up in front of the eyes, forward a short distance.

- **near** With both open hands, palms in and fingers pointing up, held up in front of the face, left hand nearer the face than the right hand, move the right hand in toward the back of the left hand.

prescribe To order treatment or medicine for a patient.

- **order** Move the extended right index finger, palm forward and finger pointing up, from in front of the mouth forward and down, ending with the finger pointing forward and the palm down.

- **medicine** With the bent middle finger of the right *5 hand* in the palm of the left *open hand*, palms facing each other, rock the right hand from side to side with a double movement while keeping the middle finger in place.

prescription 1. A written order by a physician for the preparation of a medicine. 2. Medicine so prepared.

- **doctor** Tap the fingertips of the right *D hand* on the wrist of the upturned left *open hand* with a double movement.

- **write** With the right index finger and thumb pinched together, slide the palm side of the right hand from the heel to the fingers of the upturned left *open hand.*

- **buy** Beginning with the back of the right *flattened O hand* in the palm of the left *open hand*, both palms up, move the right hand forward in an arc.

-- [sign continues]

- **medicine** With the bent middle finger of the right *5 hand* in the palm of the left *open hand*, palms facing each other, rock the right hand from side to side with a double movement while keeping the middle finger in place.

pressure or **stress** A condition of stress; strain. Same sign used for: **repress.**

- **pressure** Push the palm of the right *5 hand*, palm down, on the index-finger side of he left *S hand*, palm right, forcing the left hand downward.

pressure point Any of the places on the body that when pressed serve to curtail the flow of blood in the artery beneath that place.

- Press the fingers of the right *C hand* firmly on the left wrist.

- **stop** Hit the little-finger side of the right *open hand* on the palm of the left *open hand.*

- **blood** While wiggling the fingers, move the right *5 hand* downward with a double movement past the back of the left *open hand* held in front of the chest, both palms in and fingers pointing in opposite directions.

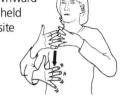

pressure See sign for BLOOD PRESSURE.

pressure sore See sign for BEDSORE.

preterm See sign for PREMATURE.

prevent

prevent To take an action for the purpose of hindering something from happening, such as a preventing a disease. Same sign used for: **blockage, obstruction.** Related form: **preventive.**

- **prevent** With the little-finger side of the right *B hand* against the index-finger side of the left *B hand*, palms facing in opposite directions, move the hands forward a short distance.

---

private room A hospital room equipped for use by one patient.

- **one** Hold the extended index finger of the right *one hand*, palm back, in front of the right shoulder.

- **person** Move both *P hands*, palms facing each other, downward along the sides of the body.

- **hospital** Bring the fingers of the right *H hand* first downward and then across from back to front on the upper left arm.

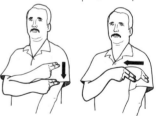

- **room** Beginning with both *R hands* in front of each side of the body, palms facing each other and fingers pointing forward, turn the hands sharply in opposite directions, ending with both palms in and fingers pointing in opposite directions.

---

problem See sign for DISORDER.

procaine[1] or **Novocaine** (*trademark*) A medication used as a local anesthetic.

- **shot** With the index finger of the right *L hand* touching the left upper arm, bend the right thumb down.

-- [sign continues] --->

- **gums** Note: Use the appropriate sign for the location where the anesthetic is administered. Move the bent index finger of the right *X hand*, palm down, from right to left along the top gum line.

- **freeze** Beginning with both *5 hands* in front of each side of the body, palms down and fingers pointing forward, pull the hands back toward the body while constricting the fingers.

procaine[2] or **Novocaine** (*trademark*) (alternate sign)

- **inject** Move the extended index finger of the right *L hand*, palm right, against the right side of the gums.

- **freeze** Beginning with both *5 hands* in front of each side of the body, palms down and fingers pointing forward, pull the hands back toward the body while constricting the fingers.

procedure A method or course of action.

- **procedure** Beginning with both *open hands* in front of the body, palms in, left fingers pointing right and right fingers pointing left, and the right hand closer to the chest than the left hand, move the right hand over the left hand and then the left hand over the right hand in an alternating movement.

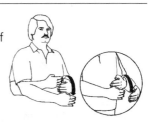

proctoscope An optical instrument with a lighted tip used to examine the interior of the rectum.

- **tube** Beginning with the index-finger sides of the both *F hands*, palms forward, together in front of the chest, move the hands apart to in front of each side of the chest.

- **anus** Point the extended right index finger first to the thumb side of the left *F hand*, palm facing forward, and then to behind the right hip.

-- [sign continues] ---➤

prognosis

- **doctor** Tap the fingertips of the right *D hand* on the wrist of the upturned left *open hand* with a double movement.

- **look-inside** Push the extended fingers of the right *V hand*, palm down, into the hole formed by the open fingers of the left *F hand*, palm right, held in front of the chest.

---

prognosis A forecasting of the course of a disease and its outcome.

- **doctor** Tap the fingertips of the right *D hand* on the wrist of the up-turned left *open hand* with a double movement.

- **your** Push the palm of the right *open hand* palm forward and fingers pointing up, toward the person being talked to.

- **opinion** Move the right *O hand*, palm left in front of the forehead, downward toward the head with a double movement.

---

progressive Of, pertaining to, or describing a worsening in the extent or severity of a disease.

- **disease** Touch the bent middle finger of the right *5 hand* to the forehead while touching the bent middle finger of the left *5 hand* to the abdomen.

-- [sign continues] -->

■ **decline** Touch the little-finger side of the right *open hand* first near the shoulder, then near the elbow, and finally near the wrist of the extended left arm.

---

prolapse A falling down of an organ or part from its normal position.

■ **prolapse** Beginning with the fingers of both *flattened O hands* on each side of the upper abdomen, move the hands downward.

---

prone[1] Lying face down.

■ **lie-down** Lay the back of the right *V hand* on the palm of the left *open hand*, both palms up.

■ **abdomen** Touch the abdomen with the fingers of the right *bent hand*.

---

prone[2] See sign for SUSCEPTIBLE.

---

prophylactic, condom, or **rubber** A device used to cover the penis as a prevention against transmitting disease or causing pregnancy.

■ **rubber** Brush the index finger side of the right *X hand*, palm left, down on the chin with a double movement.

■ **condom** Slide the fingers of the right *bent V hand*, palm in, down on the extended left index finger pointing up in front of the chest, palm right.

prophylactic treatment Cleaning of the teeth and gums to help prevent tooth decay and gum inflammation.

- **specialty** Slide the little-finger side of the right *B hand*, palm left and fingers pointing forward, along the index-finger side of the left *B hand* held in front of the chest, palm right and fingers pointing forward.

- **clean** Slide the palm of the right *open hand* from the heel to the fingers of the upturned palm of the left *open hand* with a double movement.

- **teeth** Move the curved index finger of the right *X hand* from right to left across the top front teeth.

prostate Relating to the male sex gland located at the base of the bladder or referring to a disease or enlargement of that gland.

- **disease** Touch the bent middle finger of the right *5 hand* to the forehead while touching the bent middle finger of the left *5 hand* to the abdomen.

- **inside** Move the fingers of the right *flattened O hand* downward with a short double movement in the thumb side of the left *O hand* held in front of the chest.

- **testicles** Shake both *C hands* near each other in front of the abdomen, palms up.

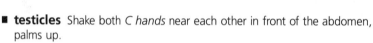

prosthesis An artificial device used as a substitute for a missing or badly functioning part of the body.

- **false** Brush the extended right index finger across the tip of the nose from right to left by bending the wrist.

- **arm** Slide the palm of the right *curved hand* along the length of the extended left arm beginning at the wrist and moving to the upper arm.

- **leg** Beginning with the left *open hand* on the upper leg, bend the leg, sliding the left hand downward toward the knee.

---

prostrate See sign for TIRED.

---

prostration See sign for EXHAUSTION.

---

protect, defend, or **guard** To cover or defend from injury or destruction.

- **protect** With the wrists of both *S hands* crossed in front of the chest, palms facing in opposite directions, move the hands forward with a short double movement.

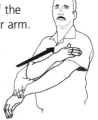

---

protocol A plan for a patient's treatment.

- **doctor** Tap the fingertips of the right *D hand* on the wrist of the upturned left *open hand* with a double movement.

-- [sign continues] -->

psoriasis

- **plan** Move both *open hands* from in front of the left side of the body, palms facing each other and fingers pointing forward, in a long smooth movement to in front of the right side of the body.

- **for** Beginning with the extended right finger touching the right side of the forehead, twist the hand forward, ending with the index finger pointing forward.

- **patient** Move the extended middle finger of the right *P hand* first down and then forward on the left upper arm.

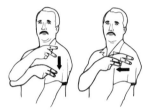

---

psoriasis A common chronic inflammation of the skin characterized by scaly patches.

- **skin** Pinch and shake the skin on the right cheek with the right *modified X hand*.

- **red** Brush the extended right index finger downward on the lips, bending the finger as it moves down.

- **scratch** Move the fingertips of the right *curved 5 hand* up and down with a repeated movement on the back of the left hand.

- **dry** Drag the index-finger side of the right *X hand*, palm down, from left to right across the chin.

psychiatrist A doctor who diagnoses and treats mental disorders. See signs for PSYCHIATRY[1,2].

psychiatry[1] The branch of medicine dealing with mental disorders. Note: Add the person marker before this sign to form the medical professional: **psychiatrist**.

- **psychiatry** Tap the middle finger of the right *P hand*, palm left, in the crook between the thumb and index finger of the left *open hand*, palm forward, with a double movement.

psychiatry[2] (alternate sign) Note: Add the person marker before this sign to form the medical professional: **psychiatrist**.

- **specialty** Slide the little-finger side of the right *B hand*, palm left and fingers pointing forward, along the index-finger side of the left *B hand* held in front of the chest, palm right and fingers pointing forward.

- **mind** Touch the index finger of the right *one hand* against the right side of the forehead.

- **analyze** With both *V hands* pointing toward each other in front of the chest, palms down, move the fingers down and apart with a double movement, bending the fingers each time.

psychoanalyst See sign for ANALYST.

psychologist A specialist in psychology. See signs for PSYCHOLOGY[1,2].

psychology[1] The science dealing with the mind and human behavior. Note: Add the person marker before this sign to form the medical professional: **psychologist**.

- **psychology** Tap the little-finger side of the right *open hand*, palm left, in the crook between the thumb and the index finger of the left *open hand*, palm forward, with a double movement.

psychology[2] (alternate sign) Note: Add the person marker before this sign to form the medical professional: **psychologist**.

- **specialty** Slide the little-finger side of the right *B hand*, palm left and fingers pointing forward, along the index-finger side of the left *B hand* held in front of the chest, palm right and fingers pointing forward.

-- [sign continues] -->

psychopath

- **behavior** Move both *B hands*, palms forward, simultaneously from side to side in front of the body with a repeated swinging movement.

psychopath or **sociopath** 1. A person who is mentally deranged, demented, or crazy. 2. Of or characteristic of insane persons. Same signh used for: **insane, psychosis.**

- **mind** Tap the index finger of the right *X hand* against the right side of the forehead with a double movement.

- **crack** Move the little-finger side of the right *open hand*, palm left, across the palm of the left *open hand*, palm up, with a jagged movement.

psychosis A severe mental disorder with symptoms such as delusions or hallucinations. See sign for PSYCHOPATH. Related form: **psychotic.**

ptomaine poisoning Food poisoning erroneously thought to be caused by ptomaine. See sign for BOTULISM.

pull-a-tooth See signs for EXTRACT.

pulled ligament See sign for SPRAIN.

pulmonary Of or affecting the lungs. See sign for LUNG.

pulsation 1. The regular beating or throbbing caused in the arteries by the beating of the heart. 2. A slow, rhythmic vibration, often accompanied with aching or pain. Same sign used for: **palpitate, throb.**

- **pulsate** Near the crook of the extended left arm, open and close the fingers of the right *C hand*, palm left, forming an *S hand* each time.

pulse The beating of the heart as reflected in the regular throbbing of the arteries.

■ **pulse** Place the fingertips of the right *flattened O hand*, palm down, on the upturned left wrist.

puncture See sign for PENETRATE.

puncture wound An injury caused by a pointed object piercing through the skin.

■ **penetrate** Insert the extended right index finger, palm in and finger pointing downward, with a deliberate movement between the middle and ring fingers of the left *open hand* held in front of the chest, palm down and fingers pointing right.

■ **spot** Place the little-finger side of the right *C hand*, palm back, on the left forearm.

■ **hurt** Beginning with both extended index fingers pointing toward each other in front of the chest, palms in, jab the fingers toward each other with a short repeated movement.

purge To clear or empty the stomach or intestines by inducing vomiting or evacuation of the bowels. Related form: **purgative**.

■ **oil** Beginning with the bent thumb and middle finger of the right *5 hand*, palm up, on each side of the little-finger side of the left *open hand*, palm right and fingers pointing forward, bring the right hand downward with a double movement, pinching the thumb and middle finger together each time.

-- [sign continues] ---➤

- **cocktail** Beginning with the thumb of the right *modified C hand* near the mouth, palm left, tip the index finger back toward the face with a double movement.

- **toilet** Shake the right *T hand*, palm forward, with a small repeated movement in front of the right shoulder.

- **back-and-forth** Move the right *10 hand*, palm left, forward and back with a repeated movement in front of the right side of the chest.

- **vomit** Beginning with the right *5 hand* near the mouth, palm left and fingers pointing forward, and the left *5 hand* forward of the right hand, palm right and fingers pointing forward, move both hands upward and forward in large arcs.

pus, matter, or **pyosis** Thick, cloudy yellowish-white fluid formed at a place of inflammation as an abscess, containing white blood cells and tissue debris.

- **skin** Pinch and shake the skin of the right cheek with the index finger and thumb of the right hand.

- **pus** Beginning with the index-finger side of the right *S hand* touching the right side of the chin, palm forward, thrust the fingers open.

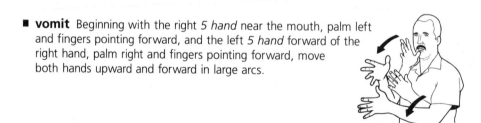

pyorrhea, gingivitis, periodontitis, or Rigg's disease

A pussy inflammation of the sockets of the teeth leading to loosening of the teeth.

■ **gums** Move the bent index finger of the right *X hand*, palm down, from right to left along the top gum line.

■ **infection** Move the right *I hand*, palm forward, from side to side with a repeated movement in front of the right shoulder.

pyosis See sign for PUS.

quadriplegia Paralysis of all four limbs or of the entire body below the neck.

- **thorax** Beginning with the thumb side of both *B hands* on upper chest, left hand below the right hand, palms down and fingers pointing in opposite directions, move the left hand downward to the waist while keeping the right hand in place.

- **freeze** Beginning with both *5 hands* in front of each side of the body, palms down and fingers pointing forward, pull the hands back toward the body while constricting the fingers.

quadruplets Four offspring born of one pregnancy.

- **baby** With the right bent arm resting on the left bent arm, swing the arms from side to side with a double movement.

- **birth** Beginning with the back of the right *open hand* against the palm of the left *open hand*, both palms in and fingers pointing in opposite directions, move the right hand down under the little-finger side of the left hand, ending with the right palm facing down.

- **four** With the palm facing forward, hold up the right *4 hand* in front of the right shoulder.

qualified[1] A characteristic or accomplishment that fits someone for a job, office, award, etc.

- **qualify** Move the right *Q hand* in a small circle and then back against the right side of the chest, palm down.

qualified[2] (alternate sign)

- **skill** Grasp the little-finger side of the left *open hand* with the curved right fingers. Then pull the right hand forward and downward while closing the fingers into the palm.

quarantine Strict isolation imposed to prevent the spread of disease.

- **disease** Touch the bent middle finger of the right *5 hand* to the forehead while touching the bent middle finger of the left *5 hand* to the abdomen.

- **stay** With the thumb of the right *10 hand* on the thumbnail of the left *10 hand*, both palms down in front of the chest, move the hands forward and downward a short distance.

- **one** Hold the extended index finger of the right *one hand*, palm back, in front of the right shoulder.

- **place** Beginning with the middle fingers of both *P hands* touching in front of the body, palms facing each other, move the hands apart in a circular movement back until they touch again near the chest.

-- [sign continues] -->

quicken

- **prevent** With the little-finger side of the right *B hand* against the index-finger side of the left *B hand*, palms facing in opposite directions, move the hands forward a short distance.

- **spread** Beginning with the fingers of both *flattened O hands* together in front of the chest, palms down, bring the hands downward and apart while opening into *5 hands*.

quicken To be in the stage of pregnancy in which the fetus gives indications of life.

- **pregnant** Beginning with both *5 hands* entwined in front of the abdomen, bring the hands forward.

- **baby** With the right bent arm resting on the left bent arm, swing the arms from side to side with a double movement.

- **crowning** With the right *S hand* cupped in the left *curved hand* in front of the body, push both hands downward with a short double movement.

quintuplets Five offspring born of one pregnancy.

- **birth** Beginning with the back of the right *open hand* against the palm of the left *open hand*, both palms in and fingers pointing in opposite directions, move the right hand down under the little-finger side of the left hand, ending with the right palm facing down.

-- [sign continues] ------------------>

■ **baby** With the right bent arm resting on the left bent arm, swing the arms from side to side with a double movement.

■ **five** With the palm facing forward, hold up the right *5 hand* in front of the right shoulder.

quiver See sign for TREMBLE.

rabies An acute, infectious, often fatal viral disease of the central nervous system that is transmitted by the bite of an infected animal.

- **animal** Beginning with the fingertips of both *bent hands* on the chest near each shoulder, roll the fingers toward each other on their knuckles with a double movement, while keeping the fingers in place.

- **bite** Bring the fingertips of the right *C hand* down to close around the index-finger side of the left *open hand*.

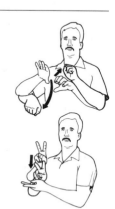

- **disease** Touch the bent middle finger of the right *5 hand* to the forehead while touching the bent middle finger of the left *5 hand* to the abdomen.

rape Sexual intercourse with a woman against her will.

- **rape** Beginning with both *curved hands* in front of the chest, palms forward, move the right hand down and the left hand up while changing the hands to *S hands*.

- **intercourse** Bring the right *V hand* downward in front of the chest to tap against the heel of the left *V hand* with a double movement, palms facing each other.

reaction or **response** A physiological response, as to a disease or an irritation.

- **medicine** With the bent middle finger of the right *5 hand* in the palm of the left *open hand*, palms facing each other, rock the right hand from side to side with a double movement while keeping the middle finger in place.

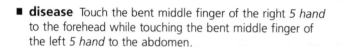

-- [sign continues] --->

- **conflict** Beginning with both extended index fingers in front of each side of the body, palms in and fingers angled toward each other, move the hands toward each other, ending with the fingers crossed.

- **report** Beginning with fingers of both *R hands* pointing up, right hand closer to the mouth than the left hand and the palms facing each other, move the hands forward and downward with a deliberate movement, ending with the palms facing down and fingers pointing forward.

- **negative** Bring the thumb side of the extended right index finger, palm down and finger pointing forward, against the palm of the left *open hand*, palm right and fingers pointing up.

- **positive** Bring the side of the extended right index finger with a double movement against the thumb side of the extended left index finger, ending with the fingers pointing at angles in opposite directions in front of the chest.

rebound **1.** To recover. **2.** To spring back from an impact. **3.** The act of rebounding.

- **rebound** Move the right *V hand* from near the right side of the head, palm facing forward and fingers pointing up, downward while bending the fingers, and at the same time raising the left *bent V hand* and extending the fingers. Repeat with an alternating movement.

receiver See sign for RECIPIENT.

recipient or **receiver** The person who is given donated blood.

- **get** Beginning with the little-finger side of the right *curved 5 hand*, palm left, on the index-finger side of the left *curved 5 hand*, palm right, bring the hands back toward the chest while closing into *S hands*.

-- [sign continues] --

recline

- **person marker** Move both *open hands*, palms facing each other, downward along the sides of the body.

---

recline See sign for LIE DOWN.

---

recover To get well again, as after an illness.

- **again** Beginning with the right *bent hand* beside the left *curved hand*, both palms up, bring the right hand up while turning it over, ending with the fingertips of the right hand touching the palm of the left hand.

- **healthy** Beginning with the fingertips of both *curved 5 hands* touching near each shoulder, bring the hands downward and forward with a deliberate movement while closing into *S hands*.

---

recovery room A specially equipped and staffed area of a hospital for observing and caring for a patient who has just undergone surgery.

- **operate** Move the thumb of the right *A hand*, palm down, across the upturned palm of the left *open hand* held in front of the chest.

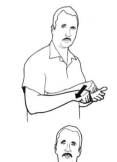

- **finish** With both *5 hands* apart in front of the body, palms up, quickly turn the hands over toward each other, ending with the palms down and fingers pointing forward.

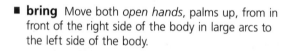

- **bring** Move both *open hands*, palms up, from in front of the right side of the body in large arcs to the left side of the body.

-- [sign continues] -->

- **body** Pat the palm side of both *open hands* first on each side of the chest and then on each side of the abdomen.

- **awake** Beginning with the index fingers and thumbs of each hand pinched together and all other fingers closed near the outside of each eye, quickly flick the index fingers and thumbs apart forming *bent L hands*.

- **room** Beginning with both *R hands* in front of each side of the body, palms facing each other and fingers pointing forward, turn the hands sharply in opposite directions, ending with both in and fingers pointing in opposite directions.

rectal Of or pertaining to the rectum. See sign for ANUS. Related form: **rectum.**

rectum The last part of the intestine linking the colon to the anus. Related form: rectal.

- **tube** Beginning with the index-finger side of the right *F hand*, palm left, on the index-finger of the left *F hand*, palm right, move the right hand up with a wiggly movement.

- **anus** Point the extended right index finger first to the thumb side of the left *F hand*, palm facing forward, and then to behind the right hip.

recurrent To occur or come back again.
Related form: **recurring.**

- **show-up** With a double movement, push the extended right index finger, palm left, upward between the index finger and middle finger of the left *open hand*, palm down.

-- [sign continues]

red blood cell

- **again** Beginning with the right *bent hand* beside the left *curved hand*, both palms up, bring the right hand up while turning it over, ending with the fingertips of the right hand touching the palm of the left hand.

red blood cell See signs for ERYTHROCYTE[1,2].

red blood corpuscle See signs for ERYTHROCYTE[1,2].

reduce See signs for DECREASE[1,2,3].

reflex[1] An involuntary movement caused as a response to a stimulus.

- **body** Pat the palm side of both *open hands* first on each side of the chest and then on each side of the abdomen.

- **part** Slide the little-finger side of the right *open hand*, palm left and fingers pointing forward, across the palm of the left *open hand*, palm up.

- **cause** Beginning with both *S hands* near the body, palms up and left hand nearer the body than the right hand, move the hands forward in an arc while opening into *5 hands*.

- **move** Beginning with both *flattened O hands* apart in front of the right side of the body, palms down, move the hands simultaneously in an arc to the left.

- **automatic** Move the extended right curved index finger back and forth on the back of the extended left index finger, both palms in.

reflex² (alternate sign)

- **elbow** Place the palm of the right open hand on the elbow of the left arm bent across the chest.

- **jerk-up** Swing the right *modified X hand* from right to left in front of the chest to strike the knuckles on the elbow of the bent left arm, causing the left arm to jerk upward.

reflux The return of the contents of the stomach or intestines to the throat. Same sign used for: **belch, burp.**

- **belch** Beginning with the right *S hand* in front of the abdomen, palm up, move the hand upward in front of the chest while flicking up the index finger.

refracture To break a bone in the same location during or after healing has occurred.

- **break** Beginning with both *S hands* in front of the body, index fingers touching and palms down, move the hands away from each other while twisting the wrists with a deliberate movement, ending with the palms facing each other.

- **bone** With a double movement, tap the back of the right *bent V hand*, palm up, on the back of the left *S hand*, palm down.

- **again** Beginning with the right *bent hand* beside the left *curved hand*, both palms up, bring the right hand up while turning it over, ending with the fingertips of the right hand touching the palm of the left hand.

regeneration The ability of some parts of the body to grow back to normal after being damaged.

- **new** Slide the back of the right *curved hand*, palm up, from the fingertips to the heel of the upturned left *open hand*.

-- [sign continues] ---➤

- **grow** Bring the right *flattened O hand*, palm in and fingers pointing up, up through the left *C hand*, palm right, while spreading the right fingers into a *5 hand*.

---

registered nurse or **RN** a graduate nurse who has passed a state board examination and has been registered and licensed to practice nursing.

- Fingerspell abbreviation: R-N

---

regress To go back to a former lower level after a period of improvement. See signs for DECLINE[1,2]. Related form: **regression.**

---

regurgitate, throw up, or **vomit** To cast up partially digested food.

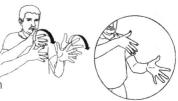

- **vomit** Beginning with the right *5 hand* near the mouth, palm left and fingers pointing forward, and the left *5 hand* forward of the right hand, palm right and fingers pointing forward, move both hands upward and forward in large arcs.

---

rehabilitate To restore or bring to a condition of good health. See sign for AID[1].

---

reject For the body to have a reaction against a transplanted organ or grafted tissue.

- **reject** Brush the fingertips of the right *open hand*, palm in, with a forward movement from the heel to the fingertips of the left *open hand*, palm up.

---

relapse A stage of illness in which the patient gets worse after having improved.

- **seem** Beginning with the right *open hand* near the right side of the head, palm forward and fingers pointing up, turn the hand so the palm faces back.

- **healthy** Beginning with the fingertips of both *curved 5 hands* touching near each shoulder, bring the hands downward and forward with a deliberate movement while closing into *S hands*.

- **disease** Touch the bent middle finger of the right *5 hand* to the forehead while touching the bent middle finger of the left *5 hand* to the abdomen.

-- [sign continues] --->

- **again** Beginning with the right *bent hand* beside the left *curved hand*, both palms up, bring the right hand up while turning it over, ending with the fingertips of the right hand touching the palm of the left hand.

relax or **rest** 1. To be still or quiet or to sleep. 2. Repose, relaxation, or sleep.

- **rest** With the arms crossed at the wrists, lay the palm of each *open hand* near the opposite shoulder.

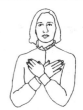

relaxant See sign for TRANQUILIZER.

release See sign for DISCHARGE[1].

relief An act or state of being freed from or experiencing reduction of pain or difficulty.

- **feel** Move the bent middle finger of the right *5 hand* upward on the chest.

- **improve** Touch the little-finger side of the right *open hand*, palm back and fingers pointing left, first to the wrist, then to the forearm, and then to the upper bent left arm.

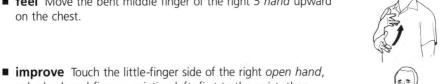

remission[1] A stage of chronic illness when a patient's condition improves.

- **disease** Touch the bent middle finger of the right *5 hand* to the forehead while touching the bent middle finger of the left *5 hand* to the abdomen.

- **show** With the extended right index finger touching the palm of the left *open hand*, palm right and fingers pointing forward, move both hands forward a short distance.

-- [sign continues] --->

- -

- **less** Move the right *bent hand*, palm down and fingers pointing left, from in front of the chest downward, stopping a few inches above the left *open hand*, palm up and fingers angled forward.

remission² (alternate sign)

- **disease** Touch the bent middle finger of the right *5 hand* to the forehead while touching the bent middle finger of the left *5 hand* to the abdomen.

- **dissolve** Beginning with both *flattened O hands* in front of the body, palms up, move the thumb of each hand smoothly across each fingertip, starting with the little fingers and ending as *10 hands* while moving the hands downward and outward to each side.

- **healthy** Beginning with the fingertips of both *curved 5 hands* touching near each shoulder, bring the hands downward and forward with a deliberate movement while closing into *S hands*.

---

remove See signs for EXCISE¹,².

---

repair To restore to sound condition after injury. See also signs for FUSION, GRAFT.

- **fix** Brush the fingertips of both *flattened O hands* across each other repeatedly as the hands move up and down in opposite directions in a double movement.

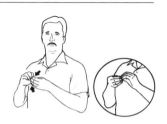

---

repress To hold in or exclude from consciousness, sometimes causing stress or other manifestations. See sign for PRESSURE.

---

reserpine See sign for TRANQUILIZER.

---

respirator A device covering the mouth or nose used in artificial respiration.

- **breathe** With the right *5 hand* in front of the chest above the left *5 hand*, fingers pointing in opposite directions and palms in, move both hands forward and back toward the chest with a double movement.

- **machine** With the fingers of both *curved 5 hands* loosely meshed together, palms in, move the hands up and down in front of the chest with a repeated movement.

respiratory Relating to the act of inhaling and exhaling or the organs responsible for breathing.

- **connect** Beginning with both *curved 5 hands* apart in front of the body, bring the hands together to intersect with each other by closing the thumb to the index finger of each hand.

- **breathe** With the right *5 hand* in front of the chest above the left *5 hand*, fingers pointing in opposite directions and palms in, move both hands forward and back toward the chest with a double movement.

respiratory failure A fatal condition in which the lungs cease to function.

- **breathe** With the right *5 hand* in front of the chest above the left *5 hand*, fingers pointing in opposite directions and palms in, move both hands forward and back toward the chest with a double movement.

- **stop** Hit the little-finger side of the right *open hand* on the palm of the left *open hand*.

respire The act of breathing. See sign for BREATHE. Related form: **respiration.**

---

response See sign for REACTION.

---

rest See sign for RELAX.

---

rest home See signs for NURSING HOME[1,2,3].

---

restorative Tending to renew or restore health.

- **help** With the little-finger side of the left *A hand* in the palm of the right *open hand*, move both hands upward in front of the chest.

- **become** With the palms of both *open hands* together, right hand on top of left, twist the wrists in opposite directions in order to reverse positions.

- **healthy** Beginning with the fingertips of both *curved 5 hands* touching near each shoulder, bring the hands downward and forward with a deliberate movement while closing into *S hands*.

---

resuscitate or **revive** To revive from apparent death or unconsciousness by used of electric paddles. Related form: **resuscitation.**

- **electric** Tap the knuckles of the index fingers of both *X hands* together with a double movement, palms in.

- **resuscitate** Beginning with both *S hands* in front of the chest, palms in, bring the little-finger sides of both hands back against the chest with a deliberate movement and bounce forward again.

---

retainer A device used to maintain the position of natural teeth. See sign for BRACES.

---

retention Storage of excess water in the body causing bloating and weight gain.

- **water** Tap the index-finger side of the right *W hand*, palm left and fingers pointing up, against the chin with a double movement.

- **enlarge** Beginning with the fingertips of both *C hands* together in front of the chest, palms facing each other, pull the hands apart.

retinitis pigmentosa or **RT** Gradual loss of peripheral vision and night blindness caused by deterioration of the retina, leading to tunnel vision or total blindness.

- Fingerspell abbreviation: R-T

revive See sign for RESUSCITATE.

Rh factor (Rh negative, Rh positive) An inherited subtype of red blood cells, that when Rh negative in the mother can cause severe reaction in her Rh positive newborn.

- **bleed** Brush the extended right index finger downward on the lips, bending the finger as it moves down. While wiggling the fingers, move the right *5 hand* from the chin downward with a double movement past the back of the left *5 hand* held in front of the chest, both palms in and fingers pointing in opposite directions.

- Fingerspell R-H: Form an *R* and then an *H* in front of the right shoulder, palm forward.

- **positive** Bring the side of the of the extended right index finger with a double movement against the thumb side of the extended left index finger, ending with the fingers pointing at angles in opposite directions in front of the chest.

- **negative** Bring the thumb side of the extended right index finger, palm down and finger pointing forward, against the palm of the left *open hand*, palm right and fingers pointing up.

rheumatism Disorder characterized by pain and stiffness in the joints or muscles.

- **joint** Keeping the fingers of both *bent V hands* entwined, palms in, move the hands up and down with a double movement.

- **swell-wrist** Beginning with the *curved 5 hand* over the left wrist, both palms down, raise the right hand a short distance.

- **swell-elbow** Beginning with the *curved 5 hand* around the left bent elbow, move the right hand down a short distance.

rheumatoid arthritis See sign for ARTHRITIS.

rhinoplasty See sign for NOSE JOB.

ribs The curved bones, 12 pairs of which form the wall of the chest, in one's torso.

- **ribs** Beginning with both *curved 5 hands* on each side of the body, palms in, move both hands toward the center of the body with a double movement.

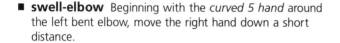

Rigg's disease See sign for PYORRHEA.

rigor, chill, or **shiver** A sudden coldness that precedes certain fevers.

- **cold** Shake both *S hands* with a slight movement in front of each side of the chest, palms facing each other.

rigor mortis The stiffening of the body after death.

- **die** Beginning with both *open hands* in front of the body, right palm down and left palm up, flip the hands to the right, turning the right palm up and the left palm down.

- **body** Pat the palm side of both *open hands* first on each side of the chest and then on each side of the abdomen.

- **stiff** With the fingertips of the right *flattened O hand* holding the fingertips of the left *open hand*, both palms in and fingers pointed toward each other, shake the hands slightly showing that they don't move.

RN See sign for REGISTERED NURSE.

---

roseola See sign for RUBELLA.

---

rot See sign for DECAY.

Rt See sign for RETINITIS PIGMENTOSA.

---

rubber See sign for PROPHYLACTIC.

---

rubella, German measles, or **roseola** A mild infection characterized by fever, cough, and a fine red rash; may damage the fetus if contracted during pregnancy.

- **German** With the little-finger side of the right *S hand* at the base of the thumb and index finger of the left *S hand*, both palms angled in, quickly open the fingers of both hands into *5 hands* with a double movement.

- **red** Brush the extended right index finger downward on the lips, bending the wrist as the finger moves down.

-- [sign continues] ---►

rupture

- **spots** Place the index-finger side of the right *F hand*, palm forward, against the right cheek in several places.

---

rupture, abdominal hernia, or hernia Protrusion of a body part, as the intestine, through the abnormally weakened wall that contains it.

- **lining** Move the right extended index finger from the index finger to the thumb of the left *C hand* held in front of the chest, palm right.

- **rupture** Push the right *S hand*, palm down, from in front of the chest past the palm side of the left *C hand*, palm right.

- **spot** Place the thumb side of the right *F hand* on the abdomen, palm down and fingers pointing left.

- **burst** Beginning with the palm sides of both *A hands* together in front of the abdomen, move the hands downward and apart while opening into *5 hands*, palms facing each other and fingers pointing down.

sac A small baglike structure that is part of an animal or plant.
- **sac** Beginning with the little fingers of both *C hands* touching, palms up, bring the hands apart and upward a short distance, ending with the palms facing each other.

saddle block See sign for EPIDURAL.

saline Salt-containing solution similar to normal body fluid that is given intravenously to help correct fluid and electrolyte imbalances.
- **salt** Alternately tap the fingers of the right *V hand* across the back of the fingers of the left *V hand*, both palms down.

- **mix** Beginning with the right *curved 5 hand* over the left *curved 5 hand*, palms facing each other in front of the chest, move the hands in circles moving in opposite directions.

- **water** Tap the index-finger side of the right *W hand*, palm left and fingers pointing up, against the chin with a double movement.

saliva[1] A liquid produced in the mouth, secreted by the salivary glands.
- **water** Tap the index-finger side of the right *W hand*, palm left and fingers pointing up, against the chin with a double movement.

-- [sign continues] --->

saliva

■ **in-mouth** Point into the open mouth with the extended right index finger, palm down.

---

saliva² (alternate sign)

■ **wet** Tap the index-finger side of the right *W hand*, palm left, against the chin. Then, beginning with both *5 hands* in front of the body, palms up, bring the hands downward while closing the fingers into *O hands* with a double movement.

■ **in-mouth** Point into the open mouth with the extended right index finger, palm down.

---

salmonellosis Acute food poisoning caused by bacteria that grow in improperly stored food, usually causing violent diarrhea and cramps. See sign for BOTULISM.

salve See sign for OINTMENT.

sanitize See sign for CLEANSE.

sarcoma See sign for CANCER².

satisfactory condition A patient's health status that meets an acceptable standard under the prevailing circumstances.

■ **healthy** Beginning with the fingertips of both *curved 5 hands* touching near each shoulder, bring the hands downward and forward with a deliberate movement while closing into *S hands*.

■ **good** Beginning with the fingertips of the right *open hand* near the mouth, palm in and fingers pointing up, bring the hand downward, ending with the back of the right hand across the palm of the left *open hand*, both palms up.

■ **enough** Push the palm side of the right *open hand*, palm down, forward across the thumb side of the left *S hand*.

scalpel or **lancet** A small, thin-bladed knife used in surgery.

- **knife** Slide the side of the extended right index finger, palm in, with a double movement at an angle down the length of the extended left index finger, palm right, turning the right palm down each time as it moves off the end of the left index finger.

- **for** Beginning with the extended right finger touching the right side of the forehead, twist the hand forward, ending with the index finger pointing forward.

- **operate** Move the thumb of the right *A hand*, palm down, across the upturned palm of the left *open hand* held in front of the chest.

scar, cicatrix, or **scar tissue** A mark on the skin that remains after injured tissue has healed.

- Fingerspell: S-C-A-R

scar tissue See sign for SCAR.

schizophrenia or **split personality** Mental illness character-ized by a distorted sense of reality, bizarre behavior, and fragmentation of the personality.

- **disease** Touch the bent middle finger of the right *5 hand* to the forehead while touching the bent middle finger of the left *5 hand* to the abdomen.

- **mind** Touch the extended right index finger the right side of the forehead.

- **schizophrenia** Move the right *S hand,* palm left, from the fore-head down in front of the face in a large jagged movement while changing to a *B hand.*

science See signs for CHEMISTRY[1,2].

---

sclera A dense white tissue that covers the portion of the eyeball not covered by the cornea. Related form: **sclerotic.**

- **part** Slide the little-finger side of the right *open hand*, palm left and fingers pointing forward, across the palm of the left *open hand*, palm up.

- **eye** Tap the extended right index finger at the outward side of the right eye with a double movement.

- **white** Beginning with the fingertips of the right *curved 5 hand* on the chest, pull the hand forward while closing the fingers into a *flattened O hand*.

---

scoliosis, kyphosis, or lordosis An abnormal lateral curvature of the spine.

- **back** Pat the fingertips of the right open hand behind the right shoulder with a double movement.

- **spine** Beginning with the little-finger side of the right *F hand* on the index-finger side of the left *F hand,* bring the right hand up with a wavy movement.

---

scratch To scrape slightly, as to relieve itching. See sign for ITCH.

---

scrotum See sign for TESTICLES.

---

sedative See sign for TRANQUILIZER.

---

see To perceive with the eyes. Same sign used for: **sight.**

- **see** Bring the fingers of the right *V hand* from pointing at the eyes, palm in, forward a short distance.

seizure A sudden attack, as experienced by people with epilepsy. See sign for GRAND MAL.

self-examination Examination of one's body for signs of illness or disease. See sign for BREAST EXAMINATION.

semen, seminal fluid, or **sperm** Male reproductive cells manufactured in testicles and ejaculated during sexual intercourse.

- **ejaculate** While touching the wrist of the right *S hand* with the left extended index finger, palms facing in opposite directions, move the right hand forward while opening into a *4 hand*, ending with the right palm left and fingers pointing forward.

- **white** Beginning with the fingertips of the right *curved 5 hand* on the chest, pull the hand forward while closing the fingers into a *flattened O hand*.

seminal fluid See sign for SEMEN.

semiprivate room A hospital room shared with one other person.

- **two** Hold up the right *2 hand*, palm forward, in front of the right shoulder.

- **person** Move both *F hands*, palms facing each other, downward along the sides of the body.

- **hospital** Bring the fingers of the right *H hand* first downward and then across from back to front on the upper left arm.

- **room** Beginning with both *R hands* in front of each side of the body, palms facing each other and fingers pointing forward, turn the hands sharply in opposite directions, ending with both palms in and fingers pointing in opposite directions.

senile See sign for DEMENTIA. Related form: **senility.**

sensation or **sense** Ability to feel or experience sensations such as sound, light, or pain. Same sign used for: **feel.** Related form: **sensory.**

- **sense** Bring the bent middle finger of the right *5 hand,* palm in, toward the body to lightly touch the left side of the chest.

sense See sign for SENSATION.

sepsis A poisoned condition resulting from the spread of an infection. Related form: **septic.**

- **blood** While wiggling the fingers, move the right *5 hand* from the chin downward with a double movement past the back of the left *5 hand* held in front of the chest, both palms in and fingers pointing in opposite directions.

- **disease** Touch the bent middle finger of the right *5 hand* to the forehead while touching the bent middle finger of the left *5 hand* to the abdomen.

septic or **putrefactive** Causing to rot from a bacterial infection.

- **not** Bring the thumb of the right *10 hand* forward from under the chin with a deliberate movement.

- **clean** Slide the palm of the right *open hand* from the heel to the fingers of the upturned palm of the left *open hand.*

set-a-fracture To put broken bones into a normal position and fix in a secure manner until healed.

- **bone** With a double movement, tap the back of the right *bent V hand*, palm up, on the back of the left *S hand*, palm down.

- **connect** Beginning with both *curved 5 hands* apart in front of the body, bring the hands together to intersect with each other by closing the thumb to the index finger of each hand.

---

sex[1] See signs for GENDER[1,2].

---

sex[2] See signs for INTERCOURSE[1,2].

---

sexual intercourse or **sexual relations** See signs for INTERCOURSE[1,2].

---

sexually transmitted disease[1]**, chlamydia, syphilis, gonorrhea,** or **venereal disease** Any disease characteristically transmitted by sexual contact.

- Fingerspell abbreviation: S-T-D

---

sexually transmitted disease[2]**, chlamydia, syphilis, gonorrhea,** or **venereal disease** (alternate sign)

- **disease** Touch the bent middle finger of the right *5 hand* to the forehead while touching the bent middle finger of the left *5 hand* to the abdomen.

- **bring** Move both *open hands*, palms up, from in front of the right side of the body in large arcs to the left side of the body.

- **during** Beginning with both extended index fingers in front of each side of the body, palms down, move them forward and upward in parallel arcs.

-- [sign continues] -->

shake

- **intercourse** Bring the right *V hand* downward in front of the chest to tap against the heel of the left *V hand* with a double movement, palms facing each other.

---

shake See sign for TREMBLE.

---

shiver See sign for RIGOR.

---

shock Condition in which the blood pressure falls below the level needed to supply blood to the body, characterized by weakness, paleness, rapid heartbeat, dry mouth, and cold sweat.
- **shock** Beginning with both index fingers touching each temple, palms forward, move the hands forward simultaneously while opening into *curved 5 hands* in front of each side of the chest, palm angled down.

---

shoot See sign for INJECT.

---

shot, hypodermic, injection, or **inoculation** An injection of a liquid medication.
- **shot** With the index finger of the right *L hand* touching the left upper arm, bend the right thumb down.

---

shoulder The part of the human body to which the arm is attached.
- **shoulder** Pat the palm of the right *curved hand*, palm down, with a single movement on the left shoulder.

---

sick See sign for DISEASE.

---

side See sign for LATERAL.

---

side effect or **adverse event** A consequence other than that intended by treatment with a drug.
- **other** Beginning with the right *10 hand* in front of the chest, palm down, flip the hand over to the right, ending with palm up.

-- [sign continues] --->

■ **effect** Beginning with the fingertips of the right *flattened O hand* on the back of the left *open hand*, both palms down, move the right hand forward while opening into a *5 hand*.

SIDS See sign for SUDDEN INFANT DEATH SYNDROME.

sight The ability to see; vision. See signs for SEE, VISION.

silent Producing no noticeable symptoms.

■ **show** With the extended right index finger touching the palm of the left *open hand*, palm right and fingers pointing forward, move both hands forward a short distance.

■ **disease** Touch the bent middle finger of the right *5 hand* to the forehead while touching the bent middle finger of the left *5 hand* to the abdomen.

■ **nothing** Beginning with both *O hands* near the chin, palms facing each other, bring the hands forward and downward while opening into *5 hands*, palms angled down and fingers pointing forward.

simple fracture A broken bone in which the skin is not broken and the bone fragments do not protrude. See also GREENSTICK, COMPLETE FRACTURE, FRACTURE, OPEN FRACTURE.

■ **break** Beginning with both *S hands* in front of the body, index fingers touching and palms down, move the hands away from each other while twisting the wrists with a deliberate movement, ending with the palms facing each other.

■ **bone** With a double movement, tap the back of the right *bent V hand*, palm up, on the back of the left *S hand*, palm down.

-- [sign continues] --►

- **not** Bring the thumb of the right *10 hand* forward from under the chin with a deliberate movement.

- **through** Slide the little-finger side of the right *open hand* between the middle finger and ring finger of the left *open hand* held up in front of the chest, palm right and fingers pointing up.

- **skin** Pinch and shake the loose skin on the back of the left *open hand* with the bent thumb and index finger of the right *5 hand*.

sinus Cavities in the skull connected with the nasal cavity.

- **sinus** Push the extended index finger of the right *one hand*, palm in and finger pointing up, upward on the right side of the nose.

skeletal system[1] or **skeleton** The bony framework of the body supporting the soft tissues and protecting the internal organs.

- **skeleton** With the hands crossed at the wrists, tap the fingers of both *bent V hands* on the opposite side of the chest.

skeletal system[2] or **skeleton** (alternate sign)

- **ribs** Beginning with both *curved 5 hands* on each side of the body, palms in, move both hands toward the center of the body with a double movement.

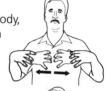

- **system** Beginning with the index-finger sides of both *S hands* touching in front of the chest, palms down, move the hands outward to in front of each shoulder and then straight down a short distance.

skeleton See signs for SKELETAL SYSTEM[1,2].

skin See signs for EPIDERMIS[1,2].

sleep apnea A brief suspension of breathing occurring repeatedly during sleep.

- **stop** Hit the little-finger side of the right *open hand* on the palm of the left *open hand*.

- **breathe** With the right *5 hand* in front of the chest above the left *5 hand*, fingers pointing in opposite directions and palms in, move both hands forward and back toward the chest with a double movement.

- **during** Beginning with both extended index fingers in front of each side of the body, palms down, move the fingers forward and upward in parallel arcs.

- **sleep** Bring the right *open hand*, palm left and fingers pointing up, in against the right cheek.

sleeping pill Medication in pill or capsule form used to induce sleep.

- **pill** Beginning with the index finger of the right *A hand* tucked under the right thumb, palm in, flick the index finger toward the mouth with a double movement.

- **for** Beginning with the extended right finger touching the right side of the forehead, twist the hand forward, ending with the index finger pointing forward.

-- [sign continues] --➤

sleepy

- **go-to-sleep** Beginning with the right *curved 5 hand* in front of the face, move the hand down while drawing the fingertips and thumb together.

sleepy or **drowsy** Feeling inclined to sleep.

- **sleepy** Beginning with the right *curved 5 hand* in front of the face, palm in and fingers pointing up, bring the fingertips downward to in front of the chin with a double movement.

smear To spread a wet, oily, or sticky substance over something.

- **smear** Beginning with the right *A hand* in front of the right side of the chest, palm left, and the left *A hand* in front of the left side of the chest, palm right, move the right hand to the left in an arc while opening both hands into *5 hands* and rubbing the right hand across the palm of the left.

smegma A thick secretion that collects beneath the foreskin of the penis or around the clitoris.

- **groin** Point to the groin area with the extended right index finger.

- **smell** Move the palm side of the right *open hand* upward in front of the nose with a double movement.

- **bad** Move the fingers of the right *open hand* from the mouth, palm in and fingers pointing up, downward while flipping the palm quickly down as the hand moves.

smell A quality that affects the sense of smell; odor. See sign for OLFACTORY.

specimen

social work An occupation focused on improving social conditions and helping troubled families. Note: Add the person marker before this sign to form the medical professional: **social worker.**

- **social-work** Hit the little-finger side of the right *S hand*, palm left, on the heel of the left open palm held in front of the body, followed by hitting the little-finger side of the right *W hand* near the left fingertips.

social worker A person who performs social work. See sign for SOCIAL WORK.

sociopath A person, such as a psychopath, whose behavior is antisocial. See sign for PSYCHOPATH.

socket See signs for JOINT[1,2].

soft spot See sign for FONTANEL.

sore[1] See sign for HURT[1].

sore[2] See signs for PAIN[1,2].

sore throat See sign for PHARYNGITIS.

sound Something heard, as noise, speech, or music. See sign for HEAR.

spasm See sign for CRAMP.

specialist A person who has a special skill in a particular branch of medicine. See sign for SPECIALTY.

specialty or **field** A field or branch of medicine in which a person has a special knowledge or skill. Note: Add the person marker before this sign to form the medical professional: **specialist.** Related form: **specialize.**

- **specialty** Slide the little-finger side of the right *B hand*, palm left and fingers pointing forward, along the index-finger side of the left *B hand* held in front of the chest, palm right and fingers pointing forward.

specimen or **culture** A sample of a substance collected for examination. See sign for BIOPSY.

- **inspect** Move the extended right index finger from near the right eye down to move from the heel to the fingers of the upturned palm of the left *open hand* held in front of the chest.

-- [sign continues] ------------------------------>

spectacles

- **analyze** With both *V hands* pointing toward each other in front of the chest, palms down, move the fingers down and apart with a double movement, bending the fingers each time.

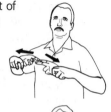

- **operate** Move the thumb of the right *A hand*, palm down, across the upturned palm of the left *open hand* held in front of the chest.

spectacles See sign for EYEGLASSES.

sperm See sign for SEMEN.

spermicide A commercially prepared cream or jelly used for birth control.

- **medicine** With the bent middle finger of the right *5 hand* in the palm of the left *open hand*, palms facing each other, rock the right hand from side to side with a double movement while keeping the middle finger in place.

- **against** Hit the fingertips of the right *bent hand* into the left *open hand*, palm right and fingers pointing forward.

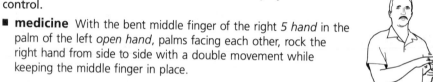

- **sperm** While touching the wrist of the right *S hand* with the left extended index finger, palms facing in opposite directions, move the right hand forward while opening into a *4 hand*, ending with the right palm left and fingers pointing forward. Beginning with the fingertips of the right *curved 5 hand* on the chest, pull the hand forward while closing the fingers into a *flattened O hand*.

sphygmomanometer An instrument used for measuring blood pressure that includes an inflatable cuff and stethoscope.

- **blood** While wiggling the fingers, move the right *5 hand* downward with a double movement past the back of the left *open hand* held in front of the chest, both palms in and fingers pointing in opposite directions.

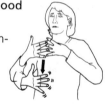

-- [sign continues] ------------------------------>

■ **pressure** With the right *C hand* grasp the upper left arm.

■ **machine** With the fingers of both *curved 5 hands* loosely meshed together, palms in, move the hands up and down in front of the chest with a repeated movement.

spinal block See sign for EPIDURAL.

spinal column See signs for SPINE[1,2].

spine[1], backbone, spinal column, vertebra, or vertebral column
A person's skeleton extending down the back from the neck to the tailbone and containing the spinal cord, which carries nerve impulses to and from the brain.

■ **back** Pat the fingertips of the right *open hand* behind the right shoulder with a double movement.

■ **spine** Beginning with the right *F hand* on the index-finger side of the left *F hand*, bring the right hand straight up.

spine[2], backbone, spinal column, vertebra, or vertebral column (alternate sign)

■ **back** With the extended right index finger of the right *one hand*, palm up, point to the lower back.

■ **spine** Beginning with the fingers of both *modified C hands* pointing toward each other in front of the chest, bring the left hand straight down.

splint

splint Wood or other supporting material arranged to hold a broken bone in place.

- **splint** Lay the bent right arm along the length of the left bent arm, right *open hand* near the crook of the left arm and the left *open hand* under the right elbow. Then reverse the arms.

split personality See sign for SCHIZOPHRENIA.

sprain, pulled ligament, or dislocation

1. To injure the ligaments around a joint without a fracture. **2.** An injury to the ligaments around a joint.

- **sprain** Beginning with both *bent V hands* in front of the chest, right palm forward and left palm in, twist the hands in opposite directions, reversing the direction of the palms.

sputum Material that is spit out; made up of saliva and mucous that is discharged from the respiratory passages.

- **white** Beginning with the fingertips of the right *curved 5 hand* on the chest, pull the hand forward while closing the fingers into a *flattened O hand*.

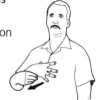

- **spit-out** Beginning with the thumb holding down the index finger of the right *A hand* in front of the mouth, palm facing forward, move the hand forward while flicking the index finger forward.

squeeze See sign for COMPRESS.

squint See sign for STRABISMUS.

stable Medically not in immediate danger or deteriorating.

- **continue** Beginning with the thumb of the right *10 hand* on the thumbnail of the left *10 hand*, both palms down in front of the chest, move the hands forward.

- **not** Bring the thumb of the right *10 hand* forward from under the chin with a deliberate movement.

-- [sign continues] -->

- **change** With the palm side of both *A hands* together, right hand above left, twist the wrists in opposite directions in order to reverse positions.

sterile[1] or **aseptic** Completely free from germs. Same sign used for: **disinfect.**

- Fingerspell: G-E-R-M

- **none** Move both *O hands*, palms forward, from in front of the chest outward to each side.

sterile[2] or **infertile** Of or describing a female who is not capable of producing offspring.

- **can't** Bring the extended index finger of the right *one hand* downward hitting the extended index finger of the left *one hand* as it moves.

- **conceive** Bring both *5 hands* from in front of each side of the body, palms in, toward each other, ending with the fingers meshed together in front of the abdomen.

sterile[3] or **infertile** (alternate sign used for males)

- **can't** Bring the extended index finger of the right *one hand* downward hitting the extended index finger of the left *one hand* as it moves.

- **cause** Beginning with both *S hands* near the body, palms up and left hand nearer the body than the right hand, move the hands forward in an arc while opening into *5 hands*.

- **baby** With the right bent arm resting on the left bent arm, swing the arms from side to side with a double movement.

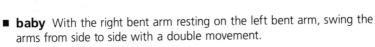

sterilization

sterilization, tubal ligation, or vasectomy
The tying of a woman's fallopian tubes to render her infertile. Related form: **sterilize**.

- **sterilize** Beginning with the index fingers of both *modified X hands* touching in front of the waist, right palm down and left palm in, pull the hands deliberately apart to each side of the waist.

---

sterilize See sign for CLEANSE.

---

stethoscope A medical instrument with earpieces and a long tube for listening to internal sounds in the body, as the heartbeat and quality of breathing.

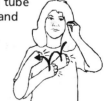

- **stethoscope** Place the palm side of the left *flattened O hand* near the right ear while touching the fingertips of the right *flattened O hand* to several places on the chest.

---

stillborn Of or describing a fetus dead at birth.

- **baby** With the right bent arm resting on the left bent arm, swing the arms from side to side with a double movement.

- **birth** Beginning with the back of the right *open hand* against the palm of the left *open hand*, both palms in and fingers pointing in opposite directions, move the right hand down under the little-finger side of the left hand, ending with the right palm facing down.

- **die** Beginning with both *open hands* in front of the body, right palm down and left palm up, flip the hands to the right, turning the right palm up and the left palm down.

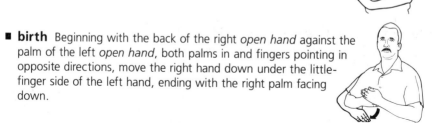

---

stimulant See sign for AMPHETAMINE.

---

stitches See sign for SUTURE.

---

stomach An organ in the abdomen for storing and digesting food. See signs for ABDOMEN[1,2].

stomachache, bellyache, or **colic** A pain in the stomach area.

- **pain** Beginning with both extended index fingers pointing toward each other in front of the body, palms up, jab the fingers toward each other with a short double movement.

stool Waste matter discharged from the intestines through the anus. See signs for BOWEL MOVEMENT[1,2].

strabismus or **squint** An abnormality in which one or both of the eyes turn inward toward the nose. Same sign used for: **cross-eyed.**

- **squint** Place the thumb sides of both G hands near the outside of each eye, palms facing each other, while squinting the eyes.

strain Bodily injury from excessive tension, effort, or use, especially one resulting from a wrench that involves undue stretching of muscles or ligaments.

- **strain** Beginning with the index-finger sides of both S hands together, palms down, twist the right hand downward.

strep throat An acute sore throat caused by streptococcus bacteria and characterized by fever and inflamed tonsils.

- **pain** With both extended index fingers pointing toward each other near the throat, palms down, jab the fingers toward each other with a short double movement.

- **infection** Move the right I hand, palm forward, from side to side with a repeated movement in front of the right shoulder.

stress See sign for PRESSURE.

stretcher A litter for carrying ill or disabled people.

- **lie-down** Lay the back of the right V hand on the palm of the left open hand, both palms up.
- **bring** Move both open hands, palms up, from in front of the left side of the body across to the right side of the body.

strychnine A poison. See sign for TOXIC.

stupor A diminished sensibility caused by disease or narcotics. See signs for PASS OUT[1,2].

sty or **hordeolum** An inflamed swelling of a skin gland on the edge of an eyelid. ·

■ **red** Brush the extended right index finger downward on the lips, bending the finger as it moves down.

■ **eye** Tap the extended right index finger at the outward side of the right eye with a double movement.

■ **swell** Beginning with the fingertips of the right *flattened O hand* touching the bottom of the right eye, pull the hand forward a short distance while opening the fingers to a *curved 5 hand*.

succumb See sign for DIE.

sucking wound A puncture wound that penetrates the lungs and permits the taking in and escape of oxygen directly through the resulting opening.

■ **lung** Rub the fingertips of both *bent hands*, palms in, up and down with a repeated movement near the center of the chest.

■ **penetrate** Insert the extended right index finger, palm in and finger pointing downward, with a deliberate movement between the middle and ring fingers of the left *open hand* held in front of the chest, palm down and fingers pointing right.

■ **spot** Place the palm side of the right *F hand* palm down and fingers pointing left, on the chest.

sudden infant death syndrome or SIDS The unexpected death of an apparently healthy infant that usually occurs during the first fourth months of life during sleeping.

- Fingerspell abbreviation: S-I-D-S

suffer¹ To endure or feel distress, pain, or grief.

- **suffer** Beginning with the thumb of the right *A hand* touching the chin, palm left, twist the hand to the left with a double movement.

suffer² (alternate sign)

- **suffer** Beginning with the thumb of the right *A hand* touching the chin, palm left, move the right hand downward and over the left hand held in front of the body, palm in, as the left *A hand* moves over the right hand.

suffocate To die from a deprivation of oxygen.

- **can't** Bring the extended index finger of the right *one hand* downward hitting the extended index finger of the left *one hand* as it moves.

- **breathe** With the right *5 hand* in front of the chest above the left *5 hand*, fingers pointing in opposite directions and palms in, move both hands forward and back toward the chest with a double movement.

suicide The taking of one's own life.

- **kill** Push the side of the extended right index finger, palm down, across the palm of the left *open hand*, palm right, with a deliberate movement.

- **myself** Tap the thumb side of the right *10 hand*, palm left, against the chest with a double movement.

sunburn A skin inflammation caused by overexposure to sunlight.

- **sun** Beginning with the right *flattened O hand* above the right shoulder, palm down, bring the right hand downward toward the face while opening into a *curved 5 hand*.

- **burn** Begin with the right *S hand*, palm up, on the back of the left wrist. Then open the right hand to a *curved 5 hand* and slide the back of the right hand toward the crook of the left arm while wiggling the right fingers with a repeated movement.

sunstroke or **heatstroke** A sudden and sometimes fatal condition caused by overexposure to the sun's rays. Related form: **sunstruck**.

- **sun** Beginning with the right *flattened O hand* above the right shoulder, palm down, bring the right hand downward toward the face while opening into a *curved 5 hand*.

- **hit-me** Beginning with the right *A hand* above the right shoulder, palm down, strike the right knuckles against the extended index finger of the left *one hand* pointing up in front of the head.

- **disease** Touch the bent middle finger of the right *5 hand* to the forehead while touching the bent middle finger of the left *5 hand* to the abdomen.

superficial, external, or **surface** Situated on or near the surface of the skin; not penetrating.

- **surface** Move the palm side of the right *open hand* in a circle on the back of the left *open hand*, both palms down in front of the chest.

supine Lying on one's back. See sign for LIE DOWN.

suppository Medication in a solid form that melts when inserted into the rectum or vagina.

■ **buttocks** Touch the extended right index finger to the right buttock.

■ **vagina** Touch the index fingers and thumbs of both *I hands*, palms in and index fingers pointing down, together in front of the body.

■ **insert-up** Insert the extended thumb of the right *10 hand*, palm left, upward into the little-finger opening of the left *A hand*, palm right, held in front of the abdomen.

■ **medicine** With the bent middle finger of the right *5 hand* in the palm of the left *open hand*, palms facing each other, rock the right hand from side to side with a double movement while keeping the middle finger in place.

---

surface See sign for SUPERFICIAL.

---

surgeon[1] A doctor who performs operations to treat diseases or injuries.

■ **doctor** Tap the fingertips of the right *D hand* on the wrist of the upturned left *open hand* with a double movement.

■ **specialty** Slide the little-finger side of the right *B hand*, palm left and fingers pointing forward, along the index-finger side of the left *B hand* held in front of the chest, palm right and fingers pointing forward.

-- [sign continues] ---▶

surgeon

- **operate** Move the thumb of the right *A hand*, palm down, across the upturned palm of the left *open hand* held in front of the chest.

---

surgeon[2] See sign for OPERATE.

---

surgery Treatment, as of a disease or injury, by a surgical procedure, such as removal of a tumor or repairing a broken limb. Related sign: **surgical.** See sign for OPERATE.

---

survive See sign for LIVE.

---

susceptible, prone, or **vulnerable** Likely to become infected by a disease.

- **disease** Touch the bent middle finger of the right *5 hand* to the forehead while touching the bent middle finger of the left *5 hand* to the abdomen.

- **easy** Brush the fingertips of the right *curved hand* upward on the back of the fingertips of the left *curved hand* with a double movement, both palms up.

- **accept** Beginning with both *5 hands* in front of the body, fingers pointing forward and palms down, pull both hands back to the chest while changing to *flattened O hands*.

- **get** Beginning with the little-finger side of the right *curved 5 hand*, palm left, on the index-finger side of the left *curved 5 hand*, palm right, bring the hands back toward the chest while closing into *S hands*.

suture or **stitches** **1.** A single loop of thread, in a connected series of such loops, put into the edges of a wound or incision to close it. **2.** To fasten with stitches.

- **closed** Bring the index fingers of both *B hands* sharply together in front of the body, palms down and fingers pointing forward.

- **sew** Bring the fingertips of the right *F hand* upward off the back of the left *open hand* with a double movement, both palms down.

swallow To take into the stomach through the mouth and throat.

- **swallow** Move the extended right index finger, palm left and finger pointing upward, in an arc from in front of the chin down the length of the neck.

swelling[1] An abnormal enlargement or protuberance, especially when caused by internal pressure or growth. Related form: **swollen.**

- **swell** With the fingertips of the right *flattened O hand* on the back of the bent left arm, raise the right hand a short distance while opening the fingers to a *curved 5 hand*.

swelling[2] (alternate sign) Related form: **swollen.**

- **puffy** Beginning with both *flattened O hands* near each side of the chin, palms facing each other, open the fingers into *curved 5 hands* near each cheek while puffing out the cheeks.

swelling[3] (alternate sign) Related form: **swollen.**

- **swollen** Beginning with the right *curved 5 hand* on the back of the left *open hand* held in front of the chest, both palms down, raise the right hand a short distance.

swollen

swollen See signs for DISTENTION, SWELLING[1,2,3].

symptom Effects of disease that only the patient can experience, such as pain, nausea, or dizziness.

- **disease** Touch the bent middle finger of the right *5 hand* to the forehead while touching the bent middle finger of the left *5 hand* to the abdomen.

- **show** With the extended right index finger touching the palm of the left *open hand*, palm right and fingers pointing forward, move both hands forward a short distance.

systemic Of or describing conditions that affect most or all of the body, in contrast to conditions that affect only a limited, or local, area.

- **full** Slide the palm of the right *open hand*, palm down, from right to left across the index-finger side of the left *S hand*, palm right.

- **body** Pat the palm side of both *open hands* first on each side of the chest and then on each side of the abdomen.

synthetic See sign for ARTIFICIAL.

syphilis See signs for SEXUALLY TRANSMITTED DISEASE[1,2].

syringe See sign for HYPODERMIC.

tablet See signs for PILL[1,2].

---

take care of See sign for MONITOR.

---

tape See signs for ADHESIVE TAPE[1,2].

---

teeth **1.** Plural of TOOTH. **2.** The set of hard bodies attached in a row to each jaw, used for chewing. Note: Add the person marker after this sign to form the medical professional: **dentist.**

- **teeth** Move the curved index finger of the right *X hand* from right to left across the top front teeth.

---

teething The period when a baby's teeth emerge, often accompanied by mild gum pain.

- **baby** With the right bent arm resting on the left bent arm, swing the arms from side to side with a double movement.

- **emerge** Move the fingers of the right *V hand*, palm back, upward between the index and middle fingers of the left *open hand* held in front of the chest, palm down.

- **teeth** Move the curved index finger of the right *X hand* from right to left across the top front teeth.

---

temperature The degree of heat of the human body.

- **temperature** Slide the back of the extended right index finger, palm in and fingers pointing left, up and down with a repeated movement on the extended index finger of the left hand, palm right and finger pointing up.

tender

tender See signs for PAIN[1,2].

tendon A tough band of connective tissue that links a muscle to some other part, such as a bone, and transmits the force exerted by a muscle.

- **muscle** Tap the fingertips of the right *M hand* against the upper part of the bent left arm with a double movement.

- **bone** With a double movement, tap the back of the right *bent V hand*, palm up, on the back of the left *S hand*, palm down.

- **tube** Beginning with the index-finger sides of the both *F hands*, palm forward, together in front of the chest, move the hands apart to in front of each side of the chest.

- **connect** Beginning with both *curved 5 hands* apart in front of the body, bring the hands together to intersect with each other by closing the thumb to the index finger of each hand.

terminal Resulting in or certain to cause death.

- **will** Move the right *open hand*, palm left and fingers pointing up, from the right side of the chin forward while tipping the fingers forward.

- **die** Beginning with both *open hands* in front of the body, right palm down and left palm up, flip the hands to the right, turning the right palm up and the left palm down.

testicles, scrotum, or **testis** The two male reproductive glands, located in the scrotum.

- **testicles** Beginning with both *C hands* in front of the abdomen, palms up, drop the hands a short distance with a double movement.

testis See sign for TESTICLES.

---

tetanus See signs for LOCKJAW[1,2].

---

therapist See sign for THERAPY[1].

---

therapy[1] or **treatment** A rehabilitation program, as for treating mental or physical disorders. Note: Add the person marker before this sign to form the medical professional: **therapist**.

■ **therapy** Beginning with the little-finger side of the right *T hand*, palm in, on the upturned palm of the left *open hand*, move both hands upward in front of the chest.

---

therapy[2] or **treatment** (alternate sign)

■ **go-to** Beginning with both extended index fingers pointing up in front of the chest, right hand closer to the chest than the left and both palms facing forward, move both hands forward simultaneously while bending the wrists so the fingers point forward.

■ **regular** Brush the little-finger side of the right *one hand* across the index-finger side of the left *one hand*, as the right hand moves in a double circular movement toward the chest.

■ **for** Beginning with the extended right finger touching the right side of the forehead, twist the hand forward, ending with the index finger pointing forward.

■ **therapy** (note: substitute purpose of therapy here, e.g., *back problem*, *speech*, etc.) Beginning with the little-finger side of the right *T hand*, palm in, on the upturned palm of the left *open hand*, move both hands upward in front of the chest.

■ **will** Move the right *open hand*, palm left and fingers pointing up, from the right side of the chin forward while tipping the fingers forward.

■ **help** With the little-finger side of the left *A hand* in the palm of the right *open hand*, move both hands upward in front of the chest.

thermometer

thermometer[1] An instrument for measuring temperature.

- **thermometer** Touch the extended right index finger, palm down and finger angled down, to the right side of the mouth.

---

thermometer[2] (alternate sign when taking one's temperature rectally)

- **insert-rectum** Move the index-finger knuckle of the right *modified X hand* to the back of the right hip.

- **shake-down** Shake the right *modified X hand*, palm in and knuckles pointing left, up and down with a repeated movement in front of the chest by twisting the wrist.

---

thorax[1] or **trunk** The upper part of the human body below the neck and above the abdomen.

- **thorax** Slide the little-finger side of the right *open hand*, palm up, from right to left with a double movement across the lower neck, and, at the same time, the left *open hand*, palm up, with a double movement from left to right across the waist.

---

thorax[2] or **trunk** (alternate sign)

- **thorax** Beginning with the thumb side of both *B hands* on the upper chest, left hand under the right hand, palms down and fingers pointing in opposite directions, move the left hand downward to the waist while keeping the right hand in place.

---

throat or **larynx** 1. The front of the neck. 2. The upper part of the passageway to the lungs and stomach, extending from the back of the mouth to below the larynx.

- **throat** Brush the extended fingertips of the right *G hand* downward along the length of the neck.

throb[1] or **pulsate** To pulsate with a steady, pronounced rhythm.

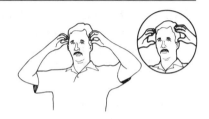

- **throb** Beginning with the fingertips of both *C hands* on each side of the head, bring the hands slightly outward to each side with a repeated movement, opening the fingers slightly each time.

throb[2] See sign for PULSATION.

thrombus A clot that forms in a blood vessel or in one of the chambers of the heart. See sign for BLOOD CLOT. Related form: **thrombosis**.

throw up See sign for REGURGITATE.

thrush An oral infection characterized by white eruptions in the mouth.

- **white** Beginning with the fingertips of the right *curved 5 hand* on the chest, pull the hand forward while closing the fingers into a *flattened O hand*.

- **inside** Move the fingers of the right *flattened O hand* downward with a short double movement in the thumb side of the right hand held in front of the chest.

- **mouth** Draw a circle around the edge of the mouth with the extended right index finger, palm down.

tine test A skin test used to indicate whether a person has been exposed to tuberculosis.

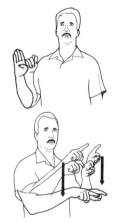

- Fingerspell: T-B

- **test** Beginning with both extended index fingers pointing forward in front of the chest, palms down, bring the hands downward while bending the index fingers into *X hands* and continuing down while extending the index fingers again.

tinnitus

tinnitus A sensation of sound, such as ringing, in the ears.

- **inside-ear** Move the fingers of the right *flattened O hand* downward with a short double movement in the thumb side of the left *O hand* held near the right ear.

- **noise** Move both *5 hands*, palms angled down, with a double shaking movement from near each ear.

- **ring** Tap the thumb side of the left extended index finger, palm right and finger pointing up, with a small repeated movement on the palm of the right *open hand* held near the right ear, palm forward.

tired[1] or **prostrate** Exhausted; fatigued; weary. Same sign used for: **lethargy**.

- **tired** Beginning with the fingers of both *bent hands* on each side of the chest, palms facing in opposite directions, roll the hands downward on the fingertips, ending with the little-finger sides of both hands touching the chest.

tired[2] See sign for EXHAUSTION.

tolerance The power of enduring or resisting the action of a drug, poison, etc.

- **medicine** Note: Substitute the sign for food, poison, etc. to indicate which the person can tolerate. With the bent middle finger of the right *5 hand* in the palm of the left *open hand*, palms facing each other, rock the right hand from side to side with a double movement while keeping the middle finger in place.

- **accept** Beginning with both *5 hands* in front of the body, fingers pointing forward and palms down, pull both hands back to the chest while changing to *flattened O hands*.

- **maximum** Beginning with the right *B hand* a few inches under the left *open hand*, both palms down and fingers pointing in opposite directions, bring the back of the right hand up to hit against the left palm.

tongue A movable muscle growing out of the floor of the mouth.

- **tongue** Touch the extended right index finger to the tongue.

tonsil A mass of tissue on each side of the throat at the back of the mouth.

- **tonsil** Place the thumb sides of both *F hands*, palms facing each other and fingers pointing up, near each other on the neck.

tonsillectomy An operation to remove one or both tonsils.

- **tonsillectomy** Beginning with the fingers of the right *V hand* touching the upper neck, palm down, bring the hand forward and upward while bending the fingers.

tonsillitis Inflammation of the tonsils.

- **infection** Move the right *I hand*, palm forward, from side to side with a repeated movement in front of the right shoulder.

- **inside** Move the fingers of the right *flattened O hand* downward with a short double movement in the thumb side of the left *curved hand* held near the neck.

- **throat** Brush the extended fingertips of the right *G hand* downward along the length of the neck.

tooth One of the hard bodies attached in a row to each jaw, used for chewing. Same sign used for: **dental**.

- **tooth** Touch a front tooth with the extended right index finger, palm down.

toothache

toothache Pain in or about a tooth.

- **pain** With both extended index fingers pointing toward each other in front of the mouth, palms down, jab the fingers toward each other with a short double movement.

toxemia or **blood poisoning** A disorder caused by bacterial substances in the blood.

- **blood** While wiggling the fingers, move the right *5 hand* downward from the chin with a double movement past the back of the left *5 hand* held in front of the chest, both palms in and fingers pointing in opposite directions.

- **infection** Move the right *I hand*, palm forward, from side to side with a repeated movement in front of the right shoulder.

- **spread** Beginning with both *flattened O hands* in front of the chest, fingers pointing down, move the hands downward and outward while opening into *5 hands.*

toxic Harmful; capable of causing damage to the body. Same sign used for: **arsenic, cyanide, strychnine.** Related form: **toxin.**

- **medicine** With the bent middle finger of the right *5 hand* in the palm of the left *open hand*, palms facing each other, rock the right hand from side to side with a double movement while keeping the middle finger in place.

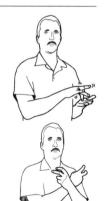

- **poison** Hold both *bent V* hands in front of opposite sides of the chest, wrists crossed and palms facing in.

tracheotomy An operation, especially to aid breathing, that requires cutting into the trachea at the neck.

- **operate** Drag the thumb of the right *A hand*, palm down, downward on the neck.

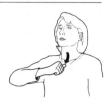

-- [sign continues] --▶

■ **hole** Place the index-finger side of the right *F hand*, palm left, against the lower part of the neck.

■ **breathe** With the right *5 hand* in front of the chest above the left *5 hand*, fingers pointing in opposite directions and palms in, move both hands forward and back toward the chest with a double movement.

traction Method of treating some condition of the bones or muscles by exerting a steady pull on the affected parts.

■ **arm** Slide the palm of the right *curved hand* along the length of the extended left arm beginning at the wrist.

■ **stretch** Beginning with the little-finger side of the left *S hand* on the index-finger side of the right *S hand*, palms facing in opposite directions and the left hand nearer the chest than the right, pull the right hand forward with a deliberate double movement.

tranquilizer, anxiolytic, paraldehyde, relaxant, reserpine, or **sedative** Medication used to help diminish anxiety and to produce calmness. See sign for DEPRESSANT.

■ **medicine** With the bent middle finger of the right *5 hand* in the palm of the left *open hand*, palms facing each other, rock the right hand from side to side with a double movement while keeping the middle finger in place.

■ **help** With the little-finger side of the left *A hand* in the palm of the right *open hand*, move both hands upward in front of the chest.

■ **rest** With the arms crossed at the wrists, place the fingers of each *R hand* near the opposite shoulder.

transfusion See sign for BLOOD TRANSFUSION.

---

transplant A living organ removed from one person and placed in the body of another.

- **heart** (Note: Substitute kind of transplant here, e.g., kidney, hair, etc.) Touch the bent middle finger of the right *5 hand* on the left side of the chest.

- **exchange** Beginning with both *modified X hands* in front of the body, right hand somewhat forward of the left hand, move the right hand back toward the body in an upward arch while moving the left hand forward with a downward arc.

---

transsexual One whose sex is changed externally by surgery.

- **change** With the palm side of both *X hands* together, left hand above right, twist the wrists in opposite directions in order to reverse positions.

- **sex** Touch the index-finger side of the right *X hand*, first near the right eye and then to the right side of the chin.

- **male** Beginning with the thumb of the right *10 hand* on the right side of the forehead, bring the hand downward while opening into a *5 hand*, ending with the thumb touching the chest.

- **become** With the palms of both *open hands* together, right hand on top of left, twists the wrists in opposite directions in order to reverse positions.

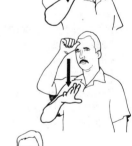

- **female** Beginning with the thumb of the right *A hand* on the chin, bring the hand downward while opening into a *5 hand*, ending with the thumb touching the chest.

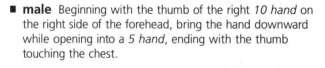

transvestite A person who enjoys the practice of dressing and acting like a person of the opposite sex.

- **male** Beginning with the thumb of the right *10 hand* on the right side of the forehead, bring the hand downward while opening into a *5 hand*, ending with the thumb touching the chest.

- **dress** Brush the thumbs of both *5 hands* downward on each side of the chest.

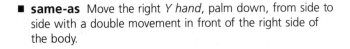

- **same-as** Move the right *Y hand*, palm down, from side to side with a double movement in front of the right side of the body.

- **female** Beginning with the thumb of the right *A hand* on the chin, bring the hand downward while opening into a *5 hand*, ending with the thumb touching the chest.

trauma Severe distress from experiencing a disastrous event outside the range of usual experience.

- **wrong** Bring the knuckles of the right *Y hand* back against the chin.

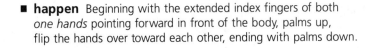

- **happen** Beginning with the extended index fingers of both *one hands* pointing forward in front of the body, palms up, flip the hands over toward each other, ending with palms down.

- **pain** Beginning with the extended index fingers of both *one hands* pointing toward each other in front of the chest, both palms in, jab the fingers toward each other with a double movement.

treatment

treatment[1] Medical application of remedies so as to effect a cure.

■ **take-care-of** With the little-finger side of the right *K hand* across the index-finger side of the left *K hand*, move the hands in a repeated flat circle in front of the body.

treatment[2] See signs for THERAPY[1,2].

tremble, quiver, or **shake** To shake involuntarily, as from fear or excitement.

■ With both *5* hands in front of the chest, palms down, move the fingers from side to side with a short repeated movement.

tremor or **Parkinson's disease** Involuntary trembling of the body.

■ **tremor** While holding the wrist of the right *open hand* with the left hand, shake the right hand slightly from side to side.

triage[1] The process of sorting injured people into groups based on their degree of need for medical treatment.

■ **decide** Move the extended right index finger from the right side of the forehead, palm left, down in front of the chest while changing into a *D hand*, ending with both *D hands* moving forward in front of the body.

■ **person** Move both *P hands*, palms facing each other, downward along the sides of the body.

■ **emergency** Shake the right *E hand*, palm forward, back and forth in front of the right shoulder.

-- [sign continues] ---➤

- **priority** Touch the middle finger of the right *P hand*, palm in, first to the thumb, then in order to each finger of the left *5 hand* held in front of the body, palm in and fingers pointing up.

triage² (alternate sign)

- **decide** Move the extended right index finger from the right side of the forehead, palm left, down in front of the chest while changing into a *D hand*, ending with both *D hands* moving forward in front of the body.

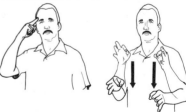

- **who** Move the extended right index finer in a small circle around the pursed lips.

- **most** Beginning with the palm sides of both *10 hands* together in front of the chest, bring the right hand upward, ending with the right hand in front of the right shoulder, palm left.

- **need** Move the bent index finger of the right *X hand* downward with a double movement in front of the right side of the body by bending the wrist down.

- **emergency** Shake the right *E hand*, palm forward, back and forth in front of the right shoulder.

triplet One of three offspring born of one pregnancy.

- **baby** With the right bent arm resting on the left bent arm, swing the arms from side to side with a double movement.

-- [sign continues] --

trunk

- **birth** Beginning with the back of the right *open hand* against the palm of the left *open hand*, both palms in and fingers pointing in opposite directions, move the right hand down under the little-finger side of the left hand, ending with the right palm facing down.

- **three** Hold up the right *3 hand*, palm forward, in front of the right shoulder.

trunk See signs for THORAX[1,2].

tubal ligation See sign for STERILIZATION.

tube See sign for VESSEL.

tuberculosis An infectious disease affecting particularly the lungs.
- Fingerspell abbreviation: T-B

tumor, growth, or **neoplasm** A swelling, usually used to refer to a cancerous growth.

- **bump** Beginning with the extended right index finger on the back of the left wrist, palm down, bring the right finger upward in a small arc, ending with the back of the right index finger on the left *open hand*, palm down.

- **not** Bring the thumb of the right *10 hand* forward from under the chin with a deliberate movement.

- **right** Bring the little-finger side of the right *one hand* down sharply on the index-finger side of the left *one hand*.

tumor marker See sign for MARKER.

turning point See signs for CRISIS[1,2].

Twelve step or **12-step** A program for recovery from addiction originating with Alcoholics Anonymous and providing 12 progressive levels toward achievement.

- **addiction** Hook the index finger of the right *X hand* in the right corner of the mouth and pull outward a short distance.

- **twelve** Beginning with the right *S hand* in front of the right shoulder, palm back, flick the index and middle fingers up.

- **step** Beginning with both *open hands* in front of the body, palms in and fingers pointing toward each other, left hand somewhat forward of the right, move the right hand forward of the left in an arc, and then the left hand forward of the right, with an alternating movement.

- **program** Move the middle finger of the right *P hand*, palm left, from the heel, over the fingertips, and the wrist of the left *open hand*, palm in and fingers pointing up.

---

twin One of two children born at the same time from the same mother. See also signs for FRATERNAL TWIN, IDENTICAL TWIN.

- **twin** Touch the index-finger side of the right *T hand*, palm left, first to the right side of the chin and then to the left side of the chin.

---

ultrasound A diagnostic method in which high-frequency sound waves are transmitted into the body and reflect back images of the organs. Related form: **ultrasonic.**

- **rub** Rub the little-finger side of the right *S hand* in a random movement around the abdomen.

- **picture** Move the right *C hand*, palm forward, from near the right side of the face downward, ending with the index-finger side of the right *C hand* against the palm of the left *open hand* held in front of the chest, palm right.

---

umbilical cord A tube providing nutrition and carrying away wastes that connects between the mother's navel and the fetus within the placenta.

- **umbilical** Beginning with the palm side of the left *F hand* on the abdomen and the index-finger side of the right *F hand* against the left index finger, move the right hand forward.

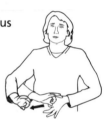

---

umbilicus, belly button, or **navel** A depression in the abdominal at the point that the umbilical cord was attached.

- **spot** Place the index-finger side of the left *F hand* on the abdomen.

---

unclean See sign for UNSTERILE.

---

unconscious[1] Not conscious; lacking awareness.

- **not** Bring the thumb of the right *10 hand* forward from under the chin with a deliberate movement.

-- [sign continues] --->

- **know** Tap the fingertips of the right *bent hand*, palm down, on the right side of the forehead.

---

unconscious[2] See sign for COMA.

---

uncontrollable Incapable of being controlled.

- **can't** Bring the extended index finger of the right *one hand* downward hitting the extended index finger of the left *one hand* as it moves.

- **control** Beginning with both *modified X hands* in front of each side of the body, right hand forward of the left hand and palms facing each other, move the hands forward and back with a repeated movement.

---

undernourished Suffering from faulty and inadequate nutrition. See sign for MALNUTRITION.

---

unnatural See signs for ABNORMAL[1,2,3].

---

unsterile or **unclean** Having, or being contaminated with, bacteria.

- **not** Bring the thumb of the right *10 hand* forward from under the chin with a deliberate movement.

- **clean** Slide the palm of the right *open hand* from the heel to the fingers of the upturned palm of the left *open hand* with a double movement.

---

upset stomach See signs for NAUSEA[1,2].

urinalysis[1] Laboratory test performed on a urine sample that helps diagnose diseases of the kidney and other parts of the body.

- **urine** Tap the middle finger of the right *P hand* against the nose with a double movement.

- **analyze** With both *V hands* pointing toward each other in front of the chest, palms down, move the fingers down and apart with a double movement, bending the fingers each time.

urinalysis[2] (alternate sign)

- **toilet** Shake the right *T hand*, palm forward, with a small repeated movement in front of the right shoulder.

- **analyze** With both *V hands* pointing toward each other in front of the chest, palms down, move the fingers down and apart with a double movement, bending the fingers each time.

urinary bladder See sign for BLADDER.

urine Yellowish liquid waste material secreted from the kidney.

- **urine** Tap the middle finger of the right *P hand* against the nose with a double movement.

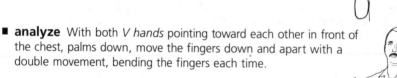

urine sample A small amount of urine collected for the purpose of laboratory analysis for possible infection or disease.

- **urine** Tap the middle finger of the right *P hand* against the nose with a double movement.

- **inside** Move the fingers of the right *flattened O hand* downward with a short double movement in the thumb side of the left *O hand* held in front of the chest.

-- [sign continues] --->

- **cup** Beginning with the little-finger side of the right *C hand*, palm left, on the palm of the left *open hand*, move the right hand up a short distance.

- **for** Beginning with the extended right finger touching the right side of the forehead, twist the hand forward, ending with the index finger pointing forward.

- **analyze** With both *V hands* pointing toward each other in front of the chest, palms down, move the fingers down and apart with a double movement, bending the fingers each time.

urologist A doctor whose specialty is the urinary tract and its treatment. See sign for UROLOGY.

urology The branch of medicine concerned with the scientific, clinical, and surgical aspects of the urinary tract. Note: Add the person marker before this sign to form the medical professional: **urologist.**

- **medical** Touch the fingertips of the right *flattened O hand* on the wrist of the upturned left *open hand*.

- **specialty** Slide the little-finger side of the right *B hand*, palm left and fingers pointing forward, along the index-finger side of the left *B hand* held in front of the chest, palm right and fingers pointing forward.

- **urine** Tap the middle finger of the right *P hand* against the nose with a double movement.

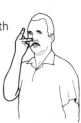
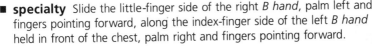
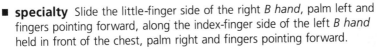
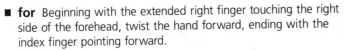
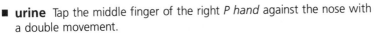

uterus

uterus[1] or **womb** The organ of the female reproductive system on which the fertilized egg attaches and develops to form a fetus.

- **uterus** Beginning with the fingertips of both *U hands* touching in front of the body, palms down, move the hands outward away from each other and downward to again touch fingertips in front of the abdomen.

---

uterus[2] or **womb** (alternate sign)

- **abdomen** Pat the abdomen with the right open hand.

- **baby** With the right bent arm resting on the left bent arm, swing the arms from side to side with a double movement.

- **grow** Bring the right *flattened O hand*, palm in and fingers pointing up, up through the left *C hand*, palm right, while spreading the right fingers into a *5 hand*.

---

vaccinate See sign for INJECT.

---

vaccination or **inoculation** Inoculation with a vaccine, a preparation for producing immunity to a specific disease.

- **vaccinate** Rub the fingertips of the right *modified X hand* downward with a double movement on the left upper arm.

---

vaccine See sign for HYPODERMIC.

---

vagina A canal between the vulva and the uterus in female mammals.

- **vagina** Touch the index fingers and thumbs of both *L hands*, palms in and index fingers pointing down, together in front of the body.

---

vaginitis Inflammation of the vagina.

- **vagina** Touch the index fingers and thumbs of both *L hands*, palms in and index fingers pointing down, together in front of the body.

- **infection** Move the right *I hand*, palm forward, from side to side with a repeated movement in front of the right shoulder.

---

valve[1] A structure in a vein or artery that slows or prevents the backward movement of blood.

- **control** Beginning with both *modified X hands* in front of each side of the body, right hand forward of the left hand and palms facing each other, move the hands forward and back with a repeated movement.

-- [sign continues] - ➤

valve

- **blood** While wiggling the fingers, move the right *5 hand* from the chin downward with a double movement past the back of the left *5 hand* held in front of the chest, both palms in and fingers pointing in opposite directions.

valve² (alternate sign)

- **heart** (Note: Substitute kind of transplant here, e.g., kidney, hair, etc.) Touch the bent middle finger of the right *5 hand* on the left side of the chest.

- **valve** Beginning with both *open hands* on the left side of the chest, fingers pointing toward each other and right fingers on top of left fingers, move the right fingers up and down with a double movement while keeping the heel of the hand in place.

- **control** Beginning with both *modified X hands* in front of each side of the body, right hand forward of the left hand and palms facing each other, move the hands forward and back with a repeated movement.

- **blood** While wiggling the fingers, move the right *5 hand* downward with a double movement past the back of the left *5 hand* held in front of the chest, both palms in and fingers pointing in opposite directions.

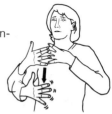

- **flow** Beginning with both *flattened O hands* together in the middle of the chest, palms in and fingers pointing down, move the hands down while opening the fingers.

---

vasectomy See sign for STERILIZATION.

ventricular fibrillation or atrial fibrillatio

A potentially fatal condition characterized by rapid, irregular contracts of the heart.

- **heartbeat** Touch the bent middle finger of the right *5 hand* on the left side of the chest. Then tap the back of the right *S hand* against the palm of the left *open hand* held in front of the chest.

- **not** Bring the thumb of the right *10 hand* forward from under the chin with a deliberate movement.

- **regular** Brush the little-finger side of the right *one hand* across the index-finger side of the left *one hand*, as the right hand moves in a double circular movement toward the chest.

vermiform appendix See signs for APPENDIX[1,2].

vertebra See signs for SPINE[1,2].

vertebral column See signs for SPINE[1,2].

vertigo[1] A disordered condition in which one feels one's surroundings whirling about.

- **ear** Point to each ear with the extended index fingers.

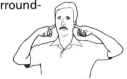

- **dizzy** Move both *C hands* in alternating circular movements near each side of the head.

vertigo[2] See sign for DIZZY.

vessel, canal, duct, tube, or vial A hollow tube in the body, such as an artery or vein, in which a body fluid is contained or circulated.

- **tube** Beginning with the little-finger side of the right *F hand*, palm left, on the index-finger side of the left *F hand*, palm right, move the right hand up with a wiggly movement.

-- [sign continues] -->

vibrator

- **for** Beginning with the extended right finger touching the right side of the forehead, twist the hand forward, ending with the index finger pointing forward.

- **blood** While wiggling the fingers, move the right *5 hand* from the chin downward with a double movement past the back of the left *5 hand* held in front of the chest, both palms in and fingers pointing in opposite directions.

vibrator A machine that causes vibrations, as one used for massage.

- **machine** With the fingers of both *curved 5 hands* loosely meshed together, palms in, move the hands up and down in front of the chest with a repeated movement.

- **vibrate** With the right *curved hand* grasping the back of the left *curved hand*, both facing down, shake the hands with a short repeated movement.

virus Any of several small germs that become alive when they enter the body, where they grow and cause a variety of infectious illnesses.

- Fingerspell: G-E-R-M

- **body** Pat the palm side of both *open hands* first on each side of the chest and then on each side of the abdomen.

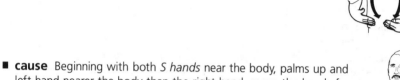

- **cause** Beginning with both *S hands* near the body, palms up and left hand nearer the body than the right hand, move the hands forward in an arc while opening into *5 hands*.

-- [sign continues] --→

362

- **disease** Touch the bent middle finger of the right *5 hand* to the forehead while touching the bent middle finger of the left *5 hand* to the abdomen.

---

visible Able to be seen. See sign for VISION.

---

vision or **sight** The act or power of seeing. Same sign used for: visible.

- **can** Move both *S hands*, palms down, downward simultaneously with a short double movement in front of each side of the body.

- **see** Move with the fingers of the right *V hand*, pointing up in front of the eyes, forward a short distance.

---

visual acuity Sharpness of vision as compared with normal ability.

- **see** Move with the fingers of the right *V hand*, pointing up in front of the eyes, forward a short distance.

- **clear** Beginning with the fingertips of both *flattened O hands* touching in front of the chest, move the hands apart while opening into *5 hands*.

---

visual field, field of vision, or **peripheral vision** The entire view encompassed by the eye when it is trained in any particular direction.

- **look** While holding the left *open hand*, palm right and fingers pointing forward, in front of the left side of the head, move the right *V hand*, palm down and fingers pointing forward, from the left palm to the right in front of the face.

-- [sign continues]

vital signs

- **wide** Hold both *open hands* in front of each side of the head, fingers and palms angled forward.

---

vital signs Essential body functions, comprised of pulse rate, body temperature, and respiration.

- **inspect** Move the extended right index finger from the nose down to strike sharply off the upturned palm of the left *open hand*, and then upward again.

- **heart** Touch the bent middle finger of the right *5 hand* on the left side of the chest.

- **pulse** Place the fingertips of the right *flattened O hand*, palm down, on the upturned left wrist.

- **temperature** Slide the back of the extended right index finger, palm in and fingers pointing left, up and down with a repeated movement on the extended index finger of the left hand, palm right and finger pointing up.

---

vitamin One of a number of chemical substances found in food that is necessary for healthy body growth, function, and tissue repair.

- **vitamin** Shake the right *V hand*, palm forward and fingers pointing up, from side to side with a small double movement in front of the right shoulder.

---

vocal cords Two narrow bands of muscular tissue in the larynx that vibrate to create the sounds of the voice.

- **voice** Move the fingertips of the right *V hand*, palm down, upward on the throat with a double movement.

-- [sign continues] -->

■ **throat** Brush the extended fingertips of the right *G hand* downward along the length of the neck.

vomit See sign for REGURGITATE.

vulnerable See sign for SUSCEPTIBLE.

vulva The external female genital organs. See sign for CLITORIS.

---

wake up To awaken from sleep or rouse someone from sleep. See sign for ALERT.

---

wakeful See sign for ALERT.

---

walker A metal framework that supports a crippled person, often used by older people who are unstable on their legs.

- **walker** With both *S hands* in front of each side of the body, palms down and palms facing each other, move the hands forward with short double movements.

---

walking stick See sign for CANE.

---

ward A room in a hospital used for more than two patients.

- **hospital** Bring the fingers of the right *H hand* first downward and then across from back to front on the upper left arm.

- **room** Beginning with both *R hands* in front of each side of the body, palms facing each other and fingers pointing forward, turn the hands sharply in opposite directions, ending with both palms in and fingers pointing in opposite directions.

- **many** Beginning with both *S hands* in front of each side of the chest, palms up, flick the fingers open quickly into *5 hands* with a double movement.

- **patient** Move the extended middle finger of the right *P hand* first down and then forward on the left upper arm.

---

weak See sign for DEBILITY.

well See sign for HEALTHY.

wen See sign for CYST.

wet dressing A moist, and sometimes medicated, bandage used to treat some skin diseases by stimulating drainage.

- **bandage** Beginning with the fingers of the right *H hand*, palm in, touching the little-finger side of the left hand, palm down, move the right hand in a circular movement completely around the left hand.

- **must** Move the best index finger of the right *X hand* downward with a deliberate movement in front of the right side of the body by bending the wrist down.

- **always** Move the extended right index finger, palm and finger angled up, in a repeated circle in front of the right side of the chest.

- **wet** Beginning with both *5 hands* in front of the body, palms up, bring the hands downward with a double movement, closing the fingers into *flattened O hands* each time.

wheelchair A chair on wheels used by invalids.

- **wheelchair** Move both extended index fingers in forward repeated circles in front of each side of the body, palms in and fingers pointing toward each other.

wheeze A high-pitched sound produced in the lungs where secretions have partially blocked air passages.

- **breathe** With the right *5 hand* in front of the chest above the left *5 hand*, fingers pointing in opposite directions and palms in, move both hands forward and back toward the chest with a double movement.

-- [sign continues] --

white blood cell

- **noise** Move both *5 hands*, palms angled down, with a double shaking movement from near each ear.

white blood cell See signs for LEUKOCYTE[1,2].

withdrawal[1] The act or process of stopping the use of an addictive drug.

- **stop** Hit the little-finger side of the right *open hand* on the palm of the left *open hand*.

- **drug** Pound the little-finger side of the right *S hand* with a double movement near the crook of the bent left arm.

- **habit** With the heel of the right *C hand* on the back of the left *S hand*, both palms down, move both hands downward while changing the right hand into an *S hand*.

withdrawal[2] See signs for COITUS INTERRUPTUS[1,2].

woman See sign for FEMALE.

womb See signs for UTERUS[1,2].

worse See signs for DECLINE[1,2].

wound[1] An injury involving cutting or breaking body tissue.

- **pain** Beginning with both extended index fingers pointing toward each other in front of the chest, right palm down and left palm in, twist the hands with a deliberate movement to turn the palms over.

-- [sign continues] --->

■ **rub** Note: Rub the area where the wound is located. Rub the fingers of the right *open hand* with a quick repeated movement on the back of the left *open hand*, both palms down.

---

wound² See sign for HURT¹.

---

wrist or **carpus** The area around the joint that connects the hand with the arm.

■ **wrist** With the bent middle finger and thumb of the right *5 hand* grasp each side of the wrist of the left *S hand*, palm down, while bending the left hand up and down.

x-ray[1] High-energy, invisible waves capable of penetrating the body and creating images of the body tissues on photographic film.

- Fingerspell: X-R-A-Y

x-ray[2] (alternate sign)

- **picture** Move the right *C hand*, palm forward, from near the right side of the face downward, ending with the index-finger side of the right *C hand* against the palm of the left *open hand* held in front of the chest, palm right.

- **body** Pat the palm side of both *open hands* first on each side of the chest and then on each side of the abdomen.

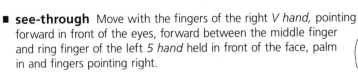

- **see-through** Move with the fingers of the right *V hand,* pointing forward in front of the eyes, forward between the middle finger and ring finger of the left *5 hand* held in front of the face, palm in and fingers pointing right.

yellow fever An acute disease caused by a virus spread by insect bites.

■ **yellow** Move the right *Y hand* with a twisting double movement in front of the right shoulder.

■ **temperature** Slide the back of the extended right index finger, palm in and fingers pointing left, up and down on the extended index finger of the left hand, palm right and finger pointing up.

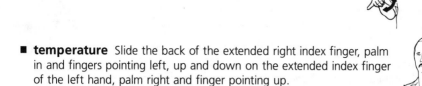

---

zoophobia Abnormal fear of animals.

- **fear** Move both *5 hands* toward each other with a short double movement in front of the chest, fingers pointing toward each other.

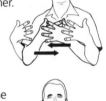

- **animal** Beginning with the fingertips of both *bent hands* on the chest near each shoulder, roll the fingers toward each other on their knuckles with a double movement, while keeping the fingers in place.
